Presented To:

_____

From:

_____

Date:

_____

ORGANIC CHRISTIANITY

NO ADDITIVES, PESTICIDES, OR INSECTICIDES

...JUST RAW GOSPEL

RON MCINTOSH

DESTINY IMAGE® PUBLISHERS, INC.

P.O. Box 310, Shippensburg, PA 17257-0310

"Promoting Inspired Lives."

This book and all other Destiny Image, Revival Press, MercyPlace, Fresh Bread, Destiny Image Fiction, and Treasure House books are available at Christian bookstores and distributors worldwide.

For a U.S. bookstore nearest you, call 1-800-722-6774.

For more information on foreign distributors, call 717-532-3040.

Reach us on the Internet: www.destinyimage.com.

ISBN 13 TP: 978-0-7684-3866-6

ISBN 13 Ebook: 978-0-7684-8968-2

For Worldwide Distribution, Printed in the U.S.A.

1 2 3 4 5 6 7 8 / 15 14 13 12

ENDORSEMENTS

Ron McIntosh is many things to many people. He is the Executive Director of Victory Bible Institute, a leading motivational speaker, a husband and father. To me, he is a close friend who has been a constant source of encouragement and prayer for my family and ministry. He genuinely cares that people walk in the fullness of faith. His latest book *Organic Christianity* reminds us that in the midst of complicated theology, evolved church doctrine, and a frantic pace of life, Jesus is with us and lovingly reminds us that His work is completed. This book unfolds the provocative revelation of grace through the completed work of Jesus Christ. I was moved by the understanding we don't have to muster up our faith, but simply appropriate by faith what God has already done by grace. *Organic Christianity* is a clear call to get away from a gospel of rules and regulations and embrace dynamic intimacy with God, through grace. God's grace is His empowerment to access the fullness of His Son in our lives. Jesus' work is amazing! Let's live fully! Thanks, Ron, for this timely reminder.

TOM NEWMAN
President, Impact Productions

Ron McIntosh has cleaned the canvas and restored the original masterpiece of the "too good to be true" Gospel!

If your Christian life is plagued by self-help phrases like:

"try harder"

"pray more"

"have more faith"

Organic Christianity is for you!

If your holiness depends on your *doing* instead of what Christ *has done*—this book is for you.

If you want *"a life that is exceptional, remarkable, amazing, unimaginable, and abundant,"* this book is for you!

If you feel unworthy, unwanted, and undeserving—THIS BOOK IS FOR YOU!

CURT BEZINQUE
Lead Pastor, Midland Christian Fellowship, Midland, TX
President of the International Ministry Network
Full Gospel Evangelistic Association

I suppose different people mean different things by the word *organic*. One of the best dictionary definitions is "simple, healthful, and close to nature." Ron McIntosh describes here precisely that kind of life for believers. He is advocating a simple faith without pretense or additives, a healthy obedience that is joy not drudgery, and a "natural" kind of supernatural living.

DR. MARK RUTLAND
President, Oral Roberts University

Ron McIntosh has captured the heart of the Gospel! In *Organic Christianity* Ron hits the nail on the head. That which is living is organic; it cannot be replaced by a synthetic. No matter how close the synthetic may be, it always has deadly side effects. Ron very clearly and concisely points the reader back to the heart of God and the Gospel. If a believer doesn't hear this message, he hasn't heard the

Gospel. For everyone who wants an answer to, "What is God saying today?" you are holding it in your hands!

DR. JAMES B. RICHARDS
Author, *Grace: The Power to Change*

In this timely, must-read book, Ron McIntosh masterfully unfolds God's liberating, transformational grace while giving essential concepts and tools so readers can personally experience God's grace at work in their lives.

Ron's latest book is packed with life-giving nuggets forged from the Scriptures and intent of God.

This book provides a prophetic framework of where the Church is and how God's amazing grace, fully understood and applied practically into our lives, is transforming it to be the powerful demonstrator of God's Kingdom and nature.

The first two chapters alone are worth getting and reading this book NOW; and with each successive chapter, my heart exploded with joy and excitement in better understanding God's amazing grace and intent toward me. Wow!

Ron skillfully provides the scriptural framework and revelation of the enormity and liberating power of God's grace and gives us a practical pathway to live in the abundance of it.

TIM REDMOND
President, Redmond Leadership Institute
Author, *Power to Create*

One way that God speaks to His people is giving the same message to many of His mouthpieces at once, emphasizing a priority word to add a building block or a course correction to His body. The enemy quickly develops counterfeit words to cause confusion. Some react to the counterfeit and throw the baby out with the bathwater, missing Heaven's point altogether. Ron McIntosh has correctly identified the current word and coming reformation...*grace* is the word. And grace is the controversy. Not overreacting to the extremes, Ron delivers the purity of the message and brings biblical clarification to the questions raised, keeping the original word on track. Stop what you are reading and read this book now!

CRAIG MCLEOD
Pastor, Life Church
Buffalo, NY

In *Organic Christianity*, Ron McIntosh delivers a message that reclaims the true heart of the Gospel diverse from a set of must follow rules. It is a must-read for those who are weary of the status quo of "religion" and seek authenticity, the extraordinary, and how to live a life fully alive.

This is a book that can revolutionize the Church as well as raise up a generation about to be lost. It's great! *This is life-changing material.* I feel it is something I want to read several times to really get it in my spirit.

KAREN HARDIN
Priority PR

DEDICATION

No one writes a book by him or herself. First, we "stand on the shoulders" of the countless people who have imparted into our lives. There are numerous people who have impacted, imparted, and given input into my life. I can never thank such people enough for their writings, teachings, and mentoring that have shaped the concepts of this writing.

While there are countless people too numerous to mention, there are also people to be counted and counted on. I want to first thank Sue Scoggin for her tireless effort and encouragement along the way to take a concept and manufacture it into written form. Thank you for doing it and doing it again so that there is a product to exhort people.

Most of all, I dedicate this work to my wife and family. There's nothing more important than family to me this side of Heaven. Your encouragement, ideas, dialogue, and love made this work an enjoyable ride. To my wife, Judy, our last years are our best years. Your belief in me helps me believe in myself. To my children, David and Shelly, Daniel, and Jonathan, you truly motivate me to follow God more. It is a wonderful life!

CONTENTS

INTRODUCTION

I was walking out of my staff meeting where I was sharing some concepts that are intertwined in this book when I heard my Resource Director shouting across the hallway. He said, "I know what you should call your next book!"

"What?" I responded, collecting my thoughts. He continued, "You should call it, 'Organic Christianity,' subtitled, 'No Additives, Pesticides, or Insecticides...Just Raw Gospel.'"

Something "organic" is free from synthetic materials or chemicals, which though intended to preserve, may be harmful to the consumer. Something organic has the inherent, inborn, constitutional characteristics from a living organism. The constitution of something is what it is made of. Thus, something organic is something in its most natural state. This book is an attempt to share the Gospel with nothing added to it. This discourse is an effort to communicate the Gospel free from religion—that it often attempts to help people, but it can hold them back from the true freedom to know their God in intimacy and true productivity, which is what they inherently desire. This is not an arrogant attempt to say that I know more than others, but to say I've noted what appears to be subtraction by addition. That is to say, when people add to the message they make it less than it is.

This true, living organism is Jesus Christ and a living vital Gospel He espouses. So much of the New Testament is dedicated to preserving and protecting the true essence of this message.

Much of its message is correcting misunderstandings and false doctrines that are not organic to its central message. Many of the books of the New Testament are debunking the beliefs of groups such as the Judaizers, Gnostics, and Antinomians. Judaizers were people from Paul's day who were Jewish converts, but believed people not only had to receive Jesus, but also had to keep the law to be right with God; it was Jesus + performance. Gnostics were people who believed, among many things, that matter was evil and only spirit was good. Therefore, Jesus could not have been the Son of God because He came in bodily form. Antinomians (meaning against the law) were people who were against the law. They were Gnostics who believed that since matter or flesh didn't count, people could in the flesh do whatever they desired. Some Antinomians even promoted indulgences of the flesh. Antinomians were people who tried to add to the message of organic Christianity. These sects, among others, attempted to dilute the essence of the true organic Gospel. Unwittingly, modern Judaizers and Gnostics have altered the life and vitality of God's Word. In many circles, the most radical message in the world has been reduced to religious prate or fodder.

This book wasn't written to "win a theological argument." It's a book about sharing ideas—principles—to make people free and fully alive. Certainly, there will be an exchange of ideas and theologies, but I'm not creating a work to win an argument. I simply want to help people. Perhaps Irenaeus, a second-century Church father, said it best: "The glory of God is man fully alive."[1] It is God's desire for you to be fully alive in your life, fully alive in your ministry, fully alive in your marriage, fully alive in your service, fully alive in your family, fully alive in your destiny, fully alive in your home, fully alive in your provision, fully alive about how you feel about yourself and God— fully alive.

This book is not just about surviving, but thriving. This book is about going from the ordinary to the extraordinary. This book is about freedom—freedom from sin and freedom to live life. This book is about finding the life you were born to live.

Somehow we have allowed the Gospel to be reduced to rules and regulations that depict what is good and bad, but we've missed the essence of the real Gospel. We've reduced our message to guilt, which leaves people languishing in the mire of "I know God *can,* but I just don't know if He *will*...for me." This is an invitation to find intimacy with God (which has, in essence, been lost) and to enter into the life His Kingdom really affords. It's time to step up to organic Christianity. It's time to be fully alive!

• •

ORGANIC THOUGHTS

1. Something organic, in terms of food, is free from chemically formulated fertilizers, growth stimulants, antibiotics, or pesticides. In broader terms, something organic is something in its purest, most natural state.

2. Jesus + Nothing = Everything

3. Adding to something that is organic makes it less than it is.

4. Reflect on this thought from Irenaeus: "The glory of God is man fully alive."

5. Are you ready for the extraordinary? It's time to be fully alive!

Chapter 1

- - - - - - - - - - - - - - - - - - -

FINDING THE LIFE YOU WERE BORN TO LIVE

Some time back, I found myself speaking in a Midwestern city. I was helping a throng of people at the conclusion of my message, when I noticed in my peripheral vision a woman patiently waiting to talk with me. When the crowd dissipated, I looked over at this seemingly despairing woman and asked, "Can I help you?"

This woman looked at me quizzically and said, "I don't know."

I responded, "Obviously, something happened tonight that put enough hope in you that caused you to wait a long time to talk with me. So, let's give it a shot."

Her eyes glanced downward to avoid eye contact as she stammered to get some words to come out of her mouth. She finally muttered a small litany of inadequacies and problems. Her list of insufficiencies included everything from being overweight to not enjoying life, to some specific failures, to criticisms from her husband, and finally to family problems.

Trying to gain her attention, I asked, "On a scale of 1 to 10, 10 being the most acceptable, how accepted do you feel?"

She pondered a long time before answering. Finally she stuttered, "I'm not sure, but no higher than a 3."

I followed up with a second question, "On the same scale, how accepted do you feel by God?"

Her eyes rolled with the agony of her response, "Less than 2; not a 1, but less than 2." Now tears were streaming down her face.

I gently caught the glance of her eyes as I responded, "It's hard to feel intimate with someone you don't feel accepted by."

She began nodding with the agony of her revelation. Again, grabbing her attention, I reflected, "I don't think you've grasped how much God loves you and that nothing can separate you from the love of God" (see Rom. 8:39). In the ensuing moments, I elaborated on God's love, grace, and righteousness. I was privileged to witness a transformation of countenance that would rival the metamorphosis of a caterpillar becoming a butterfly. Assuredly, this was the very beginning stages of a radical transformation.

This story illustrates this key principle that how you see God determines how you experience God. If you see Him as someone who slaps you down at every misstep, that is how you will experience Him. If you see God as someone you can never measure up to, that is how you will experience Him. If you see God in His gift of righteousness (that you are in right standing with Him, not based on what you've done, but based on what He has done, and you receive it by faith, standing before Him without guilt, without fear, without inferiority, and without condemnation), that is how you will experience Him.

The woman in this story saw God through the lens of never being able to measure to His standard (or anyone else's for that matter), and she was constantly languishing with, "I know God can, I just don't know if He will...for me." Her faith was wrapped in a standard she could never keep, and she found herself feeling unqualified to receive anything. For her, God's power was received by human effort rather than through believing God. Her existence was about the changed life instead of the exchanged life (see Gal. 2:20-21). Her life was about trying rather than trusting.

However, as I was speaking to her and as the revelation of God's unconditional love settled into her life, her countenance began to lift. "This is the essence of Christianity," I reflected.

Almost dumbfounded, this lifetime member of the Body of Christ looked at me whimsically and said, "So, what is Christianity?"

What seemed like an innocent question captured my attention. The more I asked Christian leaders this question, the more I got answers about it being more about "relationship" than "religion" (though their answers sounded more like religion).

CHRISTIANITY IN CRISIS

I began putting reflections together with some research. One Sunday, I found myself awakened early in the morning. I went to my favorite "reading chair" to do some reading and praying before church. Quietly, in the background, I had the television tuned in to a ministry program. In an almost serendipitous moment, I found myself for no apparent reason captured by the speaker's words. He was using searing rhetoric to talk about the impact of Christianity upon culture. He railed,

> In the Traditionalist Generation (retirees) about 65 percent were Bible-based believers. In the Baby Boomer Generation (1946–1964), Bible-based believers slipped to 35 percent. In Generation "X" (1965–1979), the perspective has further slipped to 17 percent. Finally in Mosaics, the current teen and

20-something generation, the percentage of Bible-based believers came in around 4 percent. *We are in jeopardy of losing a generation to the message of Jesus Christ!*

Oddly enough, though I had heard those "stats" before, this time I felt enraged at the proposed loss. I rose to my feet in anger, grabbed the remote, and shut off the television. As I stood to my feet fuming at such a deception, I heard these words from God in my spirit, "I'm not going to lose a generation; I'm going to raise one up."

I knew God was dealing with me about ideas to reach a post-modern (some would say a post-Church) generation. Mosaics are called so because of their eclectic mindsets. Like "Xers" before them, they are called such because there are no defining characteristics to identify them and set them apart. They are looking to try something of everything, to find anything they can embrace. Look what was "in" for "Xers": long hair, short hair, no hair, dreadlocks, no locks, Maalox®...it was all "in." Similarly, music styles were all inclusive. Horror of horrors, even disco made a comeback. In clothing styles, everything was "in." Mosaics have pushed eclecticism to a new level. They've looked at the Church and have rejected its message of rules and regulations, embracing anything that offers them a real experience.

The Church is in a (unperceived in some corridors) crisis. Everyone from youth culture to Emergents, to the House Church Movement, to certain Revivalists are all echoing that the modern Church isn't working. The real question is, *why?* Why the decrease in Bible-based believers from generation to generation? Why is 60 percent of America unchurched?[1] (Not to mention, there are those who are in church, but are not fully convinced of the efficacy of Christ's sacrifice.)

In many corridors of the Church, a generation peers in and sees that it looks like God's people all got baptized in pickle juice. The

Church has a big ole scowl on her face and says, "Do you want what I have?" There's a generation responding, "No thanks! I have enough problems of my own, and at least I don't have to obey all the rules and regulations."

The most radical message in the world has been reduced to religion. This generation perceives the Church as a religion steeped in legalism. *Legalism* is a system in which people, by their own efforts, attempt to earn the approval of God. It promotes the belief, "I have to keep enough rules and regulations to be right with God and to be blessed by Him." It has spawned a Church that has taken a simple message and made it complicated. We've submitted to a religion of trying to be right with God by a standard we can't keep in our own ability, and we have found ourselves feeling frustrated and unqualified to receive anything from our loving God.

We often find ourselves languishing in the chasm between what we say we believe and what we actually see. We have deviated from the organic message and have added something to it. It has become a Gospel that Paul calls really no Gospel at all (see Gal. 1:6-9). We have mistakenly misaligned the Gospel into the belief that God's power for life is received by right doing rather than by right believing. (Right doing, by the way, is always preceded by right believing.)

Christianity has subtly become a religion of what one author calls "meritocracy."[2] *Meritocracy* is a religion where right relationship with God is based on our merits. Organic Christianity, however, is a faith based on unmerited favor. We don't deserve it, and we can't earn it. It is an unmerited favor that leads to an experiential intimacy with God. Out of that intimacy is an empowerment to find the life we were born to live. Organic Christianity is more about the exchanged life than the changed life (see Gal. 2:20).

HOW'S THAT WORKIN' FOR YA'?

The Mosaic generation is steeped in postmodernism (relativism: there are no real absolute truths). They see an unproductive Church (in many respects) on one hand, and a set of rules and regulations (legalism) that they can't keep on the other. They feel a desire to make their lives count, but the Church is unwittingly making them feel unqualified to do so.

One day a successful, well-to-do young believer made his way into my office. Like the rich young ruler, he blasted, "I have kept all the commandments [laws, rules], yet I don't have a sense God is pleased with me." (See Matthew 19:16-22.)

Somehow I felt like I was in a Dr. Phil conference so I cracked, "How's that workin' for ya'?"

He mused, "I still feel unfulfilled, despite all my efforts."

He was struggling in his family, and the productivity of his ministry was muted. I simply said, "You've exchanged the organic Gospel for another Gospel. You've substituted *Jesus* for *Jesus plus the law*. Remember, Jesus + nothing = everything."

As I began to share about intimacy with God, love, and grace, I watched an extraordinary thing take place. In an "aha" moment, I watched as he had an epiphany! He had put himself, the recipients of his ministry, and his family under a standard they could never fulfill in themselves. Despite all his efforts, he felt alienated from God and wondered whether he was worthy to receive blessings from God.

What all these scenarios have in common is an undercurrent of frustration—the frustration of knowing God can, but wondering, *Will He...for me?* It is the frustration of trying to work the Word instead of letting the Word work in them. It is the frustration of knowing the extraordinarily abundant life Christ promises, yet seeing the gulf that exists between them and Kingdom reality.

Hunger is rising in people's hearts for the kind of Christianity that replaces this frustration and its resulting apathy with the ecstasy and extraordinarily abundant life the Scripture promises. The question becomes, what is the reason for the "disconnect" among both Christians and non-Christians with the Christian faith? It is the difference between Christianity and organic Christianity.

WHAT IS CHRISTIANITY?

Now I come full circle back to my conversation with the Midwestern woman at the start of the chapter. What is Christianity? Perhaps the better question is: What is organic Christianity? What is Christianity in its original state or plan? Culture has made it clear (so has the Church) that they don't want a Christianity, no matter how true it is, that they can't get to work. So what is organic Christianity? What makes our faith authentic and productive?

1. **Organic Christianity is not so much about the *changed* life as it is the *exchanged* life** (see Gal. 2:20-21). The more we make Christianity about *change* rather than exchange, the more we retard the Body of Christ. Change is about our effort to be right with God through our own efforts; exchange is about transformation that comes from the inside. Change comes from the outside-in; exchange comes from the inside-out. Organic Christianity is about God living His life through us (see Gal. 2:20; 1 John 4:9).

2. **Organic Christianity is not as much about living *for* God as living *through* Him.** It certainly is important to live *for* Him (see Gal. 2:16), but it is far more important to live *through* Him (see 1 John 4:9; Gal. 2:20). Living for Him accentuates our efforts, while living through Him is a divine surrender to His power to move *to* and *through* our lives (see Eph. 3:20).

3. **Organic Christianity is not so much about forgiveness of sins as it is about intimacy with God.** John 17:3 says it like this:

"Now this is eternal life: that they [the disciples] *may know You, the only true God, and Jesus Christ...."* The term *know* used here means to know experientially or intimately.[3] Forgiveness of sin is simply necessary to have intimacy with God. Intimacy with God, not forgiveness of sin, is our chief aim. If we simply communicate that we sin and we get forgiveness, we'll never have intimacy with God. Such people lack confidence to apply God's laws of productivity. I would never minimize or marginalize forgiveness of sin, but it is important to accentuate what is primary. This understanding is what helps people to be delivered from the mentality, "I know God can, but I don't know if He will...for me."

4. **Organic Christianity is not as much about the *do* as it is about the *done*** (see Eph. 2:8-9). Sometimes we spin our wheels trying to get God to do what He has already done. God has already blessed us with every spiritual (supernatural)[4] blessing (benefit, endowment, empowerment to prosper)[5] in the heavenly realm (Kingdom of Heaven). God has (past tense) given us everything we need for life and godliness (see 2 Pet. 1:3). How? By grace, unmerited by us, He placed every provision for life in His Kingdom for us to access by faith. We don't have to get Him to do what He has already done, but access what He did by grace through faith in our lives (see Eph. 2:8-9).

5. **Organic Christianity is not so much about *achieving*, as it is about *receiving*** (see 2 Pet. 1:3; Eph. 1:3). We labor to enter into His rest (see Heb. 4:10-11). Since His finished work has provided every spiritual blessing in His Kingdom, we rest in His finished work (see John 19:30). That doesn't mean we rest from work, but that we rest in our work. We don't work to earn God's blessing; we work because we are blessed.

6. **Organic Christianity is about the *Gospel*.** The term *Gospel,* according to one scholar, means "the too good to be true

news."[6] It is the goodness of God that leads people to repentance (see Rom. 2:4).

7. **Organic Christianity is not about going** *to* **victory, but coming** *from* **victory** (see Col. 2:15). This simple understanding changes believers' perspectives on how they deal with life. I'm not trying to defeat the devil; Jesus has already done that (see Col. 2:14-15). It's simply my job to learn what I possess and live accordingly.

8. **Organic Christianity is not about rules and regulations, but about the** *grace* **to live them.** John 1:16-17 says it this way, *"And of His* [Jesus] *fullness we have all received, and grace for grace. For the law was given through Moses, but grace and truth came through Jesus Christ"* (NKJV). Organic Christianity is not simply about the rules, but about the ability to keep them (their provision and fulfillment). God's grace is His empowerment to access the fullness of His Son in our lives. This is the key to going from ordinary to extraordinary. This is the key to His abundance. Here is God's provision for true authenticity and productivity.

9. **Organic Christianity is about being a** *new species* **of being.** Second Corinthians 5:17 tells us in the Greek, "If any man be in Christ, he is a new species of being."[7] When people get saved or born again, they don't simply become Christians, or better people; they become a whole new species of being. What they once were no longer exists. The key is not trying to simply be better, but renewing our minds to what we've become.

10. **Organic Christianity is not so much about** *eternal life* **as it is about** *intimacy with God* (see John 17:3). One day I had a student ask me, "What is eternal life?"

I answered by asking, "What do you think it is?"

He said, "Living forever!"

I replied, "No, everyone lives forever, it just depends on where." As Jesus prayed, *"Now this is eternal life: that they may know You, the only true God, and Jesus Christ, whom You have sent"* (John 17:3). The word *know,* as previously noted, is the term for intimacy. Eternal life is intimacy with God. It just happens to last forever. Here's the question: Would you still live for God if there was no Heaven? If you are hesitant, or if the answer is no, you've missed part of the essence of the Gospel. Having said that, I thank God for Heaven!

What is organic Christianity? It is when people become a new species of being in Christ that brings intimacy with God in a way that allows them to experience and communicate the Kingdom of God out of the overflow of their lives. These people are free and truly alive. Few people can reject something so extraordinary.

MODERN JUDAIZERS

The establishment of organic Christianity is Paul's concern in the Books of Romans and Galatians. He is concerned that certain sects (in this case, Judaizers[8]) were perverting the true essence of organic Christianity. In Galatians 1:6-9, Paul addresses this concern:

> *I am astonished that you are so quickly deserting the one who called you by the grace of Jesus Christ and are turning to a different gospel—which is really no gospel at all. Evidently some people are throwing you into confusion and are trying to pervert the gospel of Christ. But, even if we or an angel from heaven should preach a gospel other than the one we preached to you, let him be eternally condemned! As we have already said, so now I say again: If anybody is preaching to you a gospel other than what you accepted, let him be eternally condemned!*

This is more than a bad hair day with Paul. He is angry! Judaizers (Jewish converts who believed people had not only to accept Christ, but also to keep the law to be right with God and to be blessed by Him) had added to the organic Gospel and had made it other than what it was originally intended to be. Notice that Paul says, "You have deserted the one who called you by the grace of Christ and are turning to a different Gospel." A different Gospel than what? It is different from the grace of Christ! The grace of Christ is the organic Gospel of organic Christianity. People (Judaizers) were trying to throw Galatia and the Church into confusion. Judaizers were trying to get the Galatian Christians to go back to the old covenant (that salvation and right standing with God comes from obeying the law). Organic Christianity was, and is, the grace of Christ. Unquestionably, Paul uses the terms *grace* and *gospel* in this passage interchangeably. (See Galatians 1:6; Acts 20:24.) Paul bellows that these people (Judaizers) who proclaim this law-based Gospel should be eternally condemned.

Well, "Step on my blue suede shoes!" Why would he say such a thing? It is because the organic Christianity of the new covenant is grace, not law (see Rom. 6:14). By subjecting people to legalism, Judaizers were excavating the life and freedom from the Gospel for rules and regulations (see Gal. 5:1). Paul realized legalists were subjecting or perverting (twisting, changing, distorting[9]) the Gospel to a different (of another kind[10]) gospel. Paul is stating that by perverting the organic Gospel they were putting people under the old covenant and, therefore, nullifyin g the sacrifice of the shedding of Christ's blood as the *only way* to be right with God. Paul knew that if Christianity was reduced to rules and regulations, people would flounder with feelings of inadequacy and unworthiness for the blessings of God's Kingdom—just like the woman in the Midwestern city. They would always be languishing in the rubble of not feeling like they've done enough to be blessed by God. Paul is dealing with the issue that, if believers are accepted by God based on their performance rather than Jesus' sacrifice, they will always feel unqualified to receive from God.

Paul knew that Judaizers sought to reduce the Gospel to right doing rather than right believing (though right believing will always precede right doing; every action is predicated upon and preceded by a thought). He knew people could never match God's standard of perfection. James says it this way, *"For whoever keeps the whole law and yet stumbles at just one point is guilty of breaking all of it"* (James 2:10). Galatians 3:10 states,

> *All who rely on observing the law are under a curse, for it is written: "Cursed is everyone who does not continue to do everything written in the Book of the Law."*

We can't, therefore, be right with God based on our own performance, so He sent His Son to do it on our behalf, and we receive His work by faith. In so doing, He brought a freedom to access His Kingdom and to be fully alive (see Eph. 2:8-9; Matt. 7:13-14). Judaizers (and modern Judaizers) took the most radical message of all time and reduced it to religion.

A GOSPEL REVOLUTION

This is why Paul initiates the Book of Romans with:

> *For I am not ashamed of the gospel of Christ* [same phrase as Galatians 1]: *for it is the power of God unto salvation to everyone that believeth; to the Jew first, and also to the Greek. For therein is the righteousness of God revealed from faith to faith: as it is written, The just* [righteous] *shall live by faith* (Romans 1:16-17 KJV).

Many believers who embrace Christianity have never truly heard the organic Gospel. They believe that Christianity is nothing but a different set of rules and regulations, substituting Christian do's and don'ts for those of other religions. They continue to believe they must earn their way to God and the blessings of His Kingdom.

As I mentioned previously, the term *gospel* used in this passage, according to one scholar, means more than just good news. It means the "too good to be true news."[11] The Jews of the time had been raised under a works-oriented, performance-based, judgmental religious system.[12] This time of the early Church was characterized by persecuting those who preached the organic Gospel. Why? The Gospel—salvation by grace through faith (see Eph. 2:8-9)—was just too good to be true.[13]

This was the journey of Paul's life: "I must finish my course to testify to the Gospel of the grace of God" (see Acts 20:24). His quest was to testify of the good news of God's grace. Again, *gospel* and *grace* are used interchangeably.

THE NEW REFORMATION

I believe there is coming to the Church a new reformation, a re-forming back to its original state. Here's what I mean. About two and a half years ago (from this writing), I was doing a meeting in the Chicago area on revival. I was one of the speakers, along with Tommy Tenney, the vice president of Morris Cerullo Ministries, and one of the leaders from the Brownsville Revival. There was a gathering during the event of the conference speakers. The host pastor looked at me and said, "Ron, you've written a best-seller on revival. What do you think the next revival will look like?"

I glanced across the room at my pastor friend and said, "I'm not sure I'm looking for a revival. I'm looking more for a reformation."

Inquisitively, he looked at me and asked, "What's the difference?"

"For me the difference is, somehow we've taken the most radical message in the world and reduced it to religion. We've made it into rules and regulations that merely define good and bad instead of living an energetic relationship with a living God that breeds life. We've turned the too-good-to-be-true news into a formula, trying to be good enough to earn God's blessing. We need a revelation of what we already possess." The concept of *revival* indicates, after a period of unbelief and unfaithfulness, there is a period of restoration. We see that in several instances of the old covenant. In the new covenant it is more an idea of revelation. It is what Paul calls for in Ephesians 1:17, "*I keep asking that the God of our Lord Jesus Christ, the glorious Father, may give you the Spirit of wisdom and revelation, so that you may know Him better.*" What revelation does He want us to know? Who God is, what He has already done, and who He has made us to be (our identity in Christ). Revelation is a disclosure of what already exists. He wants us to know what is already ours.

Often people who talk about revival are trying to get God to do something new or trying to get Him to do what He used to do. Revelation is a disclosure of what He has already done (see Eph. 1:3), and we need to understand it and reclaim it by faith. A revival is temporary; revelation is a permanent fact we can always tap into. Look what Paul adds in verses 18-19, "*I pray also that the eyes of your heart may be enlightened in order that you may know the hope* [anticipation] *to which He has called you, the riches of His glorious inheritance in the saints and His incomparably great power for us who believe....*" We simply need to re-form our thinking to what God has already done.

Several of us began interacting on the concept of reformation. The new reformation, or a return to organic Christianity, would be just that—a re-formation. It would be a reforming back to the original intention—with nothing added to it. It would be a reclamation, a reclaiming of the Gospel at its organic roots.

Before we talk about the new reformation, maybe we should examine the original reformation(s). I believe there were three reformations, two biblical and one historical. The first reformation came through Jesus. John 1:17 says, *"For the law was given through Moses; grace and truth came through Jesus Christ."* Moses brought the law. This move from God was a parenthesis in history until the Seed (Jesus) re-formed law to God's original intent, the promise of grace. Galatians tells this in clear narration (see Gal. 3:3-25). The writer states, *"Are you so foolish? After beginning with the Spirit, are you now trying to attain your goal through human effort* [performance to please God]*"* (Gal. 3:3). He amplifies a few verses later, *"All who rely on observing the law* [human effort, performance] *are under a curse..."* (Gal. 3:10). In this verse, Paul is confirming Deuteronomy 27:26, *"Cursed* [to bring evil or injury[14]] *be he that confirmeth not all the words of this law to do them..."* (KJV).

In other words, those who trust in their own efforts to keep the law to earn God's blessing must keep every aspect of it in order to do so (see James 2:10). Paul then adds, *"Clearly no one is justified* [made righteous[15]] *before God by the law* [human effort to obey it]*..."* (Gal. 3:11). He concludes (I suggest you read all of Galatians to get the full impact) in verse 19 by saying, *"What, then, was the purpose of the law? It was added* [as a parenthesis] *because of transgressions until the Seed* [Jesus, see verse 16]*...had come...."* The law was a parenthesis until God's original intent, which was the covenant of the promise through grace, was re-established (see Gal. 3:19-25).[16]

The second reformation came through Paul. The Pauline epistles (as well as other New Testament works) were primarily written to correct misconceptions and improper additions to the organic message. Romans, Galatians, Ephesians, and Hebrews deal with the false doctrine of the Judaizers, people who tried to say the Gospel of salvation was Jesus + the law. They believed people not only had to receive Jesus, but also perform the law to be right with God. Other writers, such as Jude and John, in their epistles deal with Gnostics or Antinomians, many of whom believed in a dualism of spirit and flesh. Some even believed that what was done in the physical didn't count and did not constitute sin. It was a license to sin or to embrace lawlessness (see Jude 4; 1 John 1:8-9). Their false notions promoted lifestyles inappropriate to the Gospel and a true righteous lifestyle. Many of the efforts of the writers of the epistles were attempting to get back to the organic message.

The third reformation was a historical event attached to Martin Luther in 1517. The Catholic Church of the era promoted the idea that believers had to have a certain lifestyle to be right with God. In the 1500s, it was primarily the belief that people had to buy indulgences (the purchasing of full or partial remission of temporal punishment due to people's sins) from the church so God would forgive them. Luther was a tormented monk and scholar who felt he could never measure up to the church's (and God's) standards. Thus, he spent his life in condemnation, feeling unqualified to receive from God. In studying the Scriptures one day, he discovered justification by faith in the Book of Romans. He realized he could be right with God by faith in Jesus' finished work, not some adherence to the law. The result was the tacking of the 95 Theses on a Wittenberg church door and the birth of the Protestant Church. The far-reaching effect of the Protestant Reformation is hard to measure in its full impact for believers today. The impact of revival pales in comparison to a reformation.

Here is the core of the new reformation. The Church is fighting modern Judaizers and Gnostics that Paul tried to obliterate in his day. Today there are religious philosophies that unwittingly are trying to alter the Scripture's organic message. They extend grace to unbelievers to be saved, but once someone is born again, they tell them they must adhere to the law to be right with God. The basic tenets of Luther are still at play today. Here are the basic tenets of Luther's Reformation:

Sola Christus ("Christ alone")—It is only through the work of Jesus Christ that people may be saved. Postmodern philosophies have moved culture to a modern relativism (truth is relative to our situations). The result is salvation is procured through many sources. Many Christians mix truths from various religions, philosophies, and science and create their own unique personal religion.

Sola Scriptura ("Scripture alone")—Scripture is the final authority for salvation and sanctification. Postmodernists and Christian postmodernists have adopted eclectic sources of inspiration of truth. Relativism is pervading much of culture. The philosophy of "that might be true for you, but it's not true for me" is becoming increasingly predominant in culture. While I agree that truth can come from a variety of sources, it is necessary to create a Christian worldview of truth. What is truth? My definition of truth is conformity to the original pattern.[17] What is that original pattern for believers? *"Sanctify them by the truth; Your word is truth"* (John 17:17). Our truth cannot be real truth if it violates the original pattern. At such times, our truth is not truth.

Sola gratia ("grace alone")—Salvation comes by grace alone; it is not by works. It is not by performance or good deeds, but solely by unmerited favor of God through faith. Today, there is an emergence and a combating of grace. The debate between law (works or performance) and grace (unmerited favor) has raged for years. It's time again for a re-formation of balanced truth.

Sola fide ("faith alone")—People, through one act of believing in what God did by grace, can be justified in the sight of God for all time. Justification is by faith in God's grace. Faith is the act by which we, as believers, access what God did by grace in salvation and a place in His Kingdom unmerited by us (see Eph. 2:8-9).

Sola de Gloria ("the glory of God alone")—All things are to live and move and have their being to glorify God. It is time to stop building our own kingdoms and major on building His Kingdom.

REFORMING THE REFORMATION

Now, in lieu of these three reformations, what does a new reformation look like? This new reformation, or a return to organic Christianity, would have these basic tenets:

1. **It will be a movement of people, not just a person** (see Eph. 4:11-12). Today we live in the shadows of people who are on television, are on the covers of magazines, or are the authors of books. Although all of those endeavors are acceptable pursuits, it often leaves people with the impression that they have to get to "the person of God" to receive a touch from God. Massive healing crusades were tremendous moves of God, but often led people to think they had to get to the crusades to receive a touch from God. The 1950s healing crusades indelibly etched this image into the hearts of the Church.

In organic Christianity or this new reformation, the move of God will not simply be at the hand of a person, but all of God's people. There will always be key leaders, but their job is to equip the people to do the work of ministry (see Eph. 4:11-12). It was God's intent from the beginning for every believer to do the work of the Kingdom (see Mark 16:17-18). In this new reformation, God's people will have their identity in who they are in Christ. They will understand that when they became a new creation, God put within them, by grace, what was necessary to succeed for His Kingdom (see 2 Cor. 5:17; Eph. 1:3; 3:20; Philem. 6; Gal. 2:20; 1 John 4:9; 2 Pet. 1:3; Col. 2:10).

2. **God's people will have an intimacy with God through His incomprehensible grace.** People who try to earn God's blessing by performance feel as though they never measure up; they never feel intimate with God. The unmerited favor of grace allows people to come to the arms of a loving God (see Rom. 8:38-39). For many people, this thought throws up apprehension about a "license to sin." You'll find none of that here. Every problem in life is predicated by sin—yours,

Adam's, or someone else's. Indeed, Paul had to answer this allegation over and over again (see Rom. 3:8; 6:1,15; 1 Cor. 15:34,58b; Gal. 5:1,13). Let me say it categorically and clearly, grace *is not* license to sin (see Jude 4). In fact, it is the power over sin. Romans 6:14 says, *"For sin shall not be your master, because you are not under law, but under grace."*

That power is released out of an intimacy with God, and the law kept people from such a relationship. The unmerited favor of God promotes an intimacy that releases another side of God's manifold (multi-sided) grace (see 1 Pet. 4:10). It is the empowerment or ability of God. Indeed, the way we reign in life is through grace and righteousness (see Rom. 5:17). In the new reformation, individuals will understand that what they felt unworthy to receive, God has made available through grace, unmerited by their efforts, and that they receive it through faith. Believers are made righteous, holy, and free through what Christ did at Calvary, and they receive it by faith (see 1 Cor. 1:30). They are free to find an intimacy with God that heretofore eluded them.

3. **The new reformation will help believers discover their identity in Christ.** I define *identity* as knowing who God is, what He has already done, and who He has made us to be. First, new reformation believers won't simply know about God; they will have intimacy with God. Second, they will understand what God has already done. Ephesians 1:3 and First Peter 1:3 help us understand what He has done through the finished work at Calvary (see John 19:30). Ephesians 1:3 tells us that God's grace purchased every spiritual ("supernatural"[18]) blessing ("to bestow generosity of prosperity of a government"[19]) in the heavenly realm (God's Kingdom).

We often spend our time trying to get God to do what He has already done instead of receiving what He did by grace through faith. Third, we simply don't understand who we really are. In the next move, true intimacy with God will open our eyes to the fact that we are a new species of being (see 2 Cor. 5:17) and that God has put everything in us to be successful in life and in His Kingdom (see Gal. 2:16-20; Eph. 1:3; 3:16-20; Philem. 1:6; 2 Pet. 1:3).

4. **The upcoming reformation will help us "tweak" a definition of faith.** While what we have understood about faith is correct and valuable, we will add grace to the understanding of faith. It will not be faith in our faith, but faith in God's grace (His finished work).

5. **Lastly, this forthcoming reformation will have a more complete understanding of His Kingdom.** The Kingdom of Heaven is certainly the rule and reign of God, but it is also the location and resources of God. We can rest from working to gain blessing because God has provided everything we need for success in life and success for Him in His Kingdom (see Matt. 6:33).

CLAIMING THE NEW REFORMATION

This book is an invitation to find the life you were born to live. It is a call to shake free from the shackles of religion and claim the extraordinary life you were destined to possess. Countless believers are caught in the trap of feeling they don't measure up or qualify (see Colossians 1:12 to know you are qualified in Christ) for the blessings of the Kingdom. Multitudes of Christians are searching for a limitless Gospel, only to be confronted by the limitations of their lives. Numbers of believers are searching for "the more" (see Eph. 3:20) of the Gospel, knowing inwardly they are stumbling in mediocrity. They know they were made for victory, but they feel enslaved to things that are contrary to their convictions. People long for the intimacy with God that the Gospel promises, yet they feel estranged from Him due to their sense of inadequate performance.

In this postmodern eclectic age of beliefs, people are looking for a real Christian worldview that is both authentic (real) and productive (that works). What we need to know is that this is not simply a call to do what we've always done, or to just try harder. Indeed, the definition of insanity is to do the same thing over and over and expect different results. This is recognition that we have lost some of the essence of the organic message. It is discernment that perhaps, by adding to its original intent, we've lost some of the freedom in life that is Christianity (see Gal. 5:1). We must acknowledge that we've lost something of the essence to feel fully alive. We've lost sight that, like in the story of the prodigal son (see Luke 15:11-32), Daddy God is running to greet us with a ring (signet ring of family authority), a robe (a sign of nobility), shoes (slaves went barefoot, but not sons), and a fatted calf (a designation of abundant provision). Here's Daddy God with an unconditional love showing us how to live a life that is more wonderful than George Bailey (*It's a Wonderful Life*) could ever imagine.

People seem indelibly etched with the need to add their "do" to God's "done." In doing so, they risk missing the essence of the Gospel, which is more about intimacy with God than forgiveness of sins. The organic message is more about living *through* Him, than living *for* Him. Once we re-form the essence of His message a people (not simply a person) will arise without hesitation to take the beauty of the Gospel to a hurt and dying world (at every level). The message of *Organic Christianity* is the manifestation of God's Kingdom *to* you and *through* you. Let's look at it:

• •

ORGANIC THOUGHTS

1. Have you grasped how much God loves you? (See Romans 8:39.)

2. How you see God determines how you will experience Him. How do you see God?

3. Do you ever find yourself languishing through the lens, "I know God can, I just don't know if He will...for me?"

4. Examine your life for a moment. Do you think God blesses you based on your performance?

5. Have you ever wondered that church concepts are not working for you?

6. Has the Christian life been reduced to rules and regulations for you?

7. Is legalism (attempting by your efforts to earn God's approval) at work in your life?

8. Examine Galatians 1:6-9. Is there another conclusion you can reach other than "the Gospel is grace"?

9. Are you working the Word or letting the Word work in you?

10. Have you exchanged the organic Gospel for a Gospel of another kind?

11. Examine the ten conclusions of what is Christianity. Could the Church be in jeopardy of misconstruing the Gospel?

12. Are modern Judaizers reducing the impact of the Gospel?

13. Is your life about right doing or about right believing?

14. Do you think God could be bringing a reformation or reclamation to His Church?

15. What is your reflection on the five tenets of the new reformation?

Chapter 2

· · · · · · · · · · · · · · · · · · · ·

THE DEFINITION
OF INSANITY

f we listen carefully, we can hear the echoes from the corridors of the Church from leaders looking for new direction for the full manifestation of God's Kingdom. I have used a definition for *insanity* for many years that has become common. *Insanity is doing the same over and over again and expecting different results.* In some ways, the Church thing has become a little insane. We are in jeopardy of losing a generation, yet, we have reduced our thinking to, "If we just do what we've already done a little harder, we'll get something different than what we already have." If we want to see something we've never seen before, we have to do something we've never done before. Our message doesn't change, but we must reclaim its organic status and move forward in new methods of expression. This is a call to a new movement.

God is moving us to the kind of Christianity that replaces apathy with ecstasy and enthusiasm. Organic Christianity replaces the ordinary with the extraordinary. This is not "Burger King® Theology" that allows us to do it our way, but a call to reclaim the heart of an organic Gospel. We can't do what one of my friends says and "get stuck on stupid." The problem is that, according to one researcher, nine out of ten (88 percent) of Christian youth fall away from Christianity during the transition from high school to college.[1] If we're not careful, we become paralyzed by the ordinary. Today our Christianity legitimizes the ordinary when God made us to live the extraordinary (see John 10:10). We need a paradigm shift in the Church. A *paradigm shift* means a radical shift from one way of thinking to another. It's time to go beyond what is ordinary and normal and step into what exceeds the common measure. God made us for abundance and productivity.

Here's what I mean. Recently, I was doing a television program in Pittsburgh. The host greeted me in the "Green Room" before going "on the air." He began with what seemed like some legitimate excitement, "I just read your book, *The Greatest Secret*, and I loved it. I just wanted to ask you before we head to the set, 'What do you think are the next trends to touch and reach our culture right now?"

Almost without hesitation I responded, "Well, I see two dominant trends. The first comes out of a recent interaction I had with my middle son, who is a Youth Director at a church in Tulsa. He came over to the house for Sunday brunch after church, and I asked him simply, 'How was church this morning?'

"His response was noteworthy and took me a little off guard. He said, 'Dad, it was authentic! How was church for you?'

"I pondered for a second. I didn't know if I should say inauthentic (almost laughing at my lack of grasping a new vernacular), and I simply said, 'It was great!' We continued interacting about the details of our summary words, but later I was taken by his response. What he was saying was, 'Dad, it was real.' People want a Gospel that is genuine and pure.

"The second thought I have," I continued, "comes from a recent network marketing meeting where I was a guest speaker. The people there wanted something that worked, something that made them productive. The two trends I see right now are authenticity and productivity."

It's true that people are crying for something genuine, not mere religion, and they want something that works. No one really wants a Christianity, no matter how true it is, that they can't get to legitimately work for their lives. Mosaics (the current youth generation) may be eclectic in their beliefs, but they want to experience God, and they want to make their lives count.[2] They are bored with religion and rules, and they want a genuine encounter with a living God. They are willing to give themselves to something they can truly believe in. *Authentic* indicates something beyond a narcissistic, self-indulgent, materialistic Gospel that is often associated with the modern Church. Mosaics long for a cause that is genuine and Kingdom-focused. This quest makes Christ pre-eminent, not just our needs (see Matt. 6:33). Needs being met are a by-product, not the focus.

At the same time, our Gospel needs to be productive. As one author aptly states, "Our culture screams at us, 'productivity!'"[3] *Productivity* suggests we can bring into view our vision in order to bring forth beliefs to give rise to our dreams (and more importantly, God's dreams).[4] After all, we're blessed to be a blessing (see Gen. 12:2-3). Obviously, it is difficult to bless others without first being blessed in our own lives. If we are busy trying to survive, it's hard to thrive or to revive others with God's Kingdom. The dynamics of these concepts are difficult, but they are a necessary road for us to learn to navigate.

The problem is that so many believers struggle with a sense of feeling unqualified or disqualified to be used by God or to be blessed by Him. They know their performance doesn't always meet God's standards (don't think for a moment this statement condones sin or shortcoming—much more on how all this works later). So, they either judge each other by themselves (I'm not as bad as they are, or at least I'm not committing the "big" sins), or they languish in condemnation, disqualifying themselves from blessings or their destiny. However, we must understand that God doesn't bless good people, but those who believe (ultimately those who truly believe Him become good people). Obviously, it is not our "right doing" He blesses, but our right believing, which, by the way, produces right doing.

Sometimes in the Church we get caught up in "spiritual dyslexia." People with dyslexia see things backwards. So, instead of seeing "God," they see, "dog." Right doing that is not based on right believing is temporary at best. Remember, every action is preceded by a thought. We can't have an action without a belief or thought first. Believing is the root; action is the fruit. We have to have the former to have the latter. Organic Christianity is not behavior modification (change), but a transformation. Change comes from the outside-in; transformation comes from the inside-out. This is part of the reformation of organic Christianity.

God is about to bring a new reformation to His Church. It is a reformation that is a movement that breaks the shackles of the mere rules and regulations of religion for the pure manifestation of the Gospel. It is a Gospel of intimacy with God and real productivity from God. This is not "sloppy agape," "believe- ism," "cheap grace," or "license to sin." This is the finished work of Jesus granted to His people by grace, unmerited by them (see John 19:30). What grace has granted, we receive by faith, and it grants us the ability or empowerment (the other side of grace) to live victoriously. It's about taking what we believe and being able to see it manifested.

PRODUCTIVITY: MANIFESTING WHAT WE BELIEVE

How do we get what we believe to manifest? How do we go from where we are to where we want to be (and more importantly, to where

God wants us to be)? The fact is, everyone manifests! We either manifest scarcity or abundance, but we all manifest. The term *manifest* comes from the Latin term, *manus*, which means to make visible. Metaphorically, it gives the idea of reaching through the invisible curtain, separating the tangible from imagination, and then pulling the desired object into existence.[5]

One of the questions that organic Christianity seeks to answer is, "How do we close the gap between what we say we believe and what we actually see?" How do we take beliefs or ideas and manifest them? Organic Christianity is a call to understand the Gospel with nothing added to it. It is here that God manifests His Kingdom to His people.

There are five elements that I call the manifestation model. This is the key to going from the ordinary to extraordinary living. This is part of the new wineskin for new covenant believers (see Matt. 9:17). An old wineskin was old and brittle. When new wine was put into it, the wine would expand, and it would burst out of the old brittle wineskin. Thus, both were lost. The organic message of the new covenant cannot be contained in an old covenant wineskin. The law (old covenant) tried to fulfill and attain God's Kingdom through human effort to live for Him (see Gal. 3:3). The new wineskin (the new covenant) is God living His life and ability through humanity by faith in His grace (see Gal. 3:5-17; 1 John 4:9). Here's a synopsis of how the organic Gospel brings the manifestation of God's Kingdom:

MANIFESTATION MODEL

GRACE
- Unmerited favor
- God's ability
- Divine influence upon the heart

THE FINISHED WORK OF CHRIST
John 19:30, Gal. 2:20, 2 Pet. 1:1-11, Eph. 1:2ff

THE EXCHANGED LIFE NOT CHANGED BUT EXCHANGED
Gal. 2:20-21

IDENTITY
James 1:22

RIGHTEOUSNESS
Rom. 3:20ff, Rom. 4:3-13, 2 Cor. 5:21, 1 John 1:8, Rom. 5:17-19, Ps. 112:3,6-8, Rom. 6:1,14, 1 Cor. 15:34, Matt. 6:33, Matt. 5:6, Ps. 34:19, Ps. 37:1-6, Phil. 3:7-12

QUALIFIED
Col. 1:12-13,21-23; 2:6ff

CONFIDENCE
Deals with image

TRUTH
John 17:17, Eph. 6:14, John 8:31ff, John 3:21, John 4:23, John 14:6, John 16:7, Rom. 1:29, 1 Tim. 2:4, James 1:22

RENEWING THE MIND
Rom. 12:2, Eph. 4:23, Eph. 5:17, Col. 3:1-2, Col. 3:10, Ps. 1:1-2, Josh. 1:8, Deut. 11:18ff

ESTABLISHING THE HEART
Prov. 23:7, Prov. 4:20-23, Heb. 4:12, Prov. 7:1-3, Prov. 3:1-6, 2 Cor. 3:3ff, Jer. 31:3ff, Heb. 6:26-27, Matt. 12:34-35, Matt. 13

FAITH (BELIEVING THE TRUTH)
Rom. 12:3, Eph. 2:8-9, 2 Pet. l:l, Rom. 10:17, James 1:22, Heb. 10:32, 6:12, Heb. 11:1-6, Mark 11:24

CORRESPONDING ACTIONS
James 1:20-24, James 2:14, Matt. 7:26-27, Josh. l:8

FAITH IN GRACE NOT FAITH IN FAITH
Eph. 2:8-9

IMAGE/HUMILITY
Gen. 1:26, John 1:14-17, 2 Cor. 3:18, James 1:21-24, Rom. 8:29, 1 Cor. 15:49, 2 Cor. 4:4, Col. 1:27

GRACE: GOD'S ABILITY
Rom. 6:14-16, Heb. 12:14, Gal. 2:20-21, Rom. 5:1,17, 2 Cor. 12:7, Heb. 4:14-16

GOD'S INFLUENCE ON THE HEART
John 1:14-17, James 4:6-7, John 14:12, Rom. 6:14-15, Rom. 5:20

ENABLEMENT
Phil. 2:13, Eph. 3:20, Phil. 4:13, Rom. 5:17, Rom. 6:4

RECEIVING

Let me illustrate this before I explain it. One of my favorite stories comes out of Andy Andrews' book called, *The Traveler's Gift*. In this book, the chief character, David Ponder is an executive at a Fortune 500 company. The company is bought out by another company, and David's job is eliminated. His life begins to spiral downward. At the age of 50, he has difficulty finding a job. Since he can't find work, he eventually loses his house, car, money, and everything materially important to him. The crisis reaches a zenith when his daughter becomes sick and needs an operation that he cannot afford. Realizing he is losing all that is important to him, he contemplates suicide. He tries to call out to God, but in desperation he thinks, "I can't even pray." He contemplates further options and ponders the fact that he no longer has a purpose. Ultimately he rationalizes, "Everyone would be better off without me."

Without further conscious thought, he accelerates his automobile toward a tree and his ultimate demise. Gripping his steering wheel and racing toward his doom, he is somehow mysteriously transported back in time. In the past, he meets six or seven different people who expose the real secrets to success in life. He meets President Truman, King Solomon, Christopher Columbus, and others. The last person he meets is the archangel Gabriel. Gabriel gives him a tour of Heaven. There he sees rooms filled with money, some with inventions not yet experienced, even some with cures for diseases. There were rooms with photographs of children and stacks of food. Dazed by what he was seeing and confused by its meaning, he looks at the angel and asks, "Why am I here?"

Finally, the angel answers his question by asking another question, "In despair, why does one person take his life, while another is moved to greatness?"[6]

Reeling in confusion, David responds, "I don't know."

The angel responds, "Circumstances are rulers of the weak...but they are weapons of the wise. Circumstances do not push or pull.

They are daily lessons to be studied and gleaned for new knowledge and wisdom."[7]

Struggling to understand the panorama of his sight, he cries out, "What is this place?" Gabriel responds, "This, my friend is the place that never was....This is the place where we keep all the things about to be delivered just as the people stopped working and praying for them. The contents of this place are 'filled with the dreams and goals of the less courageous.'"[8]

In essence Andy Andrews captured the heart of Ephesians 1:3, *"...who* [God] *has blessed us in the heavenly realms with every spiritual blessing in Christ."* In other words, Christ's finished work provided every supernatural provision in His Kingdom by grace, unmerited by us, so that we can access it for our lives through faith (see Rom. 5:2; Eph. 2:8-9). This is the intrinsic and fundamental nature of this manifestation model.

Grace

The manifestation model is an intentional, sequential, and systemic progression to help us understand a loving God and His provision. It begins by understanding the often misunderstood concept of *grace*. It is often mixed up with *mercy*. *Mercy* is God not giving us what we deserve. *Grace* is God giving to us what we don't deserve. The former deals with punishment. The latter deals with His provision. *Grace* is unmerited favor.[9] In other words, God did something for us that we can't earn. Grace is encapsulated in the old acronym:

G—God's

R—Riches

A—At

C—Christ's

E—Expense

It reminds me of the old story of the man who dies and goes to Heaven. When he arrives he meets the archangel Gabriel at

Heaven's Gate. The new arrival humbly asks, "What must I do to get into Heaven?" Gabriel responds, "All you have to do is earn 100 points. You tell me all the works you've done and I'll tell you the assigned points. The better the work, the more points you'll earn."

Quite enthusiastically the man begins to share his repertoire of works. He states, "I was married to the same woman for 50 years and I was a good husband and father."

"Fine," says Gabriel. "That's worth 3 points."

"Wow, only 3 points," the man responds, incredulously.

"Well, I rarely missed any church services in 50 years and I was a tither."

Gabriel ponders and responds, "That's worth 1 point."

"Well how about this," the man interjects. "I opened a shelter and fed the homeless."

"Very good," the archangel replies. "That's worth another point."

Almost in desperation the man exclaims, "At this rate the only way a person could get in is by the grace of God."

Gabriel smiles and says, "That's 100 points, come on in."

We can't perform at a high enough level to receive God's blessings. Bottom line, we have access to everything Christ's work provided. Our provision, healing, love, joy, and peace are provided for us to access by faith. Trying to do it on our own is called *"dead works"* (Heb. 9:14 KJV). God doesn't just offer a changed life, but an exchanged life (see Gal. 2:20-21). We are not just believers doing our best to conform to His standard. Rather, when we yield to Him and His ways, He lives His life through us (our personality and giftings) to manifest His Kingdom. We don't just live *for* Him, but *through* Him (see 1 John 4:9).

It is important to note, however, that *grace* means much more than that. Peter calls it manifold grace or many-sided grace (many forms of grace) (see 1 Pet. 4:10). Yet, one researcher found less than 2 percent of believers could give more than one definition of *grace*.[10]

Grace is also the finished work of Calvary (see John 19:30; Eph. 1:2-3; 1 Pet. 1:2-3). "Unmerited favor" only tells us that it's free, but it doesn't tell us what it is. What God gave to us that was unmerited was everything His finished work has provided. *Grace* is also a divine influence upon the heart.[11] *Grace,* when accessed, grants a divine influence in our hearts, where all of Christianity is appropriated (see Prov. 4:23; 23:7; Heb. 4:12). Finally, *grace* is God's empowerment or His ability.[12] I like to say it this way: *Grace* is my ability to use God's ability to meet any need. *Grace* is empowerment to live (see Gal. 2:20-21), to overcome sin (see Rom. 6:14), and to live the extraordinary life (see 2 Pet. 1:2-3 TLB).

Righteousness

The second progression of the manifestation model is righteousness. *Righteousness* is right standing with God, not based on what we've done, but based on what Jesus did, and we receive it by faith (see Rom. 3:19-21; 4:1-8; 9:30–10:4; 2 Cor. 5:21; Phil. 3:7-21). It is our ability to stand before God without guilt, fear, inferiority, or condemnation. It is not simply our righteousness, but a righteousness that comes from God, and we receive it by faith. These two concepts of *grace* and *righteousness* are how we are to reign in life (see Rom. 5:17). These concepts, however, have been misconstrued in such a way that we are left with a hollow effect of the truth. We're often left adhering to what most Christians believe *righteousness* is: conformance to an established standard or acting in an upright manner.[13] While I affirm that we need to do right, the message of the new covenant is not about what we can do to be righteous (or right with God), but what Jesus did, and we receive it by faith. Our right doing comes out of our right believing. This in turn empowers people with the feeling of being qualified in Him and the feeling of confidence to receive from Him (see Col. 1:12).

Truth

Along with the righteousness of God in our lives, we need to next renew our mind to the truth of who God is, what He has already done, and who He has made us to be. It is essential that we understand that righteousness must precede renewing our minds to the truth. Why? It is because righteousness allows us to recognize that we are qualified to receive what Christ has provided by grace. That in turn grants us confidence to see and receive the truth of what He has provided by grace on our behalf. Once we realize what He did for us, unmerited by our performance (this, by the way, doesn't mean we don't perform), we need to renew our minds to who He is, what He has already done, and who He has made us to be in Him. This then creates our identity in Him, not simply in knowing about Him. Here grace becomes a divine influence upon the heart.

Faith

The next progression in manifesting God's Kingdom is faith. We have somehow made faith so complicated it is difficult to gauge. Do I have enough faith? How does faith come? How do I get more of it? The truth is, we already have all the faith we'll ever need (see Rom. 12:3; Eph. 2:8-9; 2 Pet. 1:1; Mark 11:24). *Faith* is simply believing the truth. It is the product of renewing our minds (and hearts) to what grace has already produced. The fact is, faith has an equivalency to trust. If people truly knew God, who He is, and what He has already done, they would have little problem believing Him or His Word. Lack of faith is the product of a lack of intimacy. Faith is learning to take God at His Word.

Somehow we have made faith about faith in our faith. We've made it into a video game. We conquer all the levels until we finally win the game. Organic faith is not so much faith in our faith, but faith in His grace. We access what God has done by grace through faith (see Eph. 2:8-9).

Grace

That brings us to the last progression, which is grace. You might be thinking, *I thought grace was the first progression.* This is the other side of what Peter calls manifold grace (see 1 Pet. 4:10). This word also connotes empowerment or ability. *Grace* is also God's ability. I like to say it this way: *Grace* is my ability to use God's ability to meet my need. It is empowerment to live the Christian life. The too-good-to-be-true news (the Gospel) is that God will live His life through you (see 1 John 4:9). This aspect of grace does not follow "a parked car." It follows faith. You will know when faith is engaged because there will be a corresponding action (see James 2:14). That action engages God's ability on your behalf. It is the ability to live and to manifest God's Kingdom.

HERE'S THE PROBLEM

The intent of organic Christianity is to return to the original intent of the New Covenant. Sometimes it's risky to encourage reconsideration of thought. But as we look at the New Testament, much of its writing is devoted to such reconsideration. Despite all of our energy to pronounce the Gospel, we are sitting on the precipice of losing a generation to the Gospel. We are witnessing far too many believers languishing in "religion" rather than experiencing the vitality of a life in Christ. There's too big a gap in what we say we believe and what we actually see. Is this organic message too good to be true? I believe it's the root to the fulfillment and destiny that all true believers desire.

The call to reformation, or perhaps better said, reclamation (reclaiming our original, organic roots) indicates something is amiss.

I began to realize in my own life that I was trying to change myself—with varying degrees of success. In desperation I began examining the Scripture for answers. Nothing is more frustrating than trying to do something about something you can't do anything about.

I realized my problem was this: I was looking at trying to operate out of the wrong system. Paul says it like this in Galatians 3:10, *"All who rely on observing the law* [to be right with God] *are under a curse, for it is written: 'Cursed is everyone who does not continue to do everything written in the Book of the Law.'"* In other words, it is impossible to be right with God by doing enough right things. God's standard is perfection (we can't just keep part of the law; we have to keep every aspect of it). So, if the standard is 100 percent and we get 99 percent, we still fail. James suggests, "If you are guilty of one aspect of the law, you're guilty of breaking all of it" (see James 2:10). However, I began to realize that of equal importance is the fact that victorious living doesn't come from an outward standard, but an inward transformation. I'm not accepted by God by my works (observing the law). I work because I'm accepted by God's grace through faith (see Gal. 3:11-14).

The argument over law and grace has been going on since the early Church. In fact, it preoccupies a large portion of New Covenant writing. So tackling this problem presents an interesting dilemma. How can the argument be won? It's not my intent to win the argument; my only intent is to help people. I'm not interested in putting someone else down to elevate myself. My sole purpose is to see people be free. Free to follow God. Free *from* sin, not *to* sin. Free to experience one's destiny. Free to find the life they were born to live. Again, Irenaeus says it best, "The glory of God is man fully alive." My intent is to help people be fully alive. The time for theological bickering and mudslinging must come to an end. What we need is honest dialogue that may indeed be filled with points and counterpoints, but the goal is not just to be right, but to help one another be free—free indeed! Grace wasn't made to be debated, but to be lived.

The "rap" on grace teachers is that they promote license to sin. I want to make it clear. I share no such notion. I believe every problem people have is rooted in sin (yours, Adam's, or someone else's). Indeed, Jude had to deal with the Antinomian notion that you could do whatever you want to when he said, *"...They are godless men* [Antinomians], *who change the grace of our God into a license for immorality..."* (Jude 4). However, Titus makes it clear that the way to overcome sin is grace (see Titus 2:11-12). Grace is not license to sin; it is liberty from sin (see Rom. 6:15). This is the hour to find freedom from sin, intimacy with God, and productivity from Him. Law can only point out sin (see Rom. 5:20; Gal. 3:19). Grace—God's empowerment or ability—conquers sin (see Titus 2:12, Rom. 6:15). People who promote law unwittingly promote sin. That is Paul's intent in writing to the Corinthians, urging them back to the organic Gospel. He says, *"...the power of sin is the law* [not grace]" (1 Cor. 15:56). It's not law that gives us power over sin; it is grace. I came full circle around to the fact that my frustration with the Christian life was that I was in the wrong system (covenant).

Let me further illustrate. Recently, I walked into a bookstore and the owner recognized me and engaged me in a conversation about a particular fictional book that used grace as its underlying tenet. He said to me reflectively, "That was without a doubt one of the best books I've ever read, but when I read something like that, I feel the need to balance it out with [another teacher who majors on law]."

I replied to him, "I understand your desire not to be out of balance, but the problem with your thinking is that when you mix law and grace, you neutralize grace and get the benefits of neither." It's part of what Paul is saying in Galatians 2:20-21:

I am crucified with Christ; nevertheless I live; yet not I, but Christ liveth in me: and the life which I now live in the flesh I live by the faith of the Son of God, who

loved me, and gave Himself for me. I do not frustrate
[negate, set aside, neutralize[14]] *the grace of God: for if*
righteousness [being right with God] *come by the law,*
then Christ is dead in vain (KJV).

We neutralize God's grace when we try to live the new covenant life under the old covenant standard. We frustrate ourselves by trying to do something about something we can't do anything about.[15] Does that mean the law has no purpose in our lives? No! In fact, the Scriptures say the law is good if used properly (see 1 Tim. 1:8). So that brings us to the issue that must be answered to allow people to find freedom in God's organic message.

THE $64,000 QUESTION

In the old game show The $64,000 Question (I'm sure now it would be The $1,000,000 Question due to inflation), people would have to answer a series of questions trying to earn the right to answer the ultimate question—the $64,000 question. The $64,000 question for us as believers is: *What is the role of law and grace?* So let's see what Scripture says about a series of related questions:

Question #1: Are we still under law today?

Many contend that Matthew 5:17-20 says we are still under law. So, let's examine this passage. Jesus said:

Do not think that I have come to abolish the Law or
the Prophets; I have not come to abolish [destroy[16]]
them but to fulfill [to make replete or complete[17]]. *I*
tell you the truth, until heaven and earth disappear,
not the smallest letter, not the least stroke of a pen will
by any means disappear from the Law until everything

is accomplished. Anyone who breaks one of the least of these commandments and teaches others to do the same will be called least in the kingdom of heaven, but whoever practices and teaches these commands will be great in the kingdom of heaven. For I tell you that unless your righteousness surpasses that of the Pharisees and teachers of the law, you will certainly not enter the kingdom of heaven.

Now there is a mouthful! Let's see if we can break this down a little. It is clear from this passage that the law is not going to pass away. In fact, I often hear people say that the reason there's so much sin in the Body of Christ is because we teach grace instead of law.

Here's the problem with that thought. It doesn't reconcile with Romans 6:14, *"Sin shall not be your master, because you are not under law, but under grace."* Mastery over sin seems to be a product of grace, not law. Paul just established in the previous chapter that the law was *"added"* so that trespass may increase (see Rom. 5:20). He also declared, *"...the power of sin is the law"* (1 Cor. 15:56). Grace, not law, conquers sin. Law can only point out the wrongdoing and condemn us, but it has no power to deliver us. When Jesus brought grace in the new covenant, He broke the nature to sin out of our lives when we were born again (see John 1:16-17). In other words, our *"old self"* (old nature) was crucified (see Rom. 6:6). We no longer have a propensity to sin. Then, some might think, *Why do I still struggle with my desire?* It is because our minds are not renewed to understand who we are in Christ. If we continue to promote law, we are actually promoting sin having dominion in our lives. It is the empowerment of grace that conquers sin. Knowing this frees us *from* sin, not *to* sin.

Sometimes in my life I felt I was singing the old Bobby Fuller Four song, *I fought the law and the law won.* Multitudes have misunderstood this concept. Even Paul had to answer critics. That's why he continues in Romans 6, *"What then? Shall we sin because we are not under law but under grace?..."* (Rom. 6:15). Let's stop there. It's clear that we're not under law, but under grace. Paul continues, *"...By no means! Don't you know that when you offer yourselves to someone to obey him as slaves, you are slaves to the one whom you obey..."* (Rom. 6:15-16). In other words, the one whom I obey is the one to whom I give access to my life. The reason I don't want to sin is I don't want the devil to have access to my life.

Paul had to deal with critics (Judaizers) of his Gospel of grace. He declared mastery over sin comes from grace, not law. It is his contention that grace is not permission or license to sin, but mastery over sin. Paul had to answer this charge over and over again (see Rom. 3:8; 6:1,14-15; 1 Cor. 15:34; Gal. 5:1,13). He concludes, "If you don't want the devil to have access to your life (as the one whom you obey), stay out of sin by means of grace" (see Rom. 6:18-23). This is echoed by Titus, *"For the grace of God that brings salvation has appeared to all men. It teaches us to say 'No' to ungodliness and worldly passions..."* (Titus 2:11-12). Grace in its full (manifold) implication is the way to say no to ungodliness.

Now let's finish Matthew 5:17. *"Do not think I have come to abolish the Law and the Prophets; I have not come to abolish them, but to fulfill them."* Obviously, Jesus is not a rival system to the Law of Moses. He didn't want to abolish it, but to fulfill it. No one on earth could fulfill the law and appease the Father's demand, so Jesus fulfilled the law on behalf of humankind. Jesus took our place under the law. He fulfilled it by His finished work at Calvary. I no longer have to make payment to what Jesus fully paid.

That brings us to the pivotal word in verse 18,

> *I tell you the truth, until heaven and earth disappear,*
> *not the smallest letter, not the least stroke of a pen, will*

by any means disappear from the Law until everything is accomplished.

It's obvious the law will always have a role. The key question is, what is its role?

We'll get there, but notice the operative word. The operative word in this passage is *until:* *"until everything is accomplished."* This phrase refers to Christ fulfilling the old covenant law, both by His obedience on earth and death at Calvary. Jesus' death becomes the defining work at Calvary (see John 19:30). At that point, we come under grace. This is why John says, *"For the law was given through Moses; grace and truth came through Jesus Christ"* (John 1:17). There are some interpreters who might question the meaning of the *until* clause, but it correlates directly to Galatians 3.

> *All who rely on observing the law* [to be right with God] *are under a curse, for it is written: "Cursed is everyone who does not continue to do everything written in the Book of the Law."* [All who trust in their performance or works of the law must keep every aspect of it to be justified before God, see James 2:10]...*The law is not based on faith; on the contrary, "The man who does these things will live by them."...The promises were spoken to Abraham and to his seed. The Scripture does not say "and to seeds," meaning many people, but "and to your seed," meaning one person, who is Christ* [the new covenant was made with Jesus, not with us]. *What I mean is this: The law, introduced 430 years later, does not set aside the covenant previously established by God and thus do away with the promise* (Galatians 3:10,12,16-17).

Wow! The original covenant was not the law; it was the promise of grace to Abraham. The law didn't set that previous covenant aside. It was God's original, organic intent. Paul goes on:

> *For if the inheritance* [of God's Kingdom] *depends on the law, then it no longer depends on a promise....* *What, then, was the purpose of the law? It was added* [see Rom. 5:20] *because of transgressions until* [here's the until again] *the Seed to whom the promise referred had until* [Jesus] (Galatians 3:18-19).

The words *added* and *until* are the operative words here and are significant. It seems the law was never God's primary way of dealing with humankind. The covenant of the promise of the grace of Christ was, and it preceded the law (see Gal. 3:18). This word *until* appears to reveal a temporary role for the law. When Christ came, He put an end to the role of law for justification (see Rom. 10:4). Anyone who advocates keeping the law to be right with God is making Christ's work void of value. The law was a 1,300-year parenthesis to lead us to Christ.

Question #2: *So, if the law still exists, what is its purpose?*

Paul continues in Galatians 3:24-25:

> *Wherefore the law was our schoolmaster to bring us unto Christ, that we might be justified by faith. But after that faith is come, we are no longer under a schoolmaster* (KJV).

The role of law was to show us our inability to keep it so it would bring us to Christ. It is here that God can impart His love and empower us to live victoriously (I can hardly wait to tell you how).

If this all sounds a bit theological and technical, it is the groundwork to lead us to organic Christianity. A legalistic Gospel has kept people from the freedom to experience the fullness of the Kingdom.

This day—this very moment—millions who should be free are living in shame, fear, and intimidation. The tragedy is they think that is the way it should be...they are victimized, existing on Death Row instead of enjoying the beauty and fresh air of abundant living.[18]

This is reinforced in Romans 5:20, *"The law was added so that the trespass might increase...."* Wow! Why would God do such a thing? The law was added to show we couldn't keep it. Paul was writing to Christians about Judaizers who had mistakenly taught that faith in Christ alone was not enough to produce justification. They felt there was some minimum standard of holiness through keeping God's law (like other religions) to bring justification. But Paul says the purpose of the law was not to strengthen us in our battle against sin, but to strengthen sin in its battle against us. Sin had already beaten us, but we didn't know it; the law brought that realization to us so we would quit trusting ourselves and call out to God for His intervention.[19]

So the purpose of the law was twofold: (1) to show us we can't keep it and to lead us to Christ (see Gal. 3:24-25) and (2) to show us a standard that mirrors walking in the Spirit. So if people say they are walking in the Spirit when they are committing adultery, they simply are not. The number of passages that mirror these ideas are too numerous to comment on (see Rom. 7:1-6; 10:4; Eph. 2:15; Col. 2:14).

First Timothy 1:8-9 amplifies all of these thoughts,

> *We know that the law is good if one uses it properly. We also know that the law is made not for the righteous but for lawbreakers and rebels, the ungodly and sinful, the unholy and irreligious...*

The law is not for us, in regard to believers, but for unbelievers. Its purpose is what it has always been, to lead people to the need of a Savior.

Finally, the author of Hebrews contrasts the two covenants by stating,

> *But the ministry Jesus has received is as superior to theirs* [the old covenant] *as the covenant of which He is mediator is superior to the old one, and it is founded on better promises. For if there had been nothing wrong with that first covenant, no place would have been sought for another. But God found fault...and said, "...I will put My laws in their minds and write them on their hearts. I will be their God, and they will be My people...." By calling this covenant "new," He has made the first one obsolete; and what is obsolete and aging will soon disappear* (Hebrews 8:6-13).

The writer of Hebrews is saying that the New Covenant is ruled from the inside-out, not the outside-in. Thus, we are not confined to Old Testament law. It is a system that's time has passed.

However, I want to further debunk this thought that grace makes people free to do what they want. Notice what Paul says in First Corinthians 9:19-21,

> *Though I am free and belong to no man, I make myself a slave to everyone, to win as many as possible. To the Jews I become like a Jew, to win the Jews. To those under the law I became like one under the law (though I myself am not under the law), so as to win those under the law. To those not having the law, I*

become like one not having the law (though I am not free from God's law but am under Christ's law), so as to win those not having the law.

A New Testament believer is not obligated to fulfill Old Testament law for justification (being right with God). Therefore, Paul refers to not being under the law. Yet he says he is under *"Christ's law."* Thus, we are not under Old Testament law, but we are under the law of Christ, which is to love God with all our hearts and to love others as ourselves (see Matt. 27:37-39; Mark 12:30-31; Rom. 13:9-10; 1 John 4:21; Gal. 6:2). If people would love God, their neighbors, and themselves, they would fulfill the law of God. *"Love does no harm to its neighbor. Therefore love is the fulfillment of the law"* (Rom. 13:10). So people under grace are free, but not free to indulge in the flesh (see Gal. 5:13). If we live any way we want, we give the devil access to our lives and will ultimately reap the consequences of such.

Question #3 (or The $64,000 Question): The law is not the key to overcoming sin; so what is the purpose or role of law?

The New Testament believer does not try to fulfill the law for justification. This is why Paul categorically states,

> *No one will be declared righteous in His sight by observing the law* [keeping all of the law by our own efforts]*; rather, through the law we become conscious of sin* [that's the role of law, to show us shortcomings to move us to Jesus]. *But now a righteousness from God, apart from law, has been made known, to which the Law and the Prophets testify* (Romans 3:20-21).

So, this leads us to some culminating and liberating conclusions. Listen to what Paul is trying to get at, in Romans 4:

> *If, in fact, Abraham was justified by works* [his performance according to the law], *he had something to boast about—but not before God. What does the Scripture say? "Abraham believed God, and it was credited to him as righteousness"* (Romans 4:2-3).

Wow! We can't boast (only if we compare ourselves to others), because it is God, in Christ, who provided the finished work. All of our efforts come short of the glory of God (see Rom. 3:23). Abraham, the founder of the Jewish nation, believed God, and it was credited to him as righteousness. The term *credited* is an accounting term that means it was entered into "the books" on his behalf.[20]

These were radical statements for the Jews and Jewish converts to Christianity. He goes on to state,

> *Now when a man works* [obedience to the law], *his wages are not credited to him as a gift, but as an obligation* [he earned it]. *However, to the man who does not work but trusts God who justifies* [makes right with God] *the wicked, his faith is credited as righteousness...righteousness apart from works:...Blessed is the man whose sin the Lord will never count against him"* (Romans 4:4-8).

Paul is suggesting that, if a person could be saved by his own efforts, God would be providing salvation as a payment of obligation or debt to anyone.[21] Of course, God is not obligated or in debt to that person. Trust in our own works voids grace, and trust in God's grace makes faith in our efforts useless.[22]

Now comes the culminating and ultimate thought on grace for organic Christianity. Just a few verses later, Paul drops this bombshell of revelation.

It was not through law that Abraham and his offspring received the promise that he would be heir of the world, but through the righteousness that comes by faith (Romans 4:13).

God made us to be heirs of this world. An heir is someone who is entitled to another's property or title.[23] God has deeded us the world. In other words, life should not dictate to us, but we dictate to life. That's why he goes on to say, *"...how much more will those who receive God's abundant provision of grace and the gift of righteousness reign in life through the one man, Jesus Christ"* (Rom. 5:17).

When we reduce Christianity to rules and regulations that define "good" people or "bad" people, we are nothing more than any other religion. "If we do this, we're good; if we do this, we're bad." I'm not saying there's no truth in this; what I am saying is this is not the essence of organic Christianity. Organic Christianity is not a set of rules to make us feel better or worse about our relationship to God. It is receiving the forgiveness of our sins by grace through faith in order that, by continued grace, we might find intimacy with God. That intimacy introduces us to being right with God through Christ's finished work. That finished work provides everything we need for life and godliness through God's grace. When we receive that provision by faith, we reign in life and inherit the world. So, it's not about the do; it's about the done. It's not about achieving; it's about receiving. It's not about the changed life; it's about the exchanged life. It's not as much about living for Him, as it is living through Him. We go from ordinary to extraordinary.

The law only points out where we fall short. Grace is the empowerment to live the extraordinary, to inherit the world. In my life, I had a significant other who communicated to me that I would never amount to anything. For years, it became self-fulfilling prophecy in my life. Every time I got ready to break through and go to another level, I would self-sabotage myself—even after I became a Christian. I was looking into the mirror of my personal belief system (see my book, *The Greatest Secret,* for this understanding in detail). My social environment, the authority figures in my life, my self-image, the repetitious information I was fed in my surroundings, and my experiences all brought me to this conclusion. As a result, I was less than capable of attaining my desired goals.

It wasn't until I looked into a new mirror (see James 1:22) of the Word of God that I started to see God and myself differently. Once I understood who God really was (and is), what He has already done, and who He made me to be, did I experience the freedom I desired, the freedom to know God (in intimacy) and the freedom to know myself. Once I experienced this freedom, I saw God's grace and righteousness that caused me to rule in life, not to be ruled by it.

So let's glimpse into our destiny to reign in life.

• •

ORGANIC THOUGHTS

1. Based on the book's definition of *insanity,* doing the same thing over and over again and expecting different results, is the Church somewhat insane?

2. Do you see your call to be blessed to be a blessing?

3. Are there times you feel disqualified from your blessing?

4. Have you focused on right doing or right believing?

5. Do you see the Gospel manifesting itself in true productivity in your life?

6. How do you interact with the five keys of the manifestation model?

7. Does understanding faith in His grace rather than faith in our faith change how you see faith?

8. Is there a gap between what people say they believe and what they actually see?

9. Have you experienced the frustration of trying to do something you are ill equipped to do?

10. Do you see the difference between conforming to an outward standard versus an inward transformation?

11. Do you see that we are free *from* sin, not free *to* sin?

12. How do you deal with overcoming sin, through law or grace?

13. How do you rule and reign in life through grace and righteousness? (See Romans 4:13; 5:17.)

Chapter 3

. . . .

GRACE: "DONE" VERSUS "DO"

It has become increasingly obvious to many that we need a radical paradigm shift in the Body of Christ. We need a new perspective. Now, remember I described a *paradigm shift* as a radical shift from one way of thinking to another. It means to exceed the common measure. It is a call to go from the ordinary (what we're used to) to the extraordinary (what we're ordained to). It's time for a new perspective.

In my last book, *The Greatest Secret*, I explained about having a new perspective by telling a story of a college girl writing home after her first semester. You might want to read this as though this was your daughter writing to you:

Dear Mom and Dad:

I haven't made many friends, but I met a boy (you're already excited). He's not going to school and can't find a job, but he is doing better now that he has been released from prison (Hmmmm!). He didn't have a place to live, so he moved in with me. After all, we're going to need a home for the baby. Dad, you'll be glad to hear it's a boy. Turn the letter over for the P.S.

You can almost feel the gamut of raw emotions as the stunned parents are interacting with this letter. You can almost see Mom beginning to cry and Dad sitting there in a daze shaking his head. All their lives they've done what they thought was best for their daughter. The Dad had worked hard so he could provide the income for his daughter to have a good education and have a good career. Now she had married a criminal and was pregnant out of wedlock. After a few minutes, they turned the letter over for the *P.S.*

P.S. None of this is true! But I did get a "C" in English and a "D" in Humanities, and I need more money.

Now that will change your perspective. Sometimes I think we can hear "stats" that don't really register. Four percent of Mosaics are Bible-based believers. Nine out of ten Christian high-schoolers leave their faith when going to college. The Church is in (to some an unperceived) crisis. Yet, I believe we are on the precipice of one of the great moves of God of our time—if we understand the time and the seasons (see 1 Chron. 12:32).

Some time back, I was doing a series of meetings in the nation of Australia. I was primarily invited as a speaker for a national youth conference, although I did numerous conferences and churches while I was there for three weeks. In the 20 days I was in Australia, I spoke something like 26 or 27 times. So, by the end of my tenure, I was exhausted.

The last day I was to be there was to be a day of respite. I was scheduled to visit some beaches and to see some kangaroos and koalas. At the last minute, my last host church heard about a leadership conference I do called I.M.P.A.C.T (an acronym meaning Invasion Ministries Producing Actual Church Transformation). So, on my last day in the country, they called a spontaneous meeting with no publicity. We packed out the church, despite the lack of communication. Thus, I found myself speaking right up to the last minute I was in the nation.

The next morning, when I prepared to leave, I found out the airlines had "messed up" my ticket. As a consequence, I flew in Coach instead of Business Class. Can I just tell you that it is twice as long in Coach as it is in Business Class? To complicate the matter, I was sitting across the aisle from a couple whose nationality is known for chatter. They talked incessantly from the time we left Melbourne until we arrived in Los Angeles, 16 hours later. No amount of talking, shushing, hushing, calling a flight attendant, or pillow-throwing quieted the situation down. So I got, at most, about one hour of sleep. Now my exhaustion was multiplied.

By the time I arrived in Los Angeles, I was committed to the fact that I couldn't "take" Coach any longer (I'm exaggerating to create some fun with this episode). When I arrived in Los Angeles, I began working out the possibility of an upgrade to First Class. Some last minute complications with the upgrade caused me to be among the last to board the plane. Finally, I found myself walking down the aisle of the First Class cabin to my window seat. Because my seat was a window seat, I had to "crawl over" the passenger on the aisle to get to my seat. As I moved past the aisle seat passenger, I noticed he was dressed casually, but expensively. He also had an expensive laptop. My impression was, "This guy has got money." But in all honesty, I didn't really care, because I didn't really want to talk with him. All I wanted to do was get home, kiss my wife, hug my kids, and read an American paper for the first time in three weeks.

Once I sat down, I settled in, catching up with the *USA Today* newspaper. No sooner had I begun to read, than my neighbor began glancing over my shoulder and commenting, "Bush this and Bush that." (George Bush was President of the United States during this time.) Within five minutes we were talking about politics, philosophy, and religion—the three things one should never speak to a stranger about, and we were talking about them within the first five minutes. It was obvious that my "seat neighbor" was astute, knowledgeable, and coming from the opposite perspective as I was. It was, however, an enjoyable and funny exchange.

There came a little lull in our conversation, and my newfound friend opened up his laptop to do some work. Glancing over at his screen saver, I noticed it was a picture of him and three Playboy bunnies. I thought to myself, who is this guy? This was a vice president of a highly successful men's magazine. I thought to myself, *How interesting.* We had a lengthy conversation about business procedures.

After another lull in conversation, he opened his briefcase. Being the shy, demure personality that I am, I peered into his briefcase. I noticed he had a couple of psychology textbooks stored in his "case." Finally, I said, "Forgive me for peering into your briefcase, but I noticed you have a couple of psychology textbooks located in there. Obviously, you're not in college because you told me you are a vice president for a highly successful company. You also told me at one time you were a vice president in the movie industry—so, you're not in college, so why do you have the psychology textbooks?"

His response was, "No, as a matter of fact I am in college. I don't really want to psychoanalyze anyone. I want to be a motivational speaker."

Then, just as though it was on cue he asked me, "What do you do for a living?"

Without hesitation I said, "I *am* a motivational speaker!"

He responded, "That's amazing; you're doing what I want to, and you're sitting here next to me—this must be fate."

I answered, "You have no idea!"

Now being the discerning man of God I am, I figured out this must be a setup from God. So I silently asked, "Father, what is my assignment here? Am I to plant, water, or harvest?" I felt impressed that my opportunity was to plant into this man's life.

We had just finished our meal, and we were in our descent into Dallas. Taking advantage of the situation, I said, "I know why you're studying psychology, but you don't know why you're studying psychology."

He said, "What?!!" I repeated myself, and he smiled as he replied, "OK, man, take your best shot. Why am I studying psychology?"

I responded humbly, but pointedly, "It is because you know what it's like to be important, but you don't know what it's like to be significant!"

He went ashen white at my response, and his exact words to my response were, "It's like you're 'reading my mail' or something. I'm on my way to Dallas to meet with [the name of the president of a major video company] to see if we can sell our videos in their stores. I make a whole lot of money doing this, but I don't feel very significant."

Now we have landed and rolled up to our gate. My newfound friend is out of his seat and getting his bag out of the overhead compartment. He hesitates for a moment, then goes into his wallet and pulls out his business card. Again, hesitating, he says, "I've never met anyone quite like you. The next time you're in Los Angeles, would you speak to our staff?"

Here's the point: What I said to that man that day is what I say to the Church right now. We've known some times of importance. God is about to take us into a time of significance.

Some might be thinking, *What is the difference between importance and significance?* One of Webster's definitions of *importance* is "acting as if having power, authority, influence or right position."[1] *Significance* means "full meaning, momentous, special or hidden meaning."[2] Importance implies value to oneself, but significance

73

implies value to others as well. God is touching a generation to touch the generation—we're blessed to be a blessing (see Gen. 12:2-3). God is bringing His people into a new revelation of intimacy with Him to manifest His Kingdom.

Why is the message about law and grace important to organic Christianity and a new move of God? Law is a formula, a principle, or guideline, but has no power to maintain the very principles it espouses. Law is deserved favor; grace is undeserved favor (see Rom. 4:2-8). The law is the demand of God; grace is the supply of God. This is a tremendously important point to grasp. People who live according to the law live under the burden of its demand. Those who live under grace live in the liberty and freedom of supply (provision). That is why people who live under demand often feel inadequate and stingy. Those who live under grace feel freedom and liberation because they understand all that they need has been provided in the Kingdom through grace unmerited by their efforts.

So, what is *grace*? Grace is unmerited favor.[3] Grace is the finished work of Jesus Christ (see Eph. 1:2-3). Unmerited favor only tells us that something has been bestowed upon us without our merit, but it doesn't tell us what it is. All that Jesus' finished work has provided in salvation has been placed in the heavenly realm (the Kingdom of Heaven) to be accessed by faith in our lives. It is also a divine influence in our lives. Later, as we discover how to write truth on the tablets of our heart, we'll see how grace begins a reign in our lives from the inside-out. Lastly, grace is empowerment or ability. It is the release of God's ability activated in our lives. I like to say it this way: *Grace is our ability to use God's ability to meet any need!* The frustration with modern Christianity is that we try to live the Christian life apart from His ability and empowerment. The key to extraordinary living is learning to appropriate the ability of God to break sin, shackles, and limitations in our lives.

This grace can't be earned (see Rom. 4:2-3). No amount of effort on our part can earn what God has done by grace. I watch the utter frustration of believers as they try to earn God's blessing by doing enough tithing, enough witnessing, enough doing, enough Bible reading, or enough praying to earn the right to be blessed. On the other hand, I do these things to understand who God is, what He has already done, and who He has made me to be. No amount of effort on our part can earn God's grace. (I will discuss the balance of work more later. We don't work to earn God's blessings; we work because we're blessed.) That's why we are made right with God through grace and righteousness and not the law.

Ephesians 2:15 says it like this:

> *By abolishing in His flesh the law with its commandments and regulations. His purpose was to create in Himself one new man out of the two, thus making peace.*

The word *abolish* is a very strong Greek word, which means "to render entirely useless (idle)."[4] A simple definition is, "to do away with, or to put an end to."[5] Paul is indicating that the old covenant that divided Jew and Gentile as a basis of relating to God is now done away with. Thus, all people can be rightly related to God in Christ. Paul further reiterates this in Galatians 2:19, *"For through the law I died to the law so that I might live for God."* In other words, deliverance from the law is not through unlawful means. The law demanded death for sin, but Jesus fulfilled its requirements by dying in our place. Now it would be unlawful to punish us according to that law once our debt was paid. That would be double jeopardy.[6]

We must come to a full understanding that Jesus fulfilled the law on our behalf (see Matt. 5:17). Let me help you understand what I am getting at in this point. I'm about to fulfill my mortgage for my house at our bank. Once I've done so, I have news for you. I'm going to stop sending my monthly payment. Why? The debt will have been fulfilled. If the lending institution demands more payment, I simply produce my title deed that reveals the balance has been paid in its entirety. It is in the same sense that Jesus paid my debt. Therefore, when the law *demands* I continue to make payment to be right with God by the works of keeping it, I point to the title deed of Christ's finished work. I don't earn it by what I *do*, but it is earned by what Christ has *done*. It's about the *done*, it's not about the *do* (in reference to being right with God). When we make the Gospel about the *do* instead of the *done,* we retard the Body of Christ. When we make the Gospel about change instead of transformation we encourage spiritual retardation. Operating out of the *do* instead of the *done* causes us to stammer in wondering, "I know God can, I'm just not sure He will...for me." Our doing (faith) comes out of understanding what God has done by grace unmerited by us. Our real frustration comes from trying to do God's part of the equation instead of trusting what He has done in Christ.

Similarly, in Romans 8:2 it states, *"Because through Christ Jesus the law of the Spirit of life set me free from the law of sin and death."* This statement is the culmination of what Paul has been saying in Romans 7:15-24. This is not Paul describing his own personal struggle: *"I do not understand what I do. For what I want to do I do not do, but what I hate I do"* (Rom. 7:15). It is the description of someone who is attempting to be right with God through the law, or as he says it, *"the law of sin and death."* Romans 8 is the beginning of the good news, that it can't be done by our human effort, but by the power of the Holy Spirit and grace (see Rom. 8:2). Romans 7:4 adds,

> *So, my brothers, you also died to the law through the body of Christ, that you might belong to another, to Him who was raised from the dead, in order that we might bear fruit to God.*

Christ's death freed us from relationship (marriage) to our *"old self"* (see Rom. 6:6), not so we could run around and do whatever we want. Rather, He broke the shackles of the law so we could experience the freedom of being rightly related in a new relationship (covenant) to live in Him. *"Christ is the end of the law..."* (Rom. 10:4) for the purpose of being right with God.

ORDAINED TO REIGN

This is the key to freedom in order to reign in life and to step into your destiny. Grace (not law) is my key to manifesting victory. Romans 5:17 says it this way,

> *...how much more will those who receive God's abundant provision of grace and of the gift of righteousness* [something we receive, not do—our doing comes out of our receiving] *reign in life through the one man, Jesus Christ.*

In other words, life doesn't dictate to us; we dictate to life. Stephen Scott wrote a book called *Mentored by a Millionaire*. In the book, his research found four classifications of people:

- *Drifters* (50% are in this category according to his research)—Drifters are people who just drift along in life. Whatever life dictates to them, they just "go with the flow."

- *Pursuers* (25%)—Pursuers are people who pursue a thing until they hit an obstacle. Once they do, they quit.

- *Achievers* (24.99%)—These are people who achieve at some levels, but not all levels.

- *Super-Achievers* (.01%)—Super-achievers are people who achieve at virtually every level.[7]

Martin Seligman, a noted psychologist from the University of Pennsylvania, states that 80 percent of people have learned helplessness.[8] Learned helplessness is a state where people feel helpless to change their circumstances. If we combine the research of these two men, we see that somewhere between 75 percent and 80 percent of people are drifting along in life, pursuing certain goals, but feeling helpless to change their lives to obtain their dreams (and God's). Jesus said, *"...I have come that they may have life, and that they may have it more abundantly"* (John 10:10 NKJV). The word *abundant* means super-abundant in quantity, superior in quality, excess, surplus, superfluous, extreme, excel, too much.[9] In other words, Jesus said, "I've come that you might have life, and have life as a super-achiever." Yet only .01 percent are there. Why?

It might be because we've never learned how to operate in the abundance of grace and the gift of righteousness. We're still living under demand (law) rather than supply (grace). Perhaps that's why John 1:16-17 says, *"And of His fullness we have all received, and grace for grace. For the law was given through Moses, but grace and truth came through Jesus"* (NKJV). It is obvious in this text that John is speaking to believers and saying that as believers we have received the fullness of God. The New International Version says it this way, *"From the fullness of His grace we have all received one blessing after another."*

What an awesome statement. According to Colossians 2:10, we are complete, lacking nothing, in Him. The rest of the Christian life is not about trying to obtain more from God, but renewing our minds to what we possess in Christ. The way that is manifested is grace upon grace. Greek scholars tell us that this phrase *grace upon grace* means "abundance or overflow from the fullness of God."[10] It is manifold grace—the many sides or various forms of grace (see 1 Pet. 4:10). It is God's unmerited favor, it is the finished work of Christ, it is the divine influence upon the heart, and it is the empowerment or the ability of God released to live our lives. We are empowered to overcome circumstances and sin. That is how we can dictate to life and not let life dictate to us. Listen to how John says it in his first epistle, "*...as He* [Jesus] *is, so are we in this world* (1 John 4:17 NKJV). We can conquer this world, life, sin, circumstances, sickness, disease, and lack (in all arenas) the way Jesus did—grace.

John adds, *"For the law was given through Moses; grace and truth came through Jesus Christ"* (John 1:17). Listen to how Martin Luther dealt with this verse. He intimates,

> The Law has indeed been given by Moses, but what avails that fact? To be sure, it is a noble doctrine and portrays a beautiful and instructive picture of man's duty to God and all mankind; it is really excellent as to the letter. Yet it remains empty; it does not enter into the heart.[11]

It is a truth without the power to keep it. Jesus brought truth and grace. He brought the revelation of the Word as truth (see John 17:17) and the power to do it. Jesus brought access to an intimacy with God through grace and righteousness (see Rom. 5:17), access to the Kingdom of Heaven through the finished work of Jesus Christ (see John 19:30; Eph. 1:3), and access to God's empowerment and ability to live and conquer. Luther continues,

> This becomes possible when we receive grace for grace [unmerited favor, so as to access His kingdom and

empowerment], that is, when we come to the enjoyment of Christ, and for the sake of him who enjoys with God fullness of grace, although our own obedience to the law is still imperfect.[12]

So instead of mere empty rules and regulations pointing out our shortcomings, we are introduced to the omnipotent world of God's Kingdom to rule and reign in life.

To me, this is the story from the movie *Doc,* starring Michael J. Fox. Fox plays the lead character as an empty-headed and shallow plastic surgeon graduate who is traveling to Los Angeles to take a job at a prestigious firm. In an attempt to avoid traffic and save time, he takes a detour through some country roads. He becomes lost through the cow pastures of the desolate countryside. In an attempt to read a map and drive at the same time, he ends up smashing into the newly constructed fence of the Justice of the Peace of a remote country town. His car is strewn all over the countryside for hundreds of yards. Two country bumpkin garage attendants are called to the scene. Purveying the wreckage of the car in every conceivable direction, with his hand scratching his head, the one attendant drawls, "I think we can fix that."

It is reminiscent of the plumber who just got his license to practice standing before Niagara Falls saying, "I think I can fix that." That is the difference between the two covenants that John is espousing in these two verses of his Gospel. This is the dilemma Organic Christianity seeks to address. It is the problem of new covenant believers trying to live victoriously through the old covenant. That is why the writer of Hebrews says, *"For if there had been nothing wrong with that first covenant, no place would have been sought for another"* (Heb. 8:7). If merely pointing out what was wrong was enough, we would have victory. We were unable to fulfill the tenets of the law (though they were good) on our own, so God sent His Son to fulfill them for us. This opened the door to intimacy with God and access to the Kingdom of Heaven so that we may live victoriously and manifest God's love to the world.

THE TOO-GOOD-TO-BE-TRUE NEWS

Before we delve into how *grace upon grace* works, let's re-establish the idea about how we use grace to live victoriously in the New Covenant from Romans 1:16-17:

> *For I am not ashamed of the gospel of Christ: for it is the power of God unto salvation to every one that believeth; to the Jew first, and also to the Greek. For therein is the righteousness of God revealed from faith to faith: as it is written, the just shall live by faith* (KJV).

Here, Paul begins by iterating, *"I am not ashamed of the gospel...."* This phrase, *"I am not ashamed"* gives us the idea of a painful feeling or sense of loss of status because of an event or activity.[13] It can mean exposure to fear or embarrassment that one's expectations may prove false. Sometimes it's a feeling of shame that prevents someone from doing or attempting something. It can be a lack of courage to stand up for something or what has been done.[14]

There is no rationale given as to why Paul might struggle with a loss of status or apprehension about the Gospel. The Book of Romans is written to restore the organic intent of the Gospel concerning Judaizers. Again, Judaizers were Jewish converts who stated people not only had to receive Jesus, but also had to keep the law to be right (righteous, justified) with God. They probably attempted to refute Paul's doctrine of justification by faith by shaming people for not keeping the law. However, Paul's response was *"I am not ashamed of the* [organic] *gospel of Christ..."* (Rom. 1:16 KJV).

This term *gospel* means "the too-good-to-be-true news." In other words, it is likely these Judaizers were saying, "This doctrine of Paul's is just too good to be true. It's not enough to be rightly related to God through faith in Christ's finished work alone. We also have to keep the tenets of the law." Paul's response was, "I'm not ashamed or embarrassed of this too-good-to-be-true news."

Why? It is the power of God unto salvation. This term *salvation* means much more than someday going to Heaven. I often tell people that being born again (see John 3:3) and receiving salvation are not the same thing. Being born again is the entrance into salvation. The term *saved* (*sodzo* in the Greek) means "to save, deliver, protect, heal, preserve, prosper, to do well to make whole."[15] Salvation is a reference to the blessings every believer is entitled to receive. This is what the organic Gospel means. Whatever believers need, it's in the Gospel. If we need healing, it's in the Gospel (by grace). If we need deliverance, it's in the Gospel. Prosperity, peace, love, joy—it's all in the Gospel. Since most believers don't understand this, they live their lives out of religion rather than the relationship with God in His Kingdom.

Paul finished his thoughts, *"...to everyone who believes ..."* (Rom. 1:16). It is by faith alone that we access the provision of the Gospel of salvation. This is what launches us into verse 17, *"For in the gospel a righteousness from God is revealed...."* Notice that it is God's righteousness, not ours. It's not something we do, but it's something He has done, and we receive it by faith. We are righteous, in right standing with the Father, by receiving it through faith in what Christ did. Paul concludes this verse with *"from faith to faith"* (Rom. 1:17 KJV). This phrase *faith to faith* describes how we are right with God. Righteousness cannot be earned; it only can be received and maintained in faith. It is not from faith to works; it is from faith to faith. The more we understand this, the more we'll live righteously.

GRACE UPON GRACE

What does John mean when he says, *"And of His fullness have all we received, and grace for grace"* (John 1:16 KJV)? When we received Christ, we were given *"fullness in Christ,"* as the NIV says in Colossians 2:10. The KJV says, *"Ye are complete in Him...."* In Christ we lack nothing. The key to the Christian life is not trying to get more of God, but learning to release more of God. We can't get any more of God, but we can renew our minds to what we already have.

John says to us in John 1:16 that God's fullness has given us grace for grace. What God has given is unmerited favor for the ability to live through Him in victory and abundance. One level of grace (unmerited favor) releases us to the next level of grace (God's empowerment or ability) to live in the blessing of God.

HOW ARE WE ORDAINED TO REIGN?

The key to living victoriously is to understand that we don't *go to* victory, but *come from* victory. Notice how Paul says it in Ephesians 2:8-9: *"For it is by grace you have been saved, through faith—and this not from yourselves, it is the gift of God—not by works, so that no one can boast."*

This is one of Paul's most pivotal passages. *"It is by grace you have been saved...."* Remember salvation is not simply going to a heavenly abode some day (though I would never marginalize the magnitude of this important revelation). It means "to save, deliver, protect, heal, preserve, to prosper, to do well, to make whole." One of the key reasons a person gets born again is not only to go to Heaven, but to get Heaven into him (the Kingdom of God is the rule and reign of God to be sure, but it also is the location and resources of God).[16] Jesus said it this way in John's Gospel, *"I tell you the truth, no one can see the kingdom of God unless he is born again"* (John 3:3). Being born again is an entrance into salvation, which allows believers to see (and gain access to) God's Kingdom or the resources of salvation. This, God does by grace, unmerited by us. It is extremely important, however, that we note that Paul says this process takes place by grace through faith. It is not by grace alone. It is by grace through faith. If people are saved by grace alone, multiple theological questions are given a platform.

Many believers have heard much about faith over the last couple of decades. To receive anything from God's Kingdom, it must be by grace through faith. To live by grace alone creates a false sense of sovereignty. That means everything is done by God alone. God's people have no real participation in the process. If it's by faith alone, it becomes a work that people produce to move God. Faith alone (much of where we've been in recent years) creates a sense of frustration in people who are trying to do God's part of this process. It certainly did for me, as an individual. I was frustrated trying to make things happen by "my faith" without any real power to do it. I was trying to "believe God" for provision, for healing, for a happy family, for resources to reach people. The fact was, it was only partially working.

The balance of this word is the process by which the Kingdom works—by grace through faith. God's finished work through His Son at Calvary provided every supernatural empowerment in the Kingdom of Heaven by grace, unmerited by us. This provision of grace is there for us to access in our lives by faith. It is not faith in our faith, but faith in His grace. God wants us to believe and receive what He has done unmerited by us.

In this first progression of the manifestation model, grace emphasizes the finished work of Christ, unmerited by us. When we emphasize grace alone, we have a false sovereignty. It's the idea that God does everything independent of us. Faith alone leaves us with the idea of trying to move God to do what we are believing for Him to do. This is going to be difficult for some readers to grasp. *We don't have to move God; He has already moved.* He moved 2,000 years ago with His finished work at Calvary. He moved 2,000 years ago and blessed us by grace (unmerited by anything we did) and placed it in the Kingdom of Heaven for us to access by faith.

I love the opportunity, among my many duties, to teach in a Bible college. While sharing this with a group of our second year students, I had a pupil who challenged this thought by asking an interrogative question: "Can you substantiate that thought?" I love the opportunity to validate practical theology. I responded by expounding on Ephesians 1:2-3:

> *Grace and peace to you from God our Father and the Lord Jesus Christ. Praise be to God and the Father of our Lord Jesus Christ, who has blessed us in the heavenly realm with every spiritual blessing in Christ.*

Now let's break this verse down in great practicality. Paul starts most of his epistles with *"Grace and peace to you."* This is far more than a greeting. He is saying *grace* be unto his readers—*grace* as unmerited favor, *grace* the finished work of Calvary, *grace* the divine influence upon the heart, *grace* the empowerment or ability of God. Then, he adds *peace,* or the ability to be unaffected by our circumstances. In other words, what God did in the finished work of Calvary, unmerited by us, is kept by us through peace. What grace has provided, peace retains.

Then he adds, *"...who [God] has blessed us...."* Notice it is in the past aorist tense. This is not something God is going to do; this is something that is already accomplished. These blessings were given first and are already ours. This term *blessed* means "benefit, largeness, bounty, or abundance."[17] *Blessed* also means "to cause to prosper."[18] One scholar described *prosperity* to me this way, it is the ability to use God's ability to meet any need (it's a grace). Thus, God blessed us and caused us to have access to the ability of God to meet any need. How? By grace! Where? In the heavenly realm!

Where's the heavenly realm? This is a Pauline expression to describe the Kingdom of Heaven. What Paul is expressing is that the benefits of the Spirit, their largeness or vastness, God's bounty and abundance, have been placed in the Kingdom of Heaven, unmerited by us (grace) for access on planet Earth.

What has He blessed us with? He has blessed us with spiritual blessings. The term *spiritual* means "supernatural."[19] Supernatural provision has been placed in the Kingdom unmerited by us. How? *"In Christ"* by the finished work of Calvary! God simply wants us to believe and receive.

Faith is not something we do, and then God responds. Faith doesn't believe God *will;* faith believes God *has.* It's not like we meet certain criteria and then it gets checked off the list so God can move:

- Had my Bible study ☑
- Spent time in prayer ☑
- Witnessed today ☑
- Paid my tithe ☑
- Walked in holiness ☑
- Did a good deed ☑

Faith is not something we do to get God to do something, but is a response to what He has already done. It bears repeating. It is not faith in our faith; it is faith in His grace. We don't have to convince God; we need to be convinced by God.

Recently, I was ministering to a crowd of about 2,000 to 2,500 people. When I gave the altar call, about 75 percent of the people came forward (1,500-plus people). When I walked off the platform to pray for people, the first person I came to, I asked, "What do you need?" This young man almost sheepishly said, "I have AIDS." Without hesitation, we prayed. (By the way, the preliminary doctor's report indicates he is healed.) The next person said, "I've got a terminal disease." Again, without hesitation, we prayed in faith. The next person I went to said he had a degenerative heart condition and was given three to six months to live. Again, we prayed. The next day at my Bible college, a student was reflective to me about the service he had witnessed. He said, "I watched as you prayed for one serious condition after another without flinching. You must be a great man of faith."

I responded, "Not really! You see my faith is not in my faith; my faith is in His grace. My confidence is in Him, not in me." This is the essence of Ephesians 2:8-9.

I love the fact that Paul adds Ephesians 2:10 to this mix, *"For we are God's workmanship, created in Christ Jesus to do good works, which God prepared in advance for us to do."* People who teach grace are often accused of saying that God has done it all; therefore, believers don't have to do any work. That's true concerning our relationship to God. We can't earn our right standing with the Father—works of righteousness or dead works (see Heb. 6:1; 9:14). However, we don't work to earn salvation; we work because we're saved. We don't work to be right with God; we work because we are right with God. We don't work to be accepted by God; we work because we are accepted by God.

It is my pleasure to make an effort to advance the message of God's amazing love. Once we experience the most fulfilling life there is, we can't help but share it with others (see Philem. 6). Organic Christianity is not simply about living *for* God, but living *through* Him (see 1 John 4:9).

PROBLEMS WITH GRACE

Ephesians 2:8-9 raises several issues of controversy that need to be addressed. The first issue is about grace promoting Ultimate Reconciliation (some would call it being a license to sin or Inclusion, which has been popularized in some circles). Second is the question, is grace promoting Antinomianism? Third is the question, is grace promoting Ultimate Reconciliation (meaning grace is against the law)? Let's examine these issues.

JAMES BOND THEOLOGY

James Bond was given license to kill. Grace teachers have been accused of giving people license to sin. I've found people sin without the license. The fact of the matter is, according to Scripture, nothing could be further from the truth. The phrase *license to sin* really originates with Jude. Jude 4 says,

> *For certain men whose condemnation was written about long ago have secretly slipped in among you. They are godless men, who change the grace of our God into a license for immorality and deny Jesus Christ our only Sovereign and Lord.*

Who were the people that Jude was referring to as godless men among them? Jude, like Paul, was defending the organic message of the Gospel. The godless men he refers to are Antinomians. Antinomians are a sect of Gnostics. Let me break down these fancy theological terms to some degree of simplicity without doing a complete analysis.

Gnostics were a group of people who often followed Paul (and other apostles) around trying to negate their teaching and to lead true believers into their sect. Gnostics believed (and still believe) in a dualism. What that means is they believed everything in the Spirit was good and everything in the flesh (meaning body) was evil. Antinomians took this a step further. They believed that whatever was done in the flesh was insignificant because the flesh was insignificant. They even said that there was no such thing as sin in a person's flesh.

This is the same issue John deals with in his first epistle, which includes the much-maligned verses of First John 1:8-9. John wrote this epistle to the unknown churches to combat Gnostic/Antinomian teaching, which was attempting to rob the Church of its organic message by promoting this insidious addition. Thus, John attacks this misconception, by noting,

> *If we claim to be without sin, we deceive ourselves, and the truth is not in us. If we confess our sins, He is faithful and just and will forgive* (John 1:8-9).

The King James Version translates the beginning of verse 8 as *"If we say that we have no sin"*—which is exactly what the Antinomians suggested. Verse 10 clarifies this by adding, *"If we claim we have not sinned, we make Him* [God] *out to be a liar and His word has no place in our lives."* This verse is not telling believers they must confess every sin to be right with God (which, by the way, is impossible—we'll deal with what is right and wrong about confession of sin later). Instead, John is telling Gnostics how to get saved. Likewise, Jude is simply rebuking Antinomians for saying that grace suggests we can live any way we want.

There is little doubt there are some so-called teachers who are justifying their sin with the doctrine of grace. Like Jude, we need to expose the lunacy of such an assertion. It does not, however, negate the legitimacy of the revelation of grace anymore than someone who abuses salvation negates the revelation of salvation.

I will say, however, that I do not agree with teachers who suggest that once you become a believer you never have to repent of sin. There are 14 verses that deal with individual believers or the Church repenting: Second Corinthians 7:9-10; 12:21; Second Timothy 2:25; Hebrews 12:17; Revelation 2:5,16,21-22; 3:13; 9:20-21; 10:9; 16:11.

There is, for the most part, in my opinion, a misconception concerning repentance. As one church leader pontificated to me, *repentance* is feeling really bad for your sin. It's true that part of the meaning of *repentance* is compunction.[20] However I know multitudes of people who grieve over what they've done, but do it again after their ritual of sorrow. *Repentance* is far more than that. Its primary meaning is "to think differently or to change your thinking."[21] There are five key steps to repentance:

FIVE STAGES TO REPENTANCE

1. **Identification**—Identify the sin, shortcoming, self-limiting belief, or boundary in your life.

2. **Antidote**—What does the Word say about who God is, what He has already done, and who He has made you to be concerning the boundaries in your life? What is God's mindset concerning limitations you are facing? For instance, if it is lack, then prosperity is the antidote. If it is lust, then love is the antidote. If your boundary is fear, perfect love casts out all fear and love is the antidote.

3. **Repetition**—Meditate on the antidote until a new mindset is created.[22]

4. **Revelation**—Repetition should continue until it creates solidification in your personal belief system.

5. **Rethinking**—Rethinking allows you to change the way you see God and change the way you see yourself. This in turn allows you to live in faith and expectancy to break barriers, sin, and the limitations seeking to limit and dominate your life.

The issue at stake is this: Repentance is primarily a course correction to stay aligned with Kingdom ways.

FIRST ISSUE: IS GRACE A LICENSE TO SIN?

Is grace a license to sin? The answer is, *absolutely not.* It's interesting to me that those who make such allegations often miss the entire point. When people say to me that grace is a license to sin, I always answer in this fashion: Why is it that when someone sins under grace it is always the problem of theology? However, if someone sins under law, it is never a problem of theology. The fact is that people don't sin because of their theology. They sin because of what is in their hearts (see Prov. 4:23; 23:7; Heb. 4:12). Proverbs 4:23 (NKJV) tells us the *"issues of life"* (*boundaries* in the Hebrew)[23] are determined by what is in our hearts. The limitations of our lives are an outgrowth of what we've cultivated in our hearts. The Scripture says it this way, *"As* [a man] *thinketh in his heart, so is he"* (Prov. 23:7 KJV). The word *thinks* in this verse means "doorkeeper or gate keeper."[24] In other words, the heart is the doorkeeper that allows dominant thoughts to get into our hearts. What is in our hearts is what we are going to do. Not maybe, not probably, not possibly; if we have something in our hearts, we are going to do it—until we know how to write on the tablets of our hearts (see Prov. 3:3; 7:3; 2 Cor. 3:3).

Here's the key point, however: What does the Scripture say about conquering sin? Romans 6:14 says, *"Sin shall not be your master...."* Obviously, we have a way to conquer sin, not to be conquered by sin. What is it? Romans 6:14 continues, *"...because you are not under law, but under grace."* It's not law, but grace, that conquers sin. First Corinthians 15:56 notes, *"...the power of sin is the law"*—not grace. Titus 2:11-12 says, *"For the grace of God that brings salvation has appeared to all men. It teaches us to say "No" to ungodliness and worldly passion...."* Again, overcoming sin is through grace.

People who teach the assertion that grace or righteousness is a blanket covering to do whatever they want are ludicrous, and they have no understanding of the organic Gospel. This is why Paul had to respond to allegations of permissiveness by noting, *"Come back to your senses as you ought, and stop sinning; for there are some who are ignorant of God—I say this to your shame"* (1 Cor. 15:34). Why would God make provisions for someone to live in the opposite manner of what His Word, His Spirit, and the fruit of the Spirit promote?

SECOND ISSUE: ANTINOMIANISM

All problems are the result of sin (Adam's, yours, or someone else's). Sin gives the devil access to your life (see Rom. 6:16). The repercussions and consequences to sin are irrefutable. If you think you're smarter than God and you have freedom to live outside of His guidelines, it's the height of idiocy. It is also a complete misunderstanding of what the Gospel is saying. The height of fulfillment and destiny are given as guidelines in the Scriptures. Anyone who thinks it is more fulfilling to live outside the guidelines of scriptural injunctions has absolutely no understanding of the Gospel.

This issue, however, has raised its ugly head since the early Church and all throughout history. Look at the reformation in Luther's day. This movement of God was predicated on Scripture alone (the organic message), grace alone (God's Kingdom is extended by grace, not our works earning us anything), faith alone (we have right standing and access to God through faith alone, not our works), and the glory of God alone (all we do should bring glory to God).

Since the "original" reformation was based on grace and faith, it created an Antinomian sentiment. Some of Luther's disciples taught Antinomianism (against the law). Luther's response was swift. Some taught that since people were justified by faith, they could engage in immorality since there was no longer any obligation to obey moral law. Most Antinomians, however, didn't adhere to "freedom to sin." Nonetheless, Luther responded by saying that the law was good as a guideline for moral living. Thus, in Luther's mind the law revealed sin and provided a rule for life, but did not establish a basis for our right standing with God. Bottom line: Grace is freedom *from* sin, not freedom *to* sin (see Gal. 5:1,13).

THIRD ISSUE: ULTIMATE RECONCILIATION

There is another increasingly dominant movement based on false premises of grace called Ultimate Reconciliation (some call it the Gospel of Inclusion or Universalism). This doctrine says that Jesus' death paid for the sins of all humankind by grace. Therefore, all people are saved—automatically. This doctrine is based on such Scriptures as First John 2:2, *"He* [Jesus] *is the atoning sacrifice for our sins, and not only for ours but also for the sins of the whole world."* This is the establishment of grace without faith. Grace is not automatic; it is received by faith.

I have had numerous conversations with leaders of various segments of Universalists. It is not my intent to chronicle a lengthy rebuttal to their erroneous claims. In essence, they have not grasped the fundamental nature of Ephesians 2:8-9. We are not saved by grace! If we were, then, indeed all people would be saved automatically. According to Paul in Ephesians 2:8, we are saved by grace through faith. In other words, what we have received by grace, unmerited by us, must be received through the vehicle of faith.

See, I may give you a gift, but if you don't open it and use it, it has no value to you. Organic Christianity is not grace alone—it is grace through faith. It is like receiving a blender. The blender is useless until it is plugged into a power source. Once it is plugged into the power source, it is fully functional. Grace is the power source that faith plugs into, which makes salvation with all of its forms functional.

Why have I spent time in diversions from the real message of freedom and full functionality in Christ? It is because so many people will try to derail the new reformation, like they did Martin Luther's historical reformation in 1517, because of misconceptions and abuse. These are mere sideshows to stop or derail organic Christianity.

So, let's go to Chapter 3½ (so to speak) to finish the thought of the first progression of the manifestation model. Let's examine how grace as unmerited favor, in the finished work of Christ, delivers us from schizophrenia as believers—people who desire the full manifestation of the Kingdom, but feel unqualified to receive. It's time to learn our true identity in Christ.

● ●

ORGANIC THOUGHTS

1. Is it time for a new perspective in the Church?

2. How does Romans 5:17 help us understand that life doesn't dictate to us, but we dictate to life?

3. Examine Stephen Scott's four classifications of people. Where are you right now?

4. What's the difference between living under law (demand) and grace (supply)?

5. Do you see yourself complete in Him, having the fullness of God? (See John 1:16-17; Colossians 2:10.)

6. What does it mean that we don't have to obtain more of God, but renew our minds to what we already have?

7. How do you understand the phrase *grace upon grace?* (See John 1:16-17.)

8. What is the difference between going to victory or coming from victory?

9. How does the understanding of Ephesians 1:3 help you access God's Kingdom?

10. Does this definition of *faith*—faith doesn't believe God will, but faith believes God has—change the way you see faith?

11. Does understanding the issues of Gnosticism and Antinomianism change how you see First John 1:8-9?

12. After reading this chapter, how do you see repentance?

13. Is it clear to you that grace is the freedom to conquer sin, not the freedom to sin?

Chapter 3½

. . . .

SPIRITUAL SCHIZOPHRENIA

Theological issues aside, why is this new reformation essential? Why is this first progression of grace as unmerited favor and the finished work of Christ important to understand? It is because it formulates the basis of an impending cataclysmic work of Christ.

Ezekiel 37 reveals what I'm trying to explain. Ezekiel 37 formulates the dual purpose of the restoration of the nation of Israel (Judah) and the reinvigoration of the Church (spiritual Israel).[1] Ezekiel 37:1-3 states:

> *The hand of the Lord was upon me, and He brought me out by the Spirit of the Lord and set me in the middle of the valley; and it was full of bones. He led me back and forth among them, and I saw a great many bones on the floor of the valley, bones that were very dry. He asked me, "Son of Man, can these bones live?" I said, "O Sovereign Lord, You alone know."*

This is a story of spiritual schizophrenia. Schizophrenia is obviously having a split personality or two personalities. Spiritual schizophrenia is a condition that says, "I know God can, I just don't know if He will...for me." It is a diagnosis that analyzes that, because we don't understand what He has already done (by grace in the new covenant), we're not sure what He will do. We've not yet gleaned the understanding that faith is not *believing God can,* but rather *believing God has* already done it. The result is schizophrenic, indecisive Christians who don't grasp what is at their disposal.

Look at where God is taking us. Ezekiel 37:1 says, *"The hand of the Lord was upon me and He brought me out by the Spirit of the Lord and set me, in the middle of a valley...."* Talk about "Beam me up, Scotty" or Star Trek, The Next Generation. Please get the picture of what is happening there: The prophet is in one place, and in the next moment, he is transported to a totally different location. Star Trek's transporter is like Romper Room or Sesame Street when compared to the Spirit.

In verses 2 and 3, in his new setting, he is confronted by a valley of dry bones. God asks him an incredibly intimidating question, *"Son of man, can these bones live?"* You might think, *Why is that intimidating?* What if these were the bones of the previous prophets who had already flunked the test?

He responds, *"...O Sovereign Lord, You alone know"* (Ezek. 37:3). He might have said it this way, "I know You can. I just don't know if You will...for me." This is a call to overcome spiritual schizophrenia. This is a call to rise up and be the people of God.

God never responds to Ezekiel's answer. He simply says, "Here is what I want you to do." *"Then He said to me, 'Prophesy to these bones and say to them, "Dry bones, hear the word of the Lord"'"* (Ezek. 37:4). Ezekial's concept of dry bones in this passage is the idea of emaciation, a wasting away, starvation or leanness. It's like Psalm 106:15, *"He gave them their request; but sent leanness into their soul"* (KJV). In other words, God is saying, "In My people's minds, wills, emotions, and imaginations, they are less than I've made them to be. They are more than they realize. Prophesy to them. Speak forth the counsel of God." Prophesy what?

> *...Prophesy to these bones and say to them, "Dry bones, hear the word of the Lord! This is what the Sovereign Lord says to these bones: I will make breath enter you, and you will come to life. I will attach tendons to you and make flesh come upon you and cover you with skin; put breath in you, and you will come to life. Then you will know that I am Lord"* (Ezekiel 37:4-6).

Wow! Now that is a mouthful! Take the lifeless people of God and declare God's intent over them. He will then breathe upon them the breath of life so that they can again become a living, vital entity. In essence, they would be delivered from spiritual schizophrenia; they would know that He is Lord (see Ezek. 37:6). In so doing, they would not only know that He can, but that He *will* move on their behalf.

The prophet did as he was commanded, and a noise, a rattling sound, took place. It was the sound of a re-formation (reformation). Bone came to bone; tendons, flesh, and skin covered them—but they were still corpses. They had all the appearance of functional bodies, but had no life in them. It's time the Church not only looks right, but has the life of God flowing in it as He intends. It's time to stop propping up a dead body and spending our efforts trying to make it look like what it's not. It's time that we are delivered from spiritual schizophrenia into a unified identity as people who understand who God is, what He has already done, and who He has made us to be.

As the prophet observes a perfect-looking, but lifeless body, he is commanded to prophesy (speaking forth the counsel of God) to the breath—*"Come from the four winds, O breath, and breathe into these slain, that they may live"* (Ezek. 37:9b). As breath entered the bodies, *"...they came to life and stood on their feet—a vast army"* (Ezek. 37:10b). It is our unadulterated call to re-form our lives, as those who name the name of Jesus, and to once again become the armed and dangerous for the Kingdom of God.

The cure for overcoming spiritual schizophrenia is becoming aware of our identity in Christ. It is God's grace that allows us to understand what God has directly done and that allows us to clearly see who we really are in Christ. God is about to unleash an army of people who know who He truly is, what He has already done, and who He has made us to be. Because we know what He has done by grace, unmerited by us and placed in the Kingdom, we can be confident He *will* manifest it by faith.

THE GOSPEL REVOLUTION

The time has come for people to know who God truly is. It's not time to know about God, but to know Him in intimacy. The army of God is being assembled for such a time as this.

Notice Paul's assertion in Romans 4:13, *"It was not through the law that Abraham and his offspring received the promise that they would be an heir of the world, but through the righteousness that comes by faith."* The law's job is only to expose deficiency. The job of grace is to expose our sufficiency in Christ to fulfill His promise.

Here in this passage, Paul says that Abraham and his offspring (literally his *seed*) are heirs of the world. In other words, this world and its resources are made for use by God's Kingdom, not the corruption of the world's system. Judaizers considered the Mosaic law as special revelation for human conduct (which it is), but also a basis for right standing before God. Therefore, Paul has to declare it is not through the law that Abraham and his offspring, including us as believers (see Gal. 3:16), received the promise. The promise is His new covenant (see Gal. 3:15-16).

The essence of covenant is this: If I exchange what I have, God exchanges what He has (the Kingdom of God with all His resources). This is important because the new covenant was not made with us; it was made with Jesus (see Gal. 3:16). If it was made with us, every time we violated it, we would negate the covenant. However, because it was made with Jesus, our basis of relating to God's covenant is based on what He did, not what we do (anyone who uses this as an excuse to sin doesn't understand God). What is the essence of the promise—we are heirs of this world (see Rom. 4:13) through "faith righteousness." The promise doesn't come through "works righteousness," but "faith righteousness." What he is saying is that life doesn't dictate to us, but we dictate to life. The world doesn't dominate us, but we dominate the world.

Now here is an essential question. When does one receive an inheritance? It comes when the benefactor dies. Who is our benefactor? It is Jesus the Christ, who died 2,000 years ago. The call of organic Christianity is to stop living beneath our privileges. We are heirs of this world, not based on our performance, but based on Christ's performance. This puts an end to spiritual schizophrenia and helps us realize we are qualified to receive what God did for us by grace through faith. The promise is ours through imputed righteousness.

This is the reason why Paul can make the assertion in Romans 5:17, *"...how much more will those who receive God's abundant provision of grace and of the gift of righteousness reign in life through the one man, Jesus Christ."* It is by grace (unmerited favor, empowerment) and righteousness (faith righteousness, not works righteousness) that we rule over our environment. The lack of this understandably has created an impotent Body of Christ that is caught between the "amen" and the "there it is." It has left schizophrenic believers knowing, "God can, but I don't know if He will...for me." The quest of organic Christianity is to rally the Body of Christ to stand to our feet a vast army, to manifest God's Kingdom in the earth (personally and corporately).

Spiritual schizophrenia, however, is not limited to faith alone. The majority of believers live in the valley of wondering whether God loves them. This is the result of perverting the organic message to that of forgiveness of sins rather than intimacy with God. Please, don't misunderstand me; I would never minimize or marginalize forgiveness of sins. This emphasis, however, has kept people from intimacy with God. The problem with law-based faith is that it makes believers live with the feeling of not believing they are qualified to receive from God or have the ability to be close to God. Law-based Christianity (legalism) leaves people feeling they've never done enough to be accepted by God. Remember, God's standard for receiving a passing grade is 100 percent—we can never make a mistake (see James 2:10). If we're 99 percent students, we might feel better when we compare ourselves to others, but we still flunk God's test. That's why our right standing (righteousness) is based on what Jesus did and we receive it by faith.

Most work-based righteousness theology creates fear. The fear is what alienates people from intimacy with God. Legalism justifies this thought by quoting things like Proverbs 1:7, *"The fear of the Lord is the beginning of knowledge...."* Whatever we may believe about what "fear"[3] means here, it is essential to understand what is being said in this passage. The fear of the Lord is the beginning, not the culmination, of knowledge.

Here's an example of what I mean. As a parent, I might say to my small child, "Don't touch the stove!" I state it in such a way (almost as a law) because I know the danger of the circumstance that a young child does not yet understand. However, eventually children will operate by their own understanding. Fear was the beginning, but not the culmination, of knowledge. So law formulates guidelines for protection, but not a basis for relating to God. When law (performance or works) becomes a basis for relating to God, I never feel qualified to be intimate with God. I always have to earn His blessing.

Let me give another example. Early on in my traveling ministry, I would often come into a town on Saturday to minister on Sunday. Usually Saturday night was a time of prayer and preparation. I usually prayed before I concluded the evening. Almost subconsciously I would look at my watch—why? So I could see when one hour had culminated. Somehow I thought if I prayed an hour I had earned the right to be anointed. How derelict is that kind of thinking? I was living on the wrong side of John 1:17 (*"for the law was given through Moses"* on one side and *"grace and truth came through Jesus Christ"* on the other). I had missed the organic message, which was that we have an anointing that abides with us always (see 1 John 2:27). I don't pray to earn God's blessing. I pray to better understand who He is, what He has already done, and who He made me to be. I pray to cultivate intimacy. It is intimacy that helps create sensitivity to Him for the moment.

Spiritual schizophrenia cultivates spiritual dyslexia. Remember, dyslexia sees things backwards. We think John 14:21 says that if we keep God's commandments, then we love God. In essence, it is just the opposite. I keep God's commandments because I love Him (see the verse for yourself).[4] Organic Christianity doesn't do good works to be accepted by God; it shows that because I am accepted it is natural to do good works.

My friend, musician and worship leader Israel Houghton, is presently on tour. His tour is called, Gospel R*evol*ution. The word *love* is accentuated by being written backward in the middle of the word. Israel's tour is built on the theme "Love God, love people." I have often written that one of the philosophies of my ministry is "Love

God! Love people! Love life!" However, none of that is possible until we let God love us. We can't give what we don't have. Tina Turner had it completely wrong when she sang "What's Love Got to Do with It." Notice how the apostle John writes it: *"There is no fear in love..."* (1 John 4:18). Here John is helping us to understand fear diminishes intimacy with God. It's hard to be intimate with someone when we don't feel accepted by that person. John continues, *"...But perfect love drives out fear, because fear has to do with punishment...* (1 John 4:18). Fear lives in anticipation of bad; love and faith live in anticipation of good. People who live in fear expect punishment and condemnation. That is why spiritual schizophrenia is rampant in the Body of Christ.

When people feel they don't measure up to God's standard, they feel unqualified to receive from God. John then amplifies, *"...The one who fears is not made perfect in love. We love because He first loved us"* (1 John 4:18-19). We are free to love God, love people, and love life when we know God has loved us unconditionally. Paul says it like this,

> *For I am convinced that neither death nor life, neither angels nor demons, neither the present nor the future, nor any powers, neither height nor depth, nor anything else in all creation will be able to separate us from the love of God that is in Christ Jesus our Lord* (Romans 8:38-39).

The way we become more than conquerors (see Rom. 8:37), the way we don't let life dictate to us, the way we become a vast army marching with the message of the Kingdom is by letting God give us His unconditional (agape) love. Organic Christianity at its root essence is believers knowing God's love. Spiritual schizophrenia is disintegrated in the love of God. The Gospel *Revolution* is a love revolution.

Most of us think we understand the love of God, but my experience in ministry would lead me to believe the majority of Christians don't understand God's unconditional love. Most believers think God's love is based on their performance. When I pray enough, study my Bible enough, tithe enough, witness enough, then I am qualified to receive from God. This is why spiritual schizophrenia is rampant. It's almost like picking daisy petals saying, "He loves me! He loves me not! He loves me...He loves me not..."

When we struggle to believe God's promises will come to pass for our lives (or others), this is rooted in unbelief. The root to our unbelief is primarily lack of experiencing the love of God. That is why Paul says that faith works by love (see Gal. 5:6).[5] This means that faith operates in the understanding of love. The heart of faith is the simple revelation that God loves us. I can trust someone whom I know loves me and wants my best (it helps that He is omnipotent).

A few years ago I had the privilege of counseling a dynamic young woman. Though she was obviously gifted, I noticed she had large mood swings in her daily routine that kept her from manifesting her full potential. Though she was an incredible person, she was not stepping into the fullness of her destiny. She was attractive, had an infectious personality, and possessed a personal dynamism. However, she was struggling with a sense of making her life count. The fluctuation of her spirit was dramatic. She was up one day and down the next. She was in one day and out the next. Though she was dynamic to a large degree, she was wallowing in mediocrity.

Relationship is the currency of the Kingdom, and as we developed a relationship, she began to open her life up to me. I discovered she had a very significant loss in her life. At a young age, her parents were pastors of a church, and tragically her dad passed away. The result was she felt abandoned and unloved by God. She was desperately trying to live for God, but she didn't feel loved by Him. Over time I became like a father figure to her. I showed her the revelation of God's love, righteousness, and grace.

We made tremendous strides in her identity in Christ, but they were marked by relapses of inconsistencies in her self-image and feeling loved by God. I helped her see she was looking into the wrong mirror and it was giving her an improper perspective (see James 1:22). As long as she looked into the mirror of her experience and not the mirror of the Word of God, it was distorting her perspective of her Heavenly Father. When we look into a mirror with a poor reflection, we receive an improper image (see 1 Cor. 13:12). I said, *"Your mirror has masked your understanding of God's lavish, unconditional love"* (see Rom. 8:35-39). The more she looked into the mirror of the Word, the freer she became, but ultimately she seemed to revert back to moods of feeling unloved.

This precious person also loved to bake. One day she brought me some chocolate chip cookies. Suddenly, a revelation hit me. I looked at her and said, "Wouldn't it be awful to bring chocolate chip cookies to someone who doesn't like chocolate chip cookies?"

She looked at me with a puzzled glance, and she meekly said, "Don't you like chocolate chip cookies?" (They're not my favorite, by the way. Maybe that's why the thought hit me.)

I said, "Actually, it has nothing to do with it. That's what you're trying to do with God. Somehow you've allowed your past to reflect to you that God must not love you, and you interpreted that as the fact that you must earn His love. In your mind, you never quite do enough to be acceptable, and you revert back to feeling low and unloved. So you are trying to offer Him what He doesn't want."

Her inquisitive look told me the light went on, but she didn't totally grasp what I was saying. I said, "You're so desperately trying to live *for* God to be acceptable to God that you've missed the fact that He simply wants to live *through* you. He loves you unconditionally."

Suddenly, the process of her feeling loved sped up exponentially. Stability settled in on her life. Today she and her husband have a thriving ministry in the Midwest.

Her desire to live for God and not through Him caused her to miss the essence of the Gospel. The love of God frees us to live in intimacy with Him. Living for Him focuses our attention on ourselves. Living through Him focuses our attention on God. The former gives concentration on rules, the latter on relationship.

This is Paul's astonishing message to the church of Ephesus. He says, *"I pray that out of His glorious riches..."* (Eph. 3:16). In the King James Version it reads *"His riches in glory."* This phrase is a revelation of Christ's finished work at Calvary being placed in glory (in the Kingdom of Heaven) by grace unmerited by us.

He continues, *"...He may strengthen you with power through His Spirit in your inner being, so that Christ may dwell in your hearts through faith..."* (Eph. 3:16-17). Jesus dwells in our lives through salvation, but He dwells in our hearts by faith. The issues, boundaries, and manifestations of life come directly from our hearts (see Prov. 4:23).

Then Paul adds this amazing addendum, *"...And I pray that you, being rooted and established in love"* (Eph. 3:17). People who are rooted and established in love don't feel unloved when circumstances go awry. Even in difficult times they know the constancy and consistency of God's unconditional love. They know that bad circumstances are not God's way of evening the score with them.

Now Paul reveals the dynamics of this revelation, *"may have power, together with all the saints, to grasp how wide and long and high and deep is the love of Christ, and to know this love that surpasses knowledge..."* (Eph. 3:18-19). This phrase contains a striking oxymoron: to know love that we can't understand. Astonishing! Astounding! The breadth, length, height, and depth of the love of Christ exceeds our comprehension, yet we are to know it in its boundless dimensions.[6] God grants to us a love we can experience, one that we should not qualify to receive, at least not based on our performance! This love is so all encompassing; it is beyond our understanding to comprehend the astonishing scope and vastness of His unconditional acceptance.

Here's the *coup de grâce* of this amazing revelation: *"...that you may be filled to the measure of all the fullness of God"* (Eph. 3:19). In other words, we will never be able to experience the fullness of God apart from knowing God's love. God's love is the key that opens the door to everything God is and everything God has.[7]

Spiritual schizophrenia ceases when we understand God's love, grace, and righteousness. Once we know who God is (love—see 1 John 4:16), what He has already done (grace—through the finished work of Christ), and who He has made us to be (the righteousness of God in Christ Jesus—see 2 Cor. 5:21), we know not only that God *can,* but also that He *will* manifest His Kingdom on our behalf. This revelation gives birth to a new intimacy with God and a rest in His finished work.

THE REST OF THE STORY

Toward the conclusion of the Civil War, on September 22, 1862, President Abraham Lincoln signed the Emancipation Proclamation. This amazing document freed all American slaves. The Civil War had been fought to advance the freedom of all Americans; now this document secured that freedom. However, there were many dynamics that occurred that stopped many slaves from living in their procured freedom. First, many slave owners kept the revelation of their slaves' newfound freedom from them. Thus, their slaves lived apart from the freedom that was rightfully theirs. Second, though some slaves understood they were freed, all they knew was slavery. Thus, many elected to remain in slavery. In both cases, though they were free, their ignorance (which is different than stupidity) kept them in slavery.

This is precisely what the devil has done to us as believers. Galatians 5:1 is our emancipation proclamation: *"It is for freedom that Christ has set us free...."* The context in this passage is speaking of the law (see Gal. 4:21-31). Our liberty, however, is much larger than the understanding of law. We are free to be loved by God, free to receive His provision, free from sin, free to live for and through God, free to have access to His Kingdom, free to be rightly related to Him—yet satan has blinded our eyes to the truth. Hosea 4:6 states, *"My people are destroyed from lack of knowledge."* The term *destroy* used here is not the typical definition of demolish or annihilate. The word used here means "to be dumb, cut off, to be undone, or to fail."[8] God's not saying His people will be utterly annihilated by lack of knowledge, but that they are "dumbed down," so to speak. God's people, by not understanding God (who He is and what He has already done), have cut themselves off from their source. People's ignorance of organic Christianity can cause them to live in religion rather than life (vitality). Unwittingly, people have changed the most radical, transforming message the world has ever known into religion. The result is a frustrated army of schizophrenic believers languishing in their barracks (church houses) instead of conquering their worlds.

The organic message of the Gospel is the key to the freedom that we innately desire. Listen to what Paul says to the Galatians,

> *I am crucified with Christ: nevertheless I live; yet not I, but Christ liveth in me: and the life which I now live in the flesh I live by the faith of the Son of God, who loved me, and gave Himself for me* (Galatians 2:20 KJV).

Organic Christianity is about the *exchanged life* more than it is about the *changed* life. It is more about God living *through* us than our living *for* Him. Our frustration in life comes when we try to do God's part. Despite what many of us have heard, *God cannot help those who help themselves.* Now, before this sets someone off, let me explain what I mean. Jesus said it like this, *"...Apart from Me you can do nothing"* (John 15:5 NKJV). I am not suggesting, as some grace advocates are accused of saying, that God did it all and we have no part in it. Our life is grace through faith. Grace is God's part; faith is our part. There is, however, nothing we can do to be right with God, but receive it.

Frustration among believers comes when we try to do God's part. That's called "flesh." The concept of acting in the flesh is multifaceted, but primarily I define it this way: It is when we try to do God's will our way. Hence comes the perversion of organic Christianity. My own problem was that I was trying to change myself. I was *trying*, not *trusting*. The law focuses on the outer person and tells us what we must do. Grace focuses on the inner person and tells us what is already done in Christ.[8] Those who focus on what Christ has done for them walk in grace.

As quoted earlier, Galatians 2:20 (though not universally translated this way) says that we live by the faith *of* the Son of God. The Christian life is not just hard to live; it's impossible—apart from Him. The only way to live victoriously is to let Christ live through us. To live the exchanged life we live through the supernatural faith of God. It is a life of faith in His grace.

He shows us why we're frustrated and how we've perverted organic Christianity. In Galatians 2:21, he notes, *"Do not frustrate the grace of God: for if righteousness come by the law, then Christ is dead in vain* (KJV)." The word *frustrate* means "to set aside, neutralize, violate, nullify or bring to nought."[10] We can actually nullify God's grace when we try to be right with God based on our own merit instead of receiving His unmerited benefit from His finished work. Paul echoes this in 2 Corinthians 6:1, *"As God's fellow workers we urge you not to receive God's grace in vain."* For the grace of God to be effective we must mix it with faith (see Gal. 2:21).

Thus, countless beleaguered, frustrated believers live in spiritual schizophrenia. However, this first progression of the manifestation model liberates Christians to be intimate with God—to know who He is, what He has done, and who He has made us to be.

WHO'S YOUR DADDY!?

I love this phrase, "Who's your Daddy!?" When I use this terminology, I'm not using it like modern vernacular, as in the movie, *Remember the Titans*. In one scene, Denzel Washington plays a coach who is bringing a few rebellious players into submission. The backdrop of the story has to do with a high school that is integrating black and whites during the 1960s. These two white players are trying to dictate to the coach a guarantee of how many white players will secure starting positions on the team. The coach chides their request and asserts his position by proclaiming, "Who's your Daddy?" to which the rebellious players mutter in response, "You are!"

The modern use of "Who's your Daddy?" is seeking to show who dominates whom. Although there may be some application in that thought process, I'm talking about understanding who our Daddy really is. I'm talking about understanding our spiritual identity. I define *identity* as knowing who God is, understanding what He has already done, and knowing who we are in Him.

I have used that phrase over and over again because so few believers understand what the Gospel says about God and who He has made us to be. *Identity* literally means "the condition or fact of being the same in all qualities." It means "sameness, oneness, or being identical."[11] Wow! Our identity in Christ means we are the same in all qualities as Christ. *"...As He is, so are we in this world"* (1 John 4:17 NKJV). We are made in the image and likeness of our God.

The terms *image* (Hebrew: *tselem*) and *likeness* (Hebrew: *demuwth*) carry the meaning "essential nature, copy, characteristics, and essence."[12] Some scholars attribute making proper use of "image" and "likeness" to having distinctive attributes.[13] Thus, it carries the idea that man is in the god-class and has the inherent tendencies of God and the ability to function in them.

We must understand that the organic Gospel is more about intimacy with God than forgiveness of sins. (I would never minimize or marginalize this important revelation concerning forgiveness of sins. The problem, however, is that when we make forgiveness of sins an end-product rather than the means to that end, it breaks entrustment with our Savior.) The organic Gospel frees us to be intimate with Christ. This in turn helps us to understand our identity. People who understand who they are turn into thriving people instead of surviving people. A thriving people reach out beyond themselves to hurting people who need what they have found. Collectively, they stand as a vast army.

This new "re-formation" will, first, be a movement of a people not just a person. Much of the Church today is about a person who is well-known and on the platform. I'm not belittling those things, but his or her job is to equip people with the understanding of who they are (in Christ). The Church is to be an organism (not just organization)—*living* stones training people to reach their true potential (see 1 Pet. 2:4). Thus, reformation will, second, be about intimacy with God. As we understand God's grace, we learn to run *to* God instead of running *from* God (see Heb. 4:16). As we learn to abide in Him and His truth abides in us, we can access unlimited provision from His Kingdom (see John 15:7). Third, this causes us to see without hindrance what our identity really is. Fourth, the new reformation will then free us to act in faith according to the provisions of grace. Fifth, we will understand God's Kingdom in its fullness, as I discussed in the last chapter.

BIBLICAL IDENTITY

So, who are we? Listen to our identity based on what God says:

Second Corinthians 5:17—*"If anyone is in Christ, he is a new creation; the old has gone* [KJV: *"he is a new creature: old things are passed away"*], *the new has come!"* The idea in this passage is that we are a new species of being. Being born again doesn't mean we're a better us—we're a new and distinct kind of variety. Our past doesn't dictate to our future.

Galatians 2:20—*"I am crucified with Christ: nevertheless I live: yet not I, but Christ liveth in me: and the life which I now live in the flesh I live by the faith of the Son of God..."* (KJV). This is the exchanged life.

Ephesians 3:20—*"Now to Him who is able to do immeasurably* [can't measure it] *more than all we ask or imagine, according to His power that is at work within us."* God can do extraordinary things without measure in and through our lives. Now note this—it is according to the power *already at work within us.* At the inception of salvation, Christ made us complete in Him (see Col. 2:10). We don't have to get something more; we need to renew our minds to what we already have (see Rom. 12:2).

Philemon 6—*"That the communication of thy faith may become effectual by the acknowledging of every good thing which is in you in Christ Jesus"* (KJV). Again, note that what we need is already in us through Christ.

First John 4:9—*"This is how God showed His love among us: He sent His one and only Son into the world that we might live through Him."* The term *through* means "in one side and out the other, in the midst of, by way or means of, from beginning to end."[14] God is living His life through ours as we abide in Him (see John 15:1-7).

Second Corinthians 5:21—*"God made Him who had no sin to be sin for us, so that in Him we might become the righteousness of God."*

We are in right standing with God, not based on what we do, but based on what He did, and we receive it by faith.

Colossians 2:10—*"And ye are complete in Him..."* (KJV). The term *complete* means "whole, entire, finished, lacking in nothing."[15] Is that how you see yourself?

First John 4:17—*"...as He is, so are we in this world"* (NKJV). We function here just as Jesus did so we can produce just as Jesus did.

Romans 4:13—*"It was not through law that Abraham and his offspring received the promise that he would be heir of the world, but through the righteousness that comes by faith."* As Abraham's offspring, we received the promise to be heirs of this world.

Colossians 1:12—*"Giving thanks to the Father, who has qualified you to share in the inheritance of the saints in the kingdom of light."* Wow! In Christ we are qualified to receive of God's Kingdom.

Ephesians 1:3—*"Praise be to the God and Father of our Lord Jesus Christ, who has blessed us in the heavenly realms with every spiritual blessing in Christ."* We must understand that access to everything we need for life has already been granted to us by grace—to be accessed by faith!

Second Peter 1:2-9—Peter starts by saying, *"Grace and peace be yours in abundance...."* This is more than just a greeting. Paul uses this same opening to communicate his heart over and over again (see the beginning of many of his epistles). He is saying grace to us. Grace is the finished work of Christ. Grace is unmerited favor. Grace is a divine influence upon the heart. Grace is God's empowerment or ability on our behalf. Grace to us in its fullness. Then he adds, *"and peace."* Peace is the ability to be unaffected by our circumstances. What grace provides, peace is the ability to keep.

This comes in abundance *"...through the knowledge of God and of Jesus our Lord"* (2 Pet. 1:2). The term *knowledge* is not the word for facts or understanding, but means "experiential and personal knowledge."[16] Grace and peace are the result of intimacy with God.

This knowledge is not just facts, but knowledge of Him (see 2 Pet. 1:3-8). This kind of knowledge is a reflection of our spiritual identity (knowing who He is).

Now, verse 3 begins this amazing revelation, *"His divine power has given us* [past tense] *everything we need for life and godliness through our knowledge of Him who called us by His own glory and goodness."* Verse 4 begins, *"Through these ...."* The *"these"* Peter refers to are His glory, His goodness, His knowledge, His grace, and His peace. This is a call to understanding our identity.

This thought is reinforced by the rest of the verse:

> *Through these He has given us His very great and precious promises, so that through them you may participate in divine nature and escape the corruption of the world caused by evil desires* (2 Peter 1:4).

Watch this amazing progression of this passage in verses 2-4: *grace* (unmerited favor, the finished work of Christ, divine influence upon the heart, and God's ability) gives way to *peace* (the ability to keep what grace has given to us), gives way to like precious *faith* (the same faith Peter used to raise Dorcas from the dead in Acts 9 is the same faith in us), gives way to *knowledge* (intimate, experiential knowledge of God), gives way to God's *divine power* (supernatural power), which gives us everything we need for *life* (vitality or the God kind of life)[17] and *godliness* (ability to be God-like). This in turn allows us to receive *knowledge* (experiential, intimate knowledge), which promotes His own *glory* (one of the meanings of glory is the view and opinion of God).[18] This is how we are led to *repentance* or rethinking (see Rom. 2:4). This in turn opens the *promises of God* to us (Kingdom laws of how the Kingdom of God operates) that allow us to participate in *divine nature* (see Gal. 2:20), which causes us to *conquer the world* (world's system). What a mouthful that is!

In other words, we understand the spiritual identity—"...*through our knowledge of Him...*" (2 Pet. 1:3)—who God is, what He has already done, and who He has made us to be. Now comes the amazing part of this revelation:

> *For if you possess these qualities in increasing measure, they will keep you from being ineffective and unproductive in your knowledge of our Lord Jesus Christ. But if anyone does not have them, he is nearsighted and blind, and has forgotten that he has been cleansed from his past sins* (1 Peter 1:8-9).

Tighten your seat belts and lock down your tray tables; this is essential to grasp. People who don't grasp their spiritual identity live in myopia, blindness, or amnesia. In other words, the best case scenario is Christians who don't know their spiritual identity live seeing just in front of themselves. The worst case scenario is believers completely blind and in the dark to what God is doing. The result is they live in amnesia like people who don't understand the meaning of their past sins being forgiven. Our spiritual identity solidifies our qualification to receive the blessing to be effective and productive.

Can you imagine waking up and suddenly having lost all of your memory? You can't remember your name, your address, your mate, your children, or your family. You can't remember your occupation or the skills you used to become successful. You would feel lost to proceed with any kind of security or competence. If you became insecure enough, you might cast off restraint and act like someone you are not. This is what Peter is describing in this passage. Believers who lose their sense of identity act like they've forgotten that their sins have been forgiven. Your spiritual identity is perhaps the most important aspect to living victoriously and successfully.

Let me ask you again, do you see yourself in reflection in these 12 passages? If the answer is no, it is because you've allowed the five elements of your personal belief system (PBS) to reflect to you something different.

PERSONAL BELIEF SYSTEM

Psychologists reveal to us that what we believe primarily comes from five elements of our PBS. These five areas are:

1. **Social Environment**—We have a tendency to believe what our environment tells us we are.

2. **Authority Figures**—We have a tendency to also believe what the most important people in our lives tell us we should believe. If that is positive, it's wonderful. If it's negative, it can limit our future.

3. **Self-image**—Psychologists tell us we can never rise above the image we have of ourselves in our hearts. If we want to change an area in our lives, we have to change how we see ourselves in that area first.

4. **Repetitious Information**—Things we are told over and over again, we believe are true whether they are or not.

5. **Experience**—We have a tendency to believe what we've experienced to be true.[19]

When any of these five areas of our PBS are established in our hearts, we have a tendency to overrule new truth. Psychologists call it "scotoma" or blind spots. These areas tend to rule out new truth.

That's why Paul tells us to *"be made new in the attitude of your minds; and to put on the new self, created to be like God in true righteousness and holiness"* (Eph. 4:23-24).

Our biggest dilemma as believers is that we are new creation realities living like our old selves. We are a new species of being, but we still think like we used to. We are not operating in the full meaning of our new identity. We have to renew our minds to reflect who we've become and to understand what we now possess.

Now note this because it is pivotal to understanding our identity. We need to be renewed in the spirit of our minds to put on the new man (self), which after God is created in righteousness and true holiness (see Eph. 4:23-24 KJV). Notice the use of the word *created*. A believer's holiness and righteousness is an accomplished fact in the new birth. If there's a true holiness and righteousness, there's a false holiness and righteousness. False holiness is the good we do to be set apart unto God. We've made *holiness* a complicated topic. It simply means "set apart" or "to separate."[20] True holiness is a gift from God that sets us apart from the world's system unto God. When the Scripture talks about a holy God, it means He is set apart from the world's system of doing things. Paul says it like this, *"...you are in Christ Jesus, who has become for us wisdom from God—that is, our righteousness, holiness and redemption"* (1 Cor. 1:30).

The writer of Hebrews notes, *"And by that will* [the new covenant in context], *we have been made* [past tense] *holy through the sacrifice of the body of Jesus Christ once for all"* (Heb. 10:10). By now there's a large gong going off in some people's heads. It's going, "Oh no, he's saying there's nothing we have to do to be holy!" That's absolutely right— and absolutely wrong! Look at verse 14, *"Because by one sacrifice He has made perfect forever those who are being made holy"* (Heb. 10:14).

Here's the new 64,000 dollar question: How can I be *being made holy* if I am already holy? It sounds like a lot of religious mumbo jumbo. Here's the simplicity of this pivotal set of verses. Hebrews is a book contrasting the two covenants. In Hebrews 10, the writer states that by means of a single sacrifice Christ brought every believer to completion (which is the meaning of the term *perfect21*) in perpetuity to those being made holy (or sanctified). That is why John 17:17 states, *"Sanctify them by the truth; your word is truth."* The more you understand the truth of your holiness, the more you will operate accordingly. In one single act at Calvary, Christ accomplished what old covenant sacrifices could never do. The old covenant was a legalistic process in which people related to God based on their performance. On the other hand, in the new covenant of grace and righteousness, I relate to God based on what Jesus did by grace, unmerited by me, and I receive it by faith. There's a massive difference in how people relate to God based on the two covenants.

That is why a preacher might rail, "Be holy as God is holy!" What does that mean? A quick purveying of any crowd will reveal we are all imperfect. Does God expect us to be like Him? He is infinitely pure! The only way we can match that standard is in Christ.

When we get saved, we are new "in Christ." "In Him" means not just producing a *changed* life, but an *exchanged* life. Now He becomes our wisdom, righteousness, holiness, and redemption. The Christian life isn't difficult to live—it is impossible in our own ability. It's only when we learn to let Jesus live through us that we can obtain victory. Instead of depending on our acts of righteousness to earn God's blessings, we must learn to accept the fact that Christ has given us His righteousness. We can't do enough to be holy in His sight, but we can live through His holiness. Now here's the great paradox: Though we are holy in His sight (see Heb. 10:10), the more we understand it, the more we will manifest what is holy in our lives (see Heb. 10:14; John 17:17). It doesn't come from sin consciousness, but from learning to be convicted of His righteousness and holiness (see Rom. 3:20-22; 1 Cor. 1:30; Heb. 10:1-2, 10-14, 16-23; John 16:7-10). The more we understand what it means to live separate unto God's system, the more the world's system pales by comparison. This is holiness.

Once we understand the Lord's system (Kingdom), it changes everything about how we approach God. Look how the writer of Hebrews shows us, as Paul Harvey would say, "the *rest* of the story."

> *Therefore, since the promise of entering His rest still stands, let us be careful that none of you be found to have fallen short of it....but the message they heard was of no value to them, because those who heard did not combine it with faith. Now we who have believed enter that rest....And yet His work has been finished since the creation of the world....for anyone who enters God's rest also rests from his own work, just as God did from His. Let us, therefore, make every effort to enter that rest..."* (Hebrews 4:1-3;10-11).

Understanding the new covenant causes us to live a life of rest, not spiritual schizophrenia. The concept of *rest* is not always what we think of in American culture. For instance, in Genesis 1, when God created the world, it says that God worked for six days and on the seventh day He rested. Let me tell you what this is not saying. This passage doesn't mean that God worked for six days and on the seventh He was "pooped," so He took a siesta. This concept of rest is more like a lawyer when he says, "I rest my case." The idea is, *He is finished.* As believers we can rest (take ease) in the finished work of Christ.

Scripturally, the concept of *rest* is equated to God's inheritance for His people (see Deut. 3:18-20; 12:9-11). For Israel, it was the Promised Land. In the same way, the writer of Hebrews is suggesting that new covenant believers "rest" in the inheritance of Christ's finished work at Calvary. The blessings of God are not *achieved* (earned); they are *received*.

However, it is worthy to note that even though, *"He that is entered into his rest, he also hath ceased from his own works, as God did from His"* (Heb. 4:10 KJV), we must also *"labuor therefore to enter into that rest..."* (Heb. 4:11 KJV). We have another oxymoron to ponder. We have to make an effort to rest. In other words, what God did by grace, unmerited by us, we must receive by faith. God's grace is His finished work that He did without "meritocracy" so I can by faith take dominion (dominance) over my environment. The reason I can rest is because it is not about faith in my faith, but faith in His grace. Therefore, I am delivered from spiritual schizophrenia. My qualification to receive is in Christ (see Col. 1:12).

If God can only bless perfect people, we all (the word *all* in Greek means "all") fall short. The Christian life is not hard; it's impossible (in our own ability). But that doesn't mean it's not easy. Talk about a paradox.

Often in leadership seminars, I'll ask people to give me their reactions to certain statements. For instance, I'll say, "Parenting is easy." It usually draws the biggest groans. People have a tendency to believe their own experience to be true for their lives. The other statement that draws large groans is, "Christianity is easy." For most people, their Christian life can be difficult and often frustrating. But listen to how Jesus said it should be,

> *Come to Me all you who are weary and burdened, and I will give you rest. Take My yoke upon you and learn from Me, for I am gentle and humble in heart, and you will find rest for your souls. For My yoke is easy and My burden is light* (Matthew 11:28-30).

CHRISTIANITY IS EASY?!

Here's the message of organic Christianity: *This Christianity "stuff" is easy.* In Matthew 11:28-30, Jesus sets out a process by which organic Christianity is rest: Come unto Jesus.

Christianity in its organic state was never made to be a religion. It's not a set of rules and regulations to determine who is good and who is bad. It is a life that is made to be about *exchange*, more than it is *change*. An exchanged life allows Christ to live through us more than our living for Him. This comes from a relationship that learns to abide in Him (see John 15:4,7). This term *abide* means "to continue, to be consistent, dwell, to stand fast, remain, or to stay."[22] This means that I consistently continue in the King and the King's system (the Kingdom of Heaven, where grace has provided every spiritual, supernatural blessing and provision). Why? Because I can't access God's system from the world's system.

The Kingdom is a system that operates in the exact opposite way of the world's system. If we want to live, we have to die. If we want to receive, we have to give. If we want to increase, we must decrease. If we want people to serve us, we must become the servant of all. We can't substitute lust for love. We don't seek to dominate people, but to serve them. The way we continue in the King and begin to see His Kingdom manifested is by dwelling in His system. The result, according to John 15:7, is that if we abide in Christ and His Word (His way of doing things in His system or Kingdom), we get what we ask for. More than anything, however, abiding is a call to intimacy. To be *intimate* means "to share one's most personal feelings or values." I believe there are four important keys to intimacy:

1. *You must know who you are.* You must understand your identity. Understanding who God is, what He has already done, and who He has made you to be, creates security in you. A secure person is not self-consumed. That is why Philemon 6 states, *"That the*

communication of thy faith may become effectual by the acknowledging of every good thing which is in you in Christ Jesus" (KJV). People are free to be other-centered when they feel personal security.

2. *Have an open line of communication.* Relationships are the currency of God's Kingdom, and communication is the key to intimate relationships. Here's where you share your wants, feelings, desires, and needs. I've often in my association with Oral Roberts heard him say it like this, "God sits where we sit and feels what we feel." Intimacy with Him is reciprocal as well. You sit where He sits, and you feel what He feels. It's this communication that makes you sensitive to His leaving.

3. *Learn to enjoy each other.* It's hard to be intimate with someone when you don't feel accepted by that person. If you don't feel you measure up to God, you'll never be intimate with Him. His unconditional love frees you to enjoy your relationship to God.

4. *Learn to be rooted and grounded in love.* That means that, in difficult or hard times, you don't assume God has rejected you. It is this intimacy that made Jesus sensitive to the leading of the Spirit. It was that intimacy that manifested God's Kingdom. Look at John 5:19:

> *Jesus gave them this answer: "I tell you the truth, the Son can do nothing by Himself; He can do only what He sees His Father doing, because whatever the Father does the Son also does."*

This is all about intimacy! Similarly, in John 5:30, Jesus said, *"By Myself I can do nothing; I judge only as I hear, and My judgment is just, for I seek not to please Myself but Him who sent Me."* Intimacy! (See also John 7:16; 8:16,26,38,47.) Look at John 14:10:

> *Don't you believe that I am in the Father, and that the Father is in Me? The words I say to you are not just*

My own. Rather, it is the Father, living in Me, who is doing His work [miracles].

Intimacy brings the supernatural.

MATTHEW 11:28-30 REVISITED

"I will give you rest"—We don't have to produce this work by our merit or effort; we simply receive by faith what God did by grace.

"Take My yoke upon you"—Ancient Israel would have understand this far more than the average American. Virtually on the side of any street they could see oxen yoked together for the purpose of carrying a load or a burden. Often a large ox would be yoked to a smaller ox. In this way, the load or burden was shared proportionately. The problem with non-organic Christianity is we are trying to do God's part of the equation. We don't have to earn the right of God's blessing. We just need to believe and receive. Obviously, sin is unbelief. Flesh is unbelief. "Operating in the flesh" happens when we try to do God's will our way. It is when we operate in the world's system instead of God's system. I can't access God's system (Kingdom) from the world's system.

"Learn from Me"—We need to be taught the truth of how the Kingdom operates. I will discuss this further in the chapter on truth.

"For I am gentle and humble in heart"—The moment we talk about humility, people envision becoming a doormat. The attitude is, *That's right; I'm so humble I let people walk all over me.* What nonsense! I once had a Greek scholar tell me that the word *humble* means "to submit to the view and opinion of" (in this case, God). As we submit to the view and opinion of God, His Kingdom will manifest itself—and we will find rest (grace) for our souls. It's what James says in his epistle, *"God opposes the proud but gives grace to the*

humble" (James 4:6b). Submitting to the view and opinion of God accesses the finished work of Christ.

"My yoke is easy and My burden is light"—Somehow when Christianity is taken out of its organic state, it becomes about rules and regulations. People live in the frustration of a legalism that has a standard to which they can never match up (see James 2:10). It creates schizophrenic believers. Organic Christianity realizes it is not about the *do*, but the *done*. It's not about *achieving*, but *receiving*. It's all about receiving by faith what God has done by grace. This Christian walk was made to be easy. This doesn't mean there won't be difficult times; it means we know every answer is found in the Kingdom by grace.

This is the true essence of Matthew 6:33, *"Seek first His kingdom and His righteousness, and all these things will be given to you as well."* Most of the time, when people expand on this verse, they say things like, "That's right. The first thing you need to do with your day is to seek God and do right by Him and He will bless you." That, however, is not the context of this verse. The context is about not worrying (as opposed to rest). *"...Do not worry about your life, what you will eat or drink; or about your body, what you will wear..."* (Matt. 6:25). Instead, seek first the Kingdom. Why? Because everything we need is in the Kingdom by grace, unmerited by us (see Eph. 1:3).

Not only are we to seek the Kingdom, but also *"His righteousness."* Why is that important? Because we are in right standing with the Father not based on what we have done, but based on what He has done, and we receive it by faith. In other words, everything we need is in the Kingdom by grace (unmerited by us—in the finished work of Christ), and we are qualified to receive it in Him. Therefore, we are at rest. This is how all these things shall be added unto us. How amazing is that?

A couple of years ago, I was teaching at a conference for pastors. There were several hundred participants at this meeting. One of the sessions I was teaching was on the topic of grace. When I was finished,

I was approached by many pastors who wanted me to come to their churches and minister. Most of these churches were fully inundated in the topic of grace. I met with about six or seven of the pastors privately. In the midst of the conversation, I looked at them and asked, "Is this stuff working for you, or are you just exchanging one theology for another?"

Here is my point. Organic Christianity is not about winning a theological argument of one theology over another. It's about reclaiming the roots of the Gospel message. It's about reclamation, a reclaiming of the original life of the New Covenant. It's about overcoming spiritual schizophrenia. It's about standing to our feet a vast army equipped with our identity, the understanding of the finished work of Jesus Christ, and the revelation to access it. And here's the kicker; it is the ability to rest while it is manifested.

I spent the first half of my Christian life trying to live the Christian life. I had some success, but I lived in the frustration of never measuring up to God's standard. I was trying instead of trusting, and the result was schizophrenic Christianity.

The next progression in the manifestation model is righteousness. When righteousness is added to grace, identity moves to qualification, and the army gets ready to march. So let's look at the next progression!

● ●

ORGANIC THOUGHTS

1. Have you ever felt spiritually schizophrenic?

2. Is it a revelation to you that the new covenant was made with Jesus and not with you? Why is this important to us as believers?

3.   Had you ever realized you are an heir of this world? What does that mean to you?

4.   Has the emphasis on forgiveness of sins caused you to miss intimacy with God?

5.   Have you ever felt you had to earn God's love?

6.   Has doubting God's love ever hindered your faith?

7.   Does knowing or understanding God's love cause you to feel you can experience the fullness of His Kingdom?

8.   How does knowing God's love affect your understanding of your identity?

9.   How do you see yourself in reflection in Second Peter 1:2-11? Have you ever suffered from spiritual myopia, blindness, or amnesia?

10. Did this chapter change your concept of holiness?

11. Is the Christian life based on Matthew 11:28-30 easy for you?

Chapter 4

. . . .

UNSTOPPABLE

Once people overcome the quagmire of the myriad of pitfalls that come from spiritual schizophrenia, new freedom and momentum are established in believers' lives. There is a feeling (and a reality) of being unstoppable once we know God is "not only able, but He will" (see Eph. 3:20). A feeling of inevitability and trust are established. It will elicit a new passion in people.

It is obvious to even the most casual observer that something is wrong in the majority of Christianity today. Francois Fenelon, in his work, "The Seeking Heart," states, "To just read the Bible, attend church and to avoid the 'big sins,' is this passionate, wholehearted love for God?"[1] Wow! When the Church abandons the organic message, it reduces the Christian faith to melancholy religion.

I've always been considered a passionate person, even before I met Christ. Once I encountered Christ, my passion and freedom exploded in my life. Since I didn't grow up in the Church, I didn't have a clue what a real faith-filled, momentous life looked like. It didn't take the Church long, however, to "help" me understand *sin-consciousness.* Thus, when I failed, which was often, I felt alienated and far from

God. My freedom and momentum dissipated to an ongoing journey to the altar to try and regain the unabated joy I knew at salvation. I lived in the maze of trying to find "Pavlov's reward" for performing at a high enough level to be accepted and right with God. I kept an unofficial tally in my head of how many things I did right and how many things I did wrong, and despite my sincerity, it always seemed I came up short. I lived in a constant state of flux between my quest for God and my shortcomings. I never really felt I measured up to God unless I could find other believers I was obviously superior to in behavior. I was studying the Word, sharing my faith, and pursuing the Kingdom, but I couldn't escape the feeling it wasn't enough and God was mad at me.

The quest of organic Christianity is not to point a fickle finger of correction alone at the Church, but to help awaken the Church to the fact that her teachings have been added to, thus making them less than they are. This is subtraction by addition. Where are the believers who will sacrifice their lives for their convictions? When Christianity is reduced to religious rules and regulations, it squelches passion. The problem with the Church is not just that the Church is passionless or lukewarm, but that we need to understand why we are this way. We suffer with lethargy because we have an inaccurate understanding of who God is. It's time to return to organic Christianity.

We need some wisdom. Here is an illustration of what I mean.

Some years back a friend of mine was invited to the White House to meet with the President. He was invited along with other religious leaders from around the nation. It was not this administration or the previous one, but the President before that. He was ushered into the Oval Office to discuss spiritual answers to national problems. I have no idea whether the meeting was a formality or whether there was real interest in the spiritual perspective. His "take on it" was it was the former, not the latter. Nevertheless, he met with the President in the Oval Office. After the meeting, he went to the White House commissary to get something to eat. While he was appropriating his food, a White House Aide recognized him. Approaching my friend, the Aide inquired, "Aren't you one of the people who just met with the President in the Oval Office on spiritual answers?"

My friend responded cheerily, "Yes, as a matter of fact, I did!"

The Aide then chided, "Well, I want you to know, I am the White House Aide who is responsible for getting the Manger Scene out of the White House at Christmas time."

It was obvious this guy was looking for a fight. It was like saying, "Your Momma wears army boots!" He was looking to "get into it." So, my friend shot up a quick prayer (and that was a good idea). Here was my friend's response. He said, "I've heard about you. I heard you got the Manger Scene out of the White House at Christmas time. But you were able to get the Manger Scene out of the White House at Christmas time for a different reason than you think. The reason you were able to get the Manger Scene out of the White House at Christmas time is...they couldn't find three wise men in this city."

I don't know how his attempt at humor was received, but here is the point: We need some wisdom today!

Wisdom says, "Stop the insanity." Doing the same thing over and over again doesn't produce different results. Wisdom says, "Break spiritual schizophrenia." When I know that God is not only able, but also that He will manifest His Kingdom on my behalf (by the way, that doesn't mean I understand everything going on around me; it just means I know I can trust God), now a feeling of being unstoppable for His Kingdom engulfs me. This then leads me to the second progression of the manifestation model: righteousness.

RIGHT STANDING WITH GOD

Unscientific research reveals that less than 10 to 20 percent of believers truly understand righteousness.[2] Before blowing this section off as meaningless prate that everyone knows, stop and look at its organic meaning.

Perhaps the best way to understand this concept is with a story that happened in my childhood. Somewhere around the fifth grade, a boy I'll call Billy beat me up. Now, it wasn't humiliating that he beat me up because Billy was a head taller than anyone else in the fifth grade. I mean, his voice had already changed—he already had hair under his arms. Billy already had his license. After all, he had a wife and three kids. All of that is an exaggeration to say, he was bigger and tougher than anyone else in the fifth grade.

Once you have been beaten up, it becomes obvious because your face has been "rearranged." So, as my family sat down for dinner that night and as the evening conversation was initiated, my dad bellowed out, "What happened to you??"

With great disdain I announced, "Billy beat me up!"

Now, I'm expecting great compassion to come from my dad. He looks at me and quite unexpectedly says, "The boy's a bully! If you don't put a stop to it, he'll bully you all the days of your life. So tomorrow I want you to deal with this."

As you might expect, this is not what I wanted to hear. I didn't *want* to confront long, tall Billy about *anything.* The next day at school was anything but a confrontation. I avoided Billy like the plague. That night when my dad came home, he asked my mom where I was. She said with a wink, "He is in his room doing his homework!"

It didn't take a rocket scientist to figure out I was only avoiding a conversation with my dad on the follow-up of his edict. He boldly entered my room, inquiring about the follow-through on his instructions. My stammering and bumbling around quickly convinced him of my inability to follow through. What happened next, however, shocked me. Without hesitation, my dad told me to go to Billy's house (which was in our neighborhood) and take care of this before dinner.

Not so subtly, he coaxed me out of the house and on my newfound quest. To make matters worse, Billy lived on my street at the top of a foreboding hill. I began my journey up the "mountain," thinking to myself, *I'm about to die.* I finally arrived, scaling the hill to the portals of his driveway. There I meandered for what seemed like a lifetime, pondering my fate. When I finally came to the conclusion that I had no other alternatives, I wandered up the driveway to my destiny.

Billy lived in an L-shaped house. The driveway led to a garage that connected to a back door. There were several steps that led to the back door. Standing at the bottom of the stairs, I stretched up to knock every so softly on the door. Immediately, he appeared at the door. Evidently, he had supernatural hearing as well. Not only was Billy a head taller than me, he was standing several steps higher, now taking on Goliath proportions. In a moment's time, he bellows, "What do you want!?"

In my mind, all I could think of was, *I want to live.* I mumbled and stammered, trying to get something to come out, but all I got was air. Suddenly, out of the corner of my eye, in my peripheral vision, I saw my dad standing by the side of his house. Unbeknownst to me, he had snuck across the street and hid himself behind the houses and followed me up the street. Once I saw my dad, everything changed. A new boldness came upon me. I roared, "Billy, you're ugly! Your Momma's ugly! Your dog is ugly, and you better never touch me again!!" (Or something like that.) As he started out the back door, he saw my dad, and he backed off—and he never did touch me again.

Here's the point. Everything changed when I knew daddy was on the scene. (Now I took some amplification to this story to help make my point.) In a strange way, this is a definition of righteousness. It is our confidence that our spiritual daddy is on the scene.

So, what is righteousness from a biblical point of view? Righteousness is right standing before God, not based on what we've done, but based on what Christ did—fulfilling all righteousness at Calvary (see

Matt. 3:15), and I receive it by faith (faith righteousness). It is being right with God. Righteousness is the ability to stand before God without guilt, without fear, and without inferiority or condemnation. It is a gift God gives to us, and it is the centerpiece that faith is built upon. We have a "right" to everything Jesus has a right or access to. Now, that's a mouthful, but I intend to substantiate it.

So, if this is clear in Scripture, why do so many people have difficulty grasping it? I believe it is because of how our culture and the dictionary define it. Their definition doesn't necessarily line up with Scripture. Here's how *Webster's* defines righteousness: "conformance to an acceptable standard, justice, doing things right, right performance, uprightness, free from sin, or being morally right."[3] Scripture focuses on faith in Christ. Culture focuses on performance. It is the acceptance of the cultural definition that has left believers in the quandary of spiritual schizophrenia and feeling unqualified before God. The Book of Romans is geared to helping people understand grace and righteousness from God's perspective. It helps people understand we are not in right standing with God based on our performance. Remember, God's standard for passing the test in order to be right with Him is 100 percent (see James 2:10). The only way to pass the test is through Christ. It is the difference between the *changed* life and the *exchanged* life.

Listen to how Paul initiates the understanding of this topic. Romans 3:19-20 states,

> *Now we know that whatever the law says, it says to those who are under the law....therefore no one will be declared righteous in His sight by observing the law; rather, through the law we become conscious of sin.*

It is impossible to be right with God through our performance of the law. The job of "law" is simply to produce guilt, and it focuses on sin. What we focus on longest becomes strongest. Noted psychologist Carl Jung states it like this: "What you resist persists." In other words, to say I'm going to quit _____ (whatever it is), I focus my attention on it and this promotes similar action. The way to overcome sin is not to focus on it, but to focus on our identity (who God is, what He has already done, and who He has made us to be), to be convicted of righteousness (see John 16:8). It is to this end, Paul continues,

> *But now a righteousness from God, apart from law, has been made known....This righteousness from God comes through faith in Jesus Christ to all who believe. There is no difference* (Romans 3:21-22).

It becomes apparent in Paul's writings that being right with God is based on *faith righteousness,* not the *works righteousness* of the law. It is equally noteworthy that God doesn't want us to be sin-conscious, but righteousness-conscious. Why? The way we overcome sin and shortcoming is by knowing who God made us to be.

This was Paul's anthem to organic Christianity. This was an incredibly radical statement to make. As I mentioned before, he was addressing the influence of Judaizers on the Church, and he left no doubt that it was never God's intent that God's people trust in the law for justification with God. The law's job was to show them the need of an intimate relationship with a loving God who has provided everything they need for life and godliness (see 2 Pet. 1:3). This is the intent of Romans 3:23, *"For all have sinned and fall short of the glory of God."* That's the purpose of the law, to cause us to run to God's open gift of faith righteousness. There's such freedom there!

Because of who I am, a Bible school director, and because of what I do, travel and speak, I am connected with multitudes of people who seek my counsel. Recently, I had a man who has spoken to massive crowds come to my office for counsel. He had some shortcomings and a failure in his life. When they occurred, he openly shared them and got counsel in his life for restoration. His past was checkered with abuse against him in his childhood. The things he has had to overcome were huge. Somehow, he overcame them and has ministered to crowds in excess of a quarter million people. Now in the midst of restoration, he sat across my desk weeping because he felt God had rejected him. He felt he was not pleasing to God.

I never gave credence to his sin or shortcoming, but I pointed out that God's nature is redemption and restoration. His sincerity was already demonstrated in his restorative process.

I looked at him and said, "Let me share with you the wonderful heart of God in the story of the prodigal son. Note the position of the father. When the prodigal came to his senses and came out of his sin and he started home (see Luke 15:17-19), the father didn't wait for the return to be complete. '...*But while he was still a long way off, his father saw him and was filled with compassion for him; he ran to his son, threw his arms around him and kissed him*' (Luke 15:20). He told the servants to get his best robe (such robes were worn by the most noted nobles), a robe that signifies righteousness (see Isa. 61:10). He also told them to bring the signet ring, representing the mark of sonship; a signet ring indicated he had authority and access to all of the family holdings. He also told the servants to bring shoes; slaves went without shoes, but not a son. And he told them to kill the fatted calf, a symbol of abundance or bounty. This is God's attitude toward us. He is waiting with open arms to restore us and liberate us from the shackles of sin."

As I was talking to this man, I spent time breaking down some of his false belief patterns (the five elements of the Personal Belief System) and how to overcome them. After reflecting on these revelations, he said, "I feel free...I feel unstoppable. I feel I want to follow God with my whole heart."

This is the revelation of righteousness. The Pharisee's response to Paul's too-good-to-be-true news was obviously, "This will encourage people to sin." Notice, however, Paul's response, *"...The power of sin is the law"* (1 Cor. 15:56). Law is not equipped to help us stop sinning anymore than a speed sign equips us to stay in the speed limit. Strength to overcome sin comes from an intimacy with God through righteousness that releases a grace or empowerment to conquer sin. This is why Paul says, *"Awake to righteousness, and sin not; for some* [of you] *have not the knowledge of God: I speak this to your shame"* (1 Cor. 15:34 KJV). Those who think grace and righteousness are freedom to sin are in the height of idiocy. Sin gives the devil access to our lives (see Rom. 6:16). Grace and righteousness are not freedom to sin, but freedom from sin (freedom to conquer it).

It is almost impossible, however, to live in this kind of victory without knowing God loves us unconditionally (agape). I'll never forget my first real revelation of God's love. I had graduated from a premier Christian university. It was my privilege to rise to the top echelon of student leadership while I attended there. I was diligent and passionate about my faith, but I did not understand God's love. I always felt God was scrutinizing my every action, and often I was found wanting.

One day before attending classes in graduate school, I sat down on our rickety furniture in our first apartment of our married life. I opened my Bible to First Corinthians 13 and Romans 8, and I read about the love of God. Suddenly, the Spirit of God began to speak to me about how much God loved me. For the first time in my young Christian life I realized, "Nothing can separate me from the love of God" (see Rom. 8:39). Jesus didn't come to judge me or condemn me (see John 3:17; 8:15), but to love me unto Himself. How we see God determines how we experience God. Through this experience, I was catapulted to a new intimacy with Him. I felt unstoppable.

Paul continues his revelation of God's righteousness in Romans 3 and 4:

> *Where, then, is boasting? It is excluded. On what principle? On that of observing the law? No, but on that of faith. For we maintain that a man is justified* [or made righteous—right with God[4]] *by faith apart from observing the law....If, in fact, Abraham was justified by works* [performing the law] *he had something to boast about—but not before God. What does the Scripture say? "Abraham believed God, and it was credited to him as righteousness." Now when a man works, his wages are not credited to him as a gift, but as an obligation. However, to the man who does not work but trusts God who justifies the wicked, his faith is credited to him as righteousness. David says the same thing when he speaks of the blessedness of the man to whom God credits righteousness apart from works* [works righteousness]: *"...Blessed is the man whose sin the Lord will never count against him"* (Romans 3:27-28; 4:2-8).

All of this is to say in great simplicity, we can't earn righteousness. God gives it as a gift by grace through faith. It is freeing to understand this revolutionary revelation. If we are saved by adherence to the law, we have something to boast about—especially in comparing ourselves to others. However, in the sight of God, not one of us has anything to brag about. In this passage, Paul tells us categorically how we become righteous. Like Abraham, we become righteous by believing God. *"Abraham believed God, and it was credited to him as righteousness"* (Rom. 4:3). According to verse 6, *"...God credits righteousness apart from works...."*

The modern Church has unwittingly left its organic roots for a religion that says, like the Marines, "I'm striving to be all I can be." The problem with works righteousness is it still takes a 100 percent grade to pass. The only way for us to be truly righteous and right with God is through Jesus Christ. When the Church combines law and grace, it creates spiritual schizophrenia.

Organic Christianity is oriented in faith righteousness. There are two roads to God. The first is self-righteousness or our works (self-effort) to do enough to please God. The second is pleasing God by trusting in the finished work of Christ.

I lived a large portion of my life in the former before I discovered the latter. I was diligently following after God. I was in the Word, seeking His face, sharing my faith, but I knew I had certain shortcomings. I would work on my sin by making an effort to sin less. Despite my efforts, I still had some shortcomings. Then, there is the game of keeping up appearances. It is fanned by exhortations to do more, give it all, sell out, get on fire, shape up, tighten up, and a myriad of other injunctions. The fact is, when comparing myself to others, I was considered passionate; however, when I compared myself to God's standard, I felt I came up short, and I suffered in varying degrees of spiritual schizophrenia.

Only when I lived out of who God says I am (my identity) did I find freedom and victory. It's only here that I feel vitally alive. Trusting in the finished work of Jesus Christ is what made me feel free and alive. Paul's exhortation is: The way we overcome sin is by understanding who we are in Christ.

Paul seems to indicate in Romans 3 and 4 that I'm not to focus on my sin (see Rom. 3:20), but to focus on who I am in Him (see Rom. 3:21-22). The way to overcome sin is through my identity in Him, not through focusing on my shortcomings. Organic Christianity is more about:

- Telling us who we are, than who we aren't.

- Understanding that God is not mad at us (see John 3:17; 8:15).

- Relationship with God, than rules.

- Understanding we are righteous by faith, not by our deeds.

- Commendation, than condemnation.

- Putting in us a new DNA (see 2 Cor. 5:17), than being saved sinners.

- God loving us unconditionally, than teaching fear.

- What we have, than what we are trying to get (see Philem. 6; Eph. 3:20).

- How much we let God love us, than how much we love God.

Organic Christianity is far more about understanding that there is not enough we can do to change ourselves, but that we simply need to mature into who He has made us to be.[5] It is essential that we understand God's unconditional love.

Paul continues, *"That God was reconciling the world to Himself in Christ, not counting men's sins against them..."* (2 Cor. 5:19). Notice it doesn't say God was reconciling some Christians to Himself. It says He was reconciling *"the world"* unto Himself. The provision for our reconciliation (to be compatible with[6]) was made before we were born again (see Rom. 5:8). He adds, *"not counting men's sins against them."* This is an accounting term meaning, "to lay to one's account." God didn't send His Son to collect our debt, but to pay our debt.[7] When we receive God's free gift (grace) of salvation by faith, He does for us what we could never do for ourselves—He offers us right standing (righteousness) with the Father as a free gift.

Paul concludes this amazing revelation with, *"God made Him who had no sin to be sin for us, so that in Him we might become the righteousness of God"* (2 Cor. 5:21). The typical Christian believes the first part of the verse without claiming the latter. Most Christians believe God bore our sins, but only a few believe He made us righteous. Righteousness is a gift we receive by faith. It is *faith righteousness,* not *works righteousness.* Paul says earlier in First Corinthians 1:30-31:

> *It is because of Him that you are in Christ Jesus, who has become for us wisdom from God—that is, our righteousness, holiness and redemption. Therefore... "Let him who boasts boast in the Lord."*

In other words, in Christ we have righteousness; we have been made joint heirs with Christ. Wow! We have access to everything He has access to.

Here's the dilemma. If I were to say to you that I would give you $10,000 if you would meet me at a certain location tonight, is there any reason you wouldn't come? You might not come if you didn't believe me. You might not come if you didn't trust me. You might not come if you didn't think you were deserving. That is exactly what is going on in the non-organic Christian world. Because people don't feel they are deserving of such blessing—because they don't feel like they're in right standing with God—they feel unqualified to receive from Him. You have to understand that you can't get more righteous as a believer than you are right now. However, you can understand it better, and you can manifest it better.

ISSUES CONCERNING RIGHTEOUSNESS

The obvious concern is that Paul and others were promoting people to sin with their doctrines of grace and righteousness. If right standing with God is more about His *done* than our *do,* what would keep people from sin? This is one of the numerous allegations made toward Paul, that his teaching on grace and righteousness promoted sin (see Rom. 3:8; 6:1,15-16; 1 Cor. 15:34; Gal. 5:1,13).

Let's view some of these allegations in lieu of organic Christianity. Romans 3:8 reveals,

> *Why not say—as we are being slanderously reported as saying and as some claim that we say—"Let us do evil that good may result"? Their condemnation is deserved.*

There were opponents to Paul who were "spinning" what he was saying. Paul's preaching of grace and righteousness led people to slander him and to suggest his teaching was encouraging people to sin. This was unequivocally untrue. It is grace that teaches us to deny ungodliness (see Titus 2:11-12). Paul not only noted this was slander, but also said these people should be condemned (this from a grace teacher).

In Romans 6:1-2, he further amplifies, *"What shall we say, then? Shall we go on sinning so that grace may increase? By no means! We died to sin; how can we live in it any longer?"* The way Paul preached grace, I guess it was inevitable (as with anyone who does) that people thought, Can we just go right on sinning since we are right with God through grace and righteousness? By no means is this what Paul is saying. He comes back to the same argument a few verses later in Romans 6:15-16:

> *What then? shall we sin, because we are not under the law, but under grace? God forbid. Know ye not, that to*

whom ye yield yourselves servants to obey, his servants
ye are to whom ye obey; whether of sin unto death, or
of obedience unto righteousness? (KJV)

Paul categorically emphasizes that grace and righteousness do not promote sin. In fact, he concludes with this rationale for why we don't sin: "Don't you know when you submit to sin, you submit to the one who authors sin?" In other words, sin gives the devil access to our lives (as indicated by the personal pronoun *whom*).

That brings us round about to First Corinthians 15:34, *"Awake to righteousness, and sin not; for some have not the knowledge of God: I speak this to your shame"* (KJV). "Wake up! Come out of your drunken stupor" is the literal Greek meaning.[8] Righteousness is not freedom to sin, but freedom from sin. Once we realize who we are (righteousness as our identity in Christ) and know what we have (the Kingdom of Heaven), there's never a reason to use the flesh. One doctoral scholar told me the best definition of "the flesh" is trying to do God's will our way.[9] The only reason we sin is to meet a need in our lives. When we do it in the flesh, we say to God, "Please stay out of this. I've got it covered." And, He does. However, once we realize who we are in Christ and what He has provided for us (see 2 Pet. 1:3; Eph. 1:3), there is no reason to seek anything but His Kingdom.

This is the essence of Matthew 6:33, *"But seek first His kingdom and His righteousness, and all these things will be given to you as well."* Everything we need is in the Kingdom (see Eph. 1:3; 2 Pet. 1:3). We seek His righteousness because we're qualified to receive what is in His Kingdom. Therefore, I don't have to worry.

In essence, the last time Paul has to deal with the allegation that grace and righteousness promote sin is Galatians 5:1,13:

It is for freedom that Christ has set us free. Stand firm,
then, and do not let yourselves be burdened again by

a yoke of slavery....You, my brothers, were called to be free. But do not use your freedom to indulge the sinful nature...

The context of this passage is freedom from the law (see Gal. 4:21-31). Paul's promotion of grace and righteousness is not promotion of sin. On the contrary, he is saying these two characteristics promote God living in us to conquer sin. However, the motivations behind our actions change. We don't live holy to be accepted by God; we live holy because we are accepted by God. Laws and regulations are valuable guidelines, but we are powerless to enforce them. It is grace and righteousness that empower us (see Rom. 5:17).

First John 1:9, *"If we confess our sins, He is faithful and just and will forgive us our sins and purify us from all unrighteousness"* has become a hot button verse in the discussion of grace. To fully understand this verse we must understand the context of this epistle written by the apostle John. John writes this letter to undisclosed churches. It is written to combat false teachers whom he calls antichrists (anti-Christian, see 1 John 2:16-18). These false teachers were by all accounts Gnostics who centered on the teaching of a man called Cerintheus.[10] We must understand the Bible was not written to us, but for us. In other words, I can't truly figure out what a passage is saying to me until I understand the original, organic intent for which it was written in the first place. Since this passage is so pivotal in many people's minds, I risk being too technical by giving its explanation because of its profound importance.

Gnostics were false teachers who infiltrated Christian churches to undermine apostolic teaching. They generally held these basic tenets:

1. **Dualism**—Simply this means they believed only the spirit was good and matter was evil. Therefore, Jesus could not be the Son of God because He came

in a human body. The very deity of Christ was at stake with this understanding. This is dealt with in 1 John 1:1-2. Some Gnostics (Doecetics) even believed Jesus only appeared to have a physical body.

2. **Salvation by enlightenment (light)**—Gnostics believed people were saved by special knowledge or revelation. This precluded the necessity of the shed blood of Jesus. John deals with this in 1 John 1:2-3;7-8.

3. **There is no such thing as sin in the flesh**—Some proponents of early Gnosticism adopted forms of Antinomianism that said there was no such thing as sin in the flesh. Some even encouraged indulgence in the flesh. Other forms of Gnostics ascribed to Asceticism which tried to suppress flesh. It is the former with which 1 John 1:8-9 attempts to deal.

Let me attempt in simplicity to lay out the meaning of 1 John 1:

1 John 1:1—The apostle states, *"That which was from the beginning, which we have heard, which we have seen with our eyes, which we have looked at and our hands have touched..."* In other words, the Gnostic teaching of "dualism" tried to convince the Church that Jesus really didn't come in the flesh. Here John said the Son of God could be seen and touched. This was the establishment of the incarnation of Christ.

1 John 1:2—Jesus not only came in the flesh, but He is the source of eternal life, not the special enlightenment.

1 John 1:3—The declaration of John and the apostles makes it clear that he has seen this and it is his desire for his readers to understand this in order that they could have fellowship with Christ and with His body of believers. This is in reference to true salvation, in order that they may be genuine Christians.

1 John 1:5-7—This is John's effort to declare the difference between true light (not Gnostic special knowledge, which they called light) and darkness (outside of fellowship with Christ). Many Gnostics felt they could indulge in sinful behavior without consequence. Gnostics claimed such fellowship could be obtained apart from the shed blood of Jesus that processes and maintains such fellowship. True Christianity does not give license to sin, but Christ's blood is what cleanses sin. The "we" phrases are an indication of the consequences if believers embrace Gnosticism.

1 John 1:8-9—Gnostic "sin" needed no expiation (atoning sacrifice) from God; it was mere action of the flesh. Many such Gnostics said there was no such thing as sin in flesh. John negated this false justification with true salvation so they would not be deceived by pseudo-gnostic Christians.

This is the organic, hermeneutical understanding of this passage.[11] My intent, however, is not to win the argument, but to help people. If your philosophy (as opposed to theology) is to say this is familial (family) response to restore broken fellowship with God, or if your framework is your soul is cleansed while your spirit remains intact, my real question is, does your explanation encourage a more godly life? Does it position you to establish His Kingdom in the earth? Does it empower you to be about the Father's business?

John is not telling believers how to have their righteousness restored; he is telling them not to be confused about Gnostic doctrine. He is saying, in context, this is true salvation.

Why is this issue pivotal to understand? If the verses are taken at face value, as most people choose to take them, they seem to imply that righteousness is lost at every sin. If this sin is not confessed, righteousness is not restored. That means, if we have unconfessed sin, we've lost our right standing with God. If it is permanently unconfessed, we are permanently out of justification with God.

Sin is not simply the "big" issues we often accentuate in church. Paul tells us, *"...everything that does not come from faith is sin"* (Rom. 14:23). That means that if God told me to get alone with Him and I watched ESPN instead, that is sin. If I get cut off in traffic on the way to work and I get angry, that is sin. Usually, when we sin in this way, we never think of those incidents again, but if we didn't confess them, we lost our right standing with God (or so the reasoning goes)— permanently. This is why I struggled off and on for two years with grasping the meaning of this passage. In essence, our unconfessed sin would necessitate the loss of any viable relationship and intimacy with God. At best we'll be left with spiritual schizophrenia; at worst, we've lost our relationship to God.

Again, the concern is that this understanding of the rebuttal of Gnostic teachings in First John 1:9 would seem to give license to the fact that every sin doesn't need to be confessed. My response is, "That would be an impossibility!" Remember, God's passing grade for our lives is 100 percent. It is not 99 percent. We have to be perfect. Therefore, we could not miss a confession of a single sin and fulfill the legalistic requirements. In essence, it is impossible to confess every sin. This is not to say that believers don't need to repent of sin. There are 12 biblical references (and 13 verses) to the Church or an individual being expected to repent (see Rom. 2:4; 2 Cor. 7:9-10; 12:24; 2 Tim. 2:25; Heb. 12:17; Rev. 2:5,16,21-22; 3:13,19; 9:20-21; 10:9; 16:11). The term, *repent*, at its root, means "to think differently, to change your thinking or to feel compunction."[12] This is important because sin gives the devil access to our lives (see Rom. 6:16). My repentance rids his access and realigns my life with God's Kingdom (system).

REIGNING IN LIFE

Righteousness is granted as a gift to make us unstoppable. Righteousness is what causes us to reign in life. Religion always tries to weigh people down with rules they can't keep, which robs them of intimacy with God. Listen to how Paul deals with this in Romans:

> *What then shall we say? That the Gentiles, who did not pursue righteousness, have obtained it, a righteousness that is by faith; but Israel, who pursued a law of righteousness, has not attained it. Why not? Because they pursued it not by faith but as if it were by works.... Since they did not know the righteousness that comes from God and sought to establish their own, they did not submit to God's righteousness. Christ is the end of the law so that there may be righteousness for everyone who believes* (Romans 9:30-32; 10:3-4).

This is one of Paul's radical statements. Judaizers were communicating that righteousness was allocated by God through the law. Paul rebuffs them, stating unequivocally that God provides righteousness by grace for all people, regardless of their actions. The lone contingency is that they believe and receive this free gift; God reckons them as righteous. Righteousness is based on faith, not actions.

This passage reveals what was true in Paul's day as well as our own. Most people are unaware of the fact there are two kinds of righteousness and only one is acceptable to God (see Rom. 10:3). If we don't understand how God establishes righteousness (faith), we come to establish our own set of rules and regulations to become right with God. We establish our own religion to regulate and control people in an effort to guide them to religious acceptability.

Finally, Paul drops the bomb, *"Christ is the end of the law so that there may be righteousness for everyone who believes"* (Rom. 10:4). Now, this verse does not say Jesus put an end to the law, but that Christ is the end of the law for the purpose of righteousness (being right with God). This means that people can no longer be righteous or justified in the sight of God by how well they perform the law.

It seems that humanity is increasingly religious. A friend of mine told me a story that encapsulates this entire issue. He was preaching at a service. At the conclusion of the meeting, a woman aggressively approached him. Her hair was in a bun and she had on no makeup whatsoever. Every conceivable inch of her body from the neck down was covered with clothes. She walked up with a scowl on her face and abruptly confronted my friend by saying, "What do you think about makeup?"

My friend thought for a moment and finally replied, "Get some!" Evidently he came from the theology of "if the barn needs painting, paint it." The point is simple. Legalistic righteousness is obsessed with compiling a set of rules that must be kept in order to be right with God. The problem is, it often results in spiritual schizophrenia.

There is little doubt in my mind that the law reveals a standard for godliness that should be emulated. However, our compliance to the law does not earn God's blessings. God's blessings only come by faith (see Rom. 4:2-13; Gal. 3:13-14).

The understanding of this pivotal revelation is the key to dominating life and not being dominated by it. Look at Romans 5:17,

> *...how much more will those who receive God's abundant provision of grace and of the gift of righteousness reign in life through the one man, Jesus Christ.*

God has broken the effects of condemnation off of our lives to liberate us. Sin has lost its power to rule over us (see Rom. 5:21), and

God in His grace and righteousness has positioned us to conquer life. Once we realize God's not mad at us, there is unbelievable (interesting choice of words) freedom to believe God.

This is the same thought and conclusion the Psalmist comes to:

> *...his righteousness endures forever....Surely he will never be shaken; a righteous man will be remembered forever. He will have no fear of bad news; his heart is steadfast, trusting in the Lord. His heart is secure, he will have no fear; in the end he will look in triumph on his foes* (Psalm 112:3,6-8).

This is why this incredible revelation is so essential. People who understand righteousness, their right standing with God by faith, will:

- *Never be shaken!* You know you're right with God. After all, you and God are a majority.

- *Never be forgotten.* In other words, you are remembered. God's not overlooking you. You are the center of His focus.

- *Have no fear of bad news.* The doctor's report, the bank statement, the counselor's statement are all swallowed up by the good news. In all worrisome situations, you seek first the Kingdom of God (everything you need is there) and His righteousness (you're right with God and, therefore, qualified to receive from Him), and all these things (that you need) shall be added unto you. Therefore, you have no fear of bad news. You can trust God.

- *Have a heart that is steadfast (fixed, constant, established, firm*[12]*), trusting in the Lord.* You may not understand everything, but you know God is working all things together for your good.

- *Have a heart that is secure (free from fear*[14]*).* You will have no fear. If God be for me who can be against me.

- *In the end, triumph over all foes.* You've read the back of the book (the Bible), and it says we win. You're one of those people who likes to read the end of the book first, and then go back to the beginning. We win!!!

I learned this lesson years ago. I was doing a series of major meetings with one of my heroes in the faith. We were building to some climactic events in major city civic auditoriums. However, over the course of time, I became uncomfortable about how we were progressing toward that end. In our disagreements, my friend decided over a series of events to terminate our working relationship.

While flying home, he garnered my attention for a conversation. He said to me, "Ron, you're a man of integrity, and you have served here well. Let's part company friends. I'll make a three-month package, and let's move on."

I felt good about it. However, within 24 hours he changed his mind, and in two weeks we severed ways and salaries. It was mid-December, we were headed into Christmas, and I was without a job or a salary. It caused some concerns for security in my household.

One Wednesday night, my wife and I attended church services. During the worship service, I sat there in a dry and lonely feeling. The strain over the last months had left me feeling spiritually withered and desolate. In the middle of the church service, I felt the presence of the Lord come upon me. It was the first time in months I had felt His presence. My first response was something like, "Where have You been?"

Then I heard His voice. I sensed God saying that I needed to give a large amount of money in the offering. I thought, "*Oh, great! I haven't heard from You in months, and the first time I hear from You, You want money!*" And I "blew it off."

I heard the voice in my spirit man a second time. Again it was a call to give a large sum of money. I "blew it off" a second time. Some moments later, I heard this voice a third time. It was urging me to give, and I knew I had to obey Him.

I turned to my wife, who is somewhat security-oriented, and said, "God wants us to give 'x' amount of money in the offering tonight." It was a lot of money for the insecure setting we were in. She thought for a moment and said, "I rebuke you, satan, in Jesus' name!" (Just so you know, that's a gross exaggeration.) She was, however, definitively hesitant. Ultimately, with great fear, trepidation, and reluctance, she wrote the check.

I cannot begin to tell you what began to happen. You just don't normally re-launch a ministry in a couple of weeks. People are usually booked months ahead of time. My phone started "ringing off the hook." Pastor friends were saying, "I know you won't be available, but could you preach for me next month?" Supernaturally, week after week, month after month was lined up with invitations. It turned out to be the most productive ministry time and the best time of financial blessing we'd ever known up until that time. I didn't earn God's blessing, but I responded in faith to His integrity.

Here's what I learned: The righteous will never be shaken. They are secure; they will have no fear; in the end, they will triumph over their foes.

Let me finish this chapter with this passage from Philippians:

But whatever was to my profit I now consider loss for the sake of Christ. What is more, I consider everything a loss compared to the surpassing greatness of knowing Christ Jesus my Lord, for whose sake I have lost all things. I consider them rubbish, that I may gain Christ and be found in Him, not having a righteousness of my own that comes from the law, but that which is through faith in Christ—the righteousness that comes from God and is by faith. I want to know Christ and the power of His resurrection and the fellowship of sharing in His sufferings....Only let us live up to what we have already attained (Philippians 3:7-11, 16).

Before Paul met Christ, he was caught up in his many accomplishments in the Jewish religion (see Phil. 3:2-6). Everything, however, paled in comparison to intimately knowing His Lord and Savior and understanding that he was right with Him through faith in His finished work. Paul had tried to establish his own righteousness and realized the futility of his efforts. He knew his efforts were worthy only of being thrown on the dung pile. The righteousness that gives people right relationship with God is the righteousness *of* God and *by* faith.

Paul's quest culminated in *knowing* Christ. This Greek term is a Jewish idiom for sexual union between a man and wife. Paul's chief aim was not to know about Christ, but to be intimately united with Him. His goal was to live in the fullness that he already possessed (see Phil. 3:16). This is what made him unstoppable.

Understanding the concept of organic Christianity is to understand the Gospel with nothing added to it.

Jesus + Nothing = Everything

Righteousness is our ability to be right with God by faith in Christ's finished work. Yet, religion is bent to add to it. Let me give an example.

Back in the 1980s there were a series of falls among noted ministers. It was notable and serious. Every major news outlet was actively reporting any new activity. The *Nightline* television program ran a primetime special with a number of key Christian leaders. The host asked what should be done to deal with these precipitous "falls." One leader said, "These people should be removed from ministry for six months." The next leader said they should be removed for one year. Another said, three years. It finally escalated until someone said they should be removed from ministry permanently. As the show was closing, the host looked at the consortium of experts and noticed everyone had contributed to the conversation except the noted Baptist preacher from Los Angeles, Dr. E.V. Hill. Noting they were running out of time, the host said, "Dr. Hill, you're the only one who hasn't said anything. I'll give you the last word." E.V. Hill paused for a moment and then drawled, "Well...I'll tell you one thing; if I ever sin, I'm not telling these boys about it." Everyone laughed (it is a serious matter), and the show ended.

The point is not to make light of sin, but to note the legalistic bent of the Church to establish a righteousness of its own. Sin is consequential and not to be marginalized, but restoration is a lost art. (There needs to be a book written on it that is not punitive, but restorative. That, by the way, doesn't preclude tough love—emphasis on *love*—when needed.)

DR. LAURA THEOLOGY

Here is the point of all of this pontificating. Once people understand grace and righteousness, they reign in life (see Rom. 5:17). That means we take authority, rule, dominance, prevalence, and sway over life. The question is, if this is true, how does it work?

This is the quest of *Organic Christianity*. Christianity in its original state causes people to operate this way. Once we understand

God's grace (unmerited favor), → it leads to the understanding of the finished work—all that God has provided for us, unmerited by us (see Eph. 1:3). → This awakens us to the exchanged life, not simply a changed life. → This in turn solidifies our identity (who God is, what He has already done, and who He has made us to be). → This ignites freedom in our lives (God is not mad at us). → This in turn gives credence to our righteousness (right standing with God as a gift we receive by faith). → This gives us a sense that we are qualified with God (we're not disqualified). → This lends to confidence. → Such confidence makes us feel unstoppable.

At the risk of sounding like Dr. Laura, "So, go take on your day!" The manifestation model is sequential. So our righteousness positions us now to receive truth. The truth does set us free! So let's look next at truth.

ORGANIC THOUGHTS

1. Do you feel unstoppable?

2. Have people tried to reduce you to sin-consciousness?

3. Does the principle of righteousness help you to see you are qualified to receive from God?

4. What did you see in God's attitude toward you as we examined the story of the prodigal son?

5. Can you put your "arms around" the fact that God's love for you is unconditional?

6. Does the revelation of grace and righteousness cause you to feel free from sin?

7. Does the revelation of Matthew 6:33 cause you to walk in more peace in your life?

8. Is your life more reflective of *works righteousness* or *faith righteousness*?

9. Do you sometimes live in spiritual schizophrenia because you don't understand faith righteousness? Do you find a need to follow human-made rules, in order to be right with God, that rob you of spiritual momentum?

Chapter 5

. . . .

THE TRUTH REALLY
DOES SET YOU FREE

During my sophomore year at a recognized Christian university, I was exposed to my first theological debate. A professor who made a major impact on my life was challenged to a debate by a colleague at a different institution on a book he had recently written. I was fascinated at the prospect of the theological banter.

I showed up a little early to a packed-out room. As I was greeting friends and introducing myself to people I didn't know, I began to recognize an interesting phenomena. All the people who supported my professor were seated on the right side of the room. All the people who supported his opponent were sitting on the left side of the room. Both groups' positions correlated to the positions of their perspective leader on the platform.

The debate itself was engaging and lively, but not hostile. It was clear to me my professor was the decisive winner. After the debate was over, however, I noticed the most interesting phenomena of all. Not one single person changed positions or perspectives, according to my unofficial observation.

I pondered the results of this event for some time, and it occurred to me that people hear through a filter of their own personal belief system. As a result, they filter in or they filter out new information according to what they already believe. Psychologists call this "scotoma," or blind spots. That is why two people can view the exact same passage, and one can see grace and the other can see law. Philosophy often dictates theology rather than theology dictating philosophy of life. That is when I realized that debates, especially theological debates, are useless. We don't need more debate; we need more dialogue.

Debates promote defense of your position; dialogue promotes an exchange of ideas in pursuit of truth. Here's what I mean. Some time back, I was sitting on the front row of my home church when I received a tap on my shoulder. An engaging woman humbly asked, "Are you Ron McIntosh?"

I replied, "I am!"

With enthusiasm she responded, "I read your book, *The Quest for Revival,* and it was one of the greatest books I've ever read." She paused and then continued, "Do you believe everything in that book just the way you wrote it?"

I smiled as I replied, "No, as a matter of fact, I don't." Her shocked response revealed some disappointment to my reply. I explained, "I am in complete concurrence with the majority of the book, but in about 10 percent of the book, I've grown in my revelation." This calmed her fears and opened up a thought. Every move of God is predicated by a re-emphasis of an organic thought. Such a move necessitates a change in thinking. Such a change is always resisted by the status quo. Ultimately the status quo gives way to changes of momentum, and reformation becomes reconciliation. Change for good is not enacted by debate, but by dialogue.

A friend of mine was sitting in a meeting when "debate" over a grace book ensued. One vehement woman jumped to her feet and screamed, "If you promote this book, you are sending people to hell!" Needless to say, she initiated debate, not dialogue.

GRACE IS RISKY!

There's little doubt that some people use grace to justify sinful lifestyles today as they did in New Testament days (see Jude 4). The idea that grace allows us to live any way we want is ludicrous. Romans 8:7 says it like this: *"The carnal mind* [literally "the flesh"[1]] *is enmity against God..."* (NKJV). The word *enmity* means "extreme opposition, hatred, the quality of being an enemy."[2] To live in the flesh (any way we want) puts us in opposition and hatred and makes God an enemy to our ways (not to us). Does that sound like something we want? Have at it! There are always those who want to find license to sin. I have heard people who have justified sin in the name of grace. Jesus said, *"I tell you the truth, everyone who sins is a slave to sin"* (John 8:34). Sinning continually makes us slaves to sin's edicts. How can any believer suggest that living the opposite of a godly lifestyle is justifiable?

Freedom affords such opportunity. It is essential to note, however, that people don't sin because of their theology. People sin because of what is in their hearts (see Prov. 4:23; 23:7; Jer. 17:9). Heart justification will use any means to justify their actions, even theology. However, we can never negate truth because of other people's abuse. We don't negate the truth of salvation because someone abuses it. Neither do we invalidate grace because someone misuses or insults unjustly what is true.

After that debate in my sophomore year of college, I subtly committed myself to the pursuit of truth based on the hermeneutical principles of interpretation rather than by preconceived philosophy. Why? Because the key is freedom. I found that God is very concerned about our freedom. Galatians 5:1 says, *"It is for freedom that Christ has set us free. Stand firm, then, and do not let yourselves be burdened again by a yoke of slavery."* Paul seems to say he wants us to be free for no other reason than to be free. The context of this passage (see Gal. 4:21-31) is that Paul is comparing our being under the law to being a descendant of a slave woman, Hagar. The result is, she is not an heir of the promises of God. The law was given to kill (see 2 Cor. 3:7) and condemn (see 2 Cor. 3:9). The law strengthened sin (see 1 Cor. 15:56) and made sin come alive (see Rom. 7:9). The law gave sin the opportunity to deceive us and work all manner of lust in us (see Rom. 7:8,11). The point is that the law strengthened sin in us and enslaved us.

Paul now says we are free. Paul also notes that we are to *stand firm in this freedom*. This phrase means we are to hold our ground, and not be entangled in slavery (to the law) again. We are to persevere to maintain our freedom. Obviously, we have a part to play in our freedom. Galatians 2:4 says,

> *This matter arose* [keeping the law in circumcision, see Gal. 2:3] *because some false brothers had infiltrated our ranks to spy on the freedom we have in Christ Jesus and to make us slaves.*

Judaizers in Galatia had infiltrated the Church in an attempt to make believers adhere, once again, to the law in order to be right with God. They were ancient "peeping toms" spying out the freedom of the Galatian believers.

> *Then said Jesus to these Jews which believed on Him, If ye continue in My Word, then are ye My disciples indeed; and ye shall know the truth, and the truth shall make you free. They answered Him, We be Abraham's seed, and were never in bondage to any*

man: how sayest Thou, Ye shall be made free? Jesus answered them, Verily, verily I say unto you, Whosoever commiteth sin is the servant of sin....If the Son therefore shall make you free, ye shall be free indeed" (John 8:31-36 KJV).

Again, this word *know* (in verse 32) means "to know intimately or experientially." When we know truth in His Word, it makes us free. Revelation knowledge of truth frees us. The Jews (and Jewish believers) thought it was their right by birth. The apostle is sharing that the true seed of Abraham is one of faith (see Gal. 3:16,29). No one is an heir of God by natural birth, but through the Messiah who delivered humankind from sin. Sin brings death, not life. Real freedom comes from the truth.

What is freedom? Freedom means "not enslaved, not under control of some arbitrary person, able to think without arbitrary restriction, to be unhindered, unhampered."[3] The opposite of freedom is not as much slavery as it is control. There are simultaneous movements afoot. One seeks to control; the other seeks to free. Those who seek to control don't believe free people are capable of making right decisions on their own (not just spiritually, but politically as well). They fear free people will sin and bring hurt to their lives. The problem is this: these people will never experience the worst in life, but neither will they experience the best in life. In the movement toward freedom, the leaders acknowledge some mistakes will be made, but they recognize the best in life comes from being free to experience it. Control always puts a mediator between people and their savior. Control robs people of intimacy with God. Freedom comes from only one source: truth.

The question is this: Is freedom a liberty worth fighting over or for? Listen to the words of Patrick Henry addressing the Virginia convention in March, 1775, on America's quest for freedom:

If we wish to be free, we must fight! ...I repeat, sir, we must fight! An appeal to arms and to the God of Hosts is all that is left to us. It is vain sir, to extenuate the matter. The gentlemen may cry, "Peace, Peace!" But there is no peace... Why stand here idle?...Is life so dear or peace so sweet as to be purchased at the price of chains and slavery? Forbid it, Almighty God! I know not what course others may take, but as for me, give me liberty or give me death![4]

What a searing, soul-rending speech Patrick Henry made. We applaud it as an expression of the heart of America. Yet, if we're not careful, the Church seeks to quench the liberty we innately know is our destiny. The organic message of the Gospel is freedom. Remember, freedom is only truly experienced in truth. Other freedoms are invalidated by their source, and they ultimately corrupt. This is not freedom to sin. Such insanity ultimately leads to various forms of destruction. This is freedom to experience God, to experience His Kingdom, to experience life more abundantly. False freedom renders people slaves to the very thing they seek to escape (see Rom. 6:16). Truth really does set people free. Free indeed!

TRUTH UNDER ASSAULT

It is truth, however, that is under assault today. We are living in a postmodern world where all truth is relative. Relativism is a philosophy in which all truth is relative to a person's situation or philosophy. Situational ethics is a derivation of relativism that states that our standard of truth is determined by the situation and, therefore, is different from person to person. There are no absolute values. Values are not based on principle as much as on an individual's point of view, and are applicable in limited contexts. Thus, truth is relative to a personal frame of reference. Often relativism suggests that all points of view are equally valid, where absolutism argues that there is only one valid point of view.

This may all seem like philosophical banter or mumbo jumbo until we see the result in culture. According to George Barna, Mosaics or Millenialists (the current teen and 20-something generation) are philosophically caught up in eclectic relativism. Here are the key characteristics for youth culture:

1. Eclectic lifestyle is embraced (everything is in, baby).

2. They are non-linear thinkers (logic is not primary).

3. They have fluid relations (up-and-down families).

4. Values are cut-and-paste (it's borrowed, as well as personalized, spirituality).

5. They embrace the "whatever works" philosophy—particularly for "me" (that's why relativism rules).

6. They are technology-fueled (it's the main source of information).

7. They're looking for experience (experimentation rules).

8. Self-expression is key.

9. Value is set in clusters (three to six people), not cliques.

10. There are no absolutes (they are comfortable with contradictions in values and philosophies).

Whether people understand it or not, philosophy and theology rule the day! Whether we are cognizant of what philosophy or theology we have, it dictates the values we operate by in life. So, what is truth? According to Scripture, it is John 17:17, *"Sanctify them by the truth; Your word is truth."* I would define *truth* this way. It is "conforming to an original pattern, rule, or standard."[5] *Truth* is "something reliable, certain in accordance to fact, real, genuine, trustworthy."[6] Truth adheres to an original, trustworthy pattern. In the case of believers, it's the Word of God. Any truth, therefore, that doesn't conform to the Word is not truth.

We know that truth liberates and elevates people (see John 8:32). James tells us what to do with truth,

> *But be doers of the Word [obey the message], and not merely listeners to it, betraying yourselves [into deception by reasoning contrary to the Truth]* (James 1:22 AMP).

Any philosophy that violates God's standard promotes deception and ultimately various forms of destruction. That is why Mosaics typically will say things like, "That may be true for you, but not for me." Relativism seeks to obliterate any standard for truth. It blurs any sense of right and wrong. That's why *Organic Christianity* seeks to gain the original intent of Scripture to propagate truth that sets people free to experience the fullness of God.

Thus, truth must conform to an original standard. This definition, however, is not complete because it is open to interpretation and a wide variety of applications. It must also define the standard. In the Christian worldview, truth is the Word of God (see John 17:17). Such truth should bring validation and productivity of the source. When it does not, deterioration is the result.

What is the "rest of the story" for the post-modernism philosophy?

- 64 percent of Mosaics are more likely to use profanity in public, as opposed to 19 percent of Boomers.

- Mosaics are nine times more likely to have sex outside of marriage than were boomers (38 percent compared to 4 percent).

- Mosaics are six times more likely to lie than Boomers (25 percent compared to 9 percent).

- Mosaics are three times more likely to gossip than Boomers (26 percent compared to 10 percent).

- Mosaics are two times more likely to view pornography than Boomers (33 percent compared to 16 percent).

- Mosaics are two times more likely to retaliate by action than Boomers (12 percent compared to 5 percent).[7]

You can argue with the reliability of these trends, but most reasonable people would conclude that relativism and postmodernism are undermining the moral fabric of culture. For the Christian worldview and organic Christianity, it is Genesis 3:1 all over again. This passage states,

Now the serpent was more crafty than any of the wild animals the Lord God had made. He said to the woman, "Did God really say, 'You must not eat from any tree in the garden'?"

The real issue for organic Christianity is to understand what influences culture, and more importantly, what influences believers that influences culture. If we live in a world that states, "Did God really say...?" then every Christian becomes schizophrenic by nature.

THE REAL PROBLEM

The real problem is that we, as believers, are not fully persuaded of what is true. Look at Romans 4:20-21:

He did not waver through unbelief regarding the promise of God, but was strengthened in his faith... being fully persuaded that God had the power to do what He had promised.

This passage refers to 100-year-old Abraham and 90-year-old Sarah having a baby. I can just see Abraham saying to Sarah, "God said I'd be the father of many nations." And, Sarah responds, "Yeah? I've got a headache. You better not touch me." Though humanly it was impossible to have a child at that age, Abraham, in hope, believed God and became the father of many nations (see Rom. 4:18). In spite of a humanly impossible situation, Abraham did not waver through unbelief. The truth is, we often doubt that God will perform what He promised for us. Most believers are circumstantial Christians. Noted psychologist Martin Seligman, in his book *Learned Optimism,* suggests that 80 percent of people suffer from something he calls "learned helplessness." The idea behind learned helplessness is we feel helpless to change our circumstances. Life is dictating to us by the circumstances of our lives. Indeed, those are facts, but the point of this passage is that truth is greater than facts! Putting faith in God's truth will cause us to conquer facts.

Take note of what Abraham did in verse 19:

> *Without weakening in his faith, he faced not the fact [KJV: "considered not his own body"] that his body was as good as dead—since he was about a hundred years old....*

In other words, Abraham saw the facts but he put his faith in the truth, and truth overcame facts. Paul concludes his exposure of the devil's main tool of strategy by giving the answer to the deception:

> *We demolish arguments and every pretension that sets itself up against the knowledge of God,* [How?] *and we take captive every thought to make it obedient to Christ* (2 Corinthians 10:5).

The point of understanding truth is that whatever we focus on is what our hearts will believe; whatever we neglect is what our hearts will disbelieve. What we focus on longest becomes strongest. When we focus on our problems, all the reasons why the truth is impossible will begin to manifest in our personal belief system. The result is that we believe our problems are bigger than God. However, when we keep our minds stayed on the truth of God's Word, nothing is too difficult for God.

BATTLEFIELD OF THE MIND

Organic Christianity is not about getting more of God; we already have all of God we're ever going to get (see Eph. 3:20; Philem.

6; Col. 2:10). It is about renewing our minds to what we already possess. Organic Christianity is less about the facts of life and more about the truth of God's promises that conquers those facts. The key is to become fully persuaded of what is truth.

I've already devoted an entire book to this topic (*The Greatest Secret*), and I'm not interested in replicating that work, but I want to provide some essentials to guiding us, as believers, to a true authenticity and productivity (a Christianity that works).

The real battleground is the battleground of the mind. The devil's strategy is encapsulated in Second Corinthians 10:3-5:

> *For though we live in the world, we do not wage war as the world does. The weapons we fight with are not the weapons of the world. On the contrary, they have divine power to demolish strongholds. We demolish arguments and every pretension that sets itself up against the knowledge of God and we take captive every thought to make it obedient to Christ.*

I'm going to expose the devil's strategy in order to bring revelation to our lives. Quite simply, Paul tells us the devil sets up strongholds, arguments, and pretenses against the knowledge of God. The devil's stratagem is to dilute God's knowledge or truth by these three "weapons" of the mind. He wants to distort truth with contrary "facts." So what are strongholds, arguments, and pretenses?

- *Stronghold*—anything we feel powerless to change, though it is contrary to the Word of God.

- *Argument*—two contrary opinions. The original Greek word means "reasoning or logic hostile to the faith."[8]

- *Pretense*—a "fact" based on a false assumption.

The main battlefield for the Christian faith is the battlefield of the mind. The main weapon the enemy uses is double-mindedness (see James 1:7). His main strategy is to cause double-mindedness by using information or circumstances contrary to faith. The double-minded person vacillates between two opinions. James tells us that double-minded people are unstable in all their ways and can receive nothing from God. Peter indicates that everything for life and godliness is given to us by the knowledge of God (see 2 Pet. 1:3). If the devil can create an opaque truth, he keeps Christians from any real success in their faith. That is why the real issue comes down to being fully persuaded of the truth (see Rom. 4:21).

MIRROR, MIRROR, ON THE WALL

The question becomes, "How do I take every thought captive and become fully persuaded?" James 1:22-24 holds the answer:

> *But be doers of the Word and not hearers only, deceiving your own selves. For if anyone be a hearer only and not a doer, he is like the man who looks into the mirror and after looking at himself, goes away and immediately forgets what he looks like* (author's combination of KJV and NIV).

People who hear the Word of God (and do not understand it, which is clearly one of the main reasons for not applying it) and do not apply it are like people who forget the image in the mirror of themselves. One of the first things most people do early in the morning is to look in the mirror. Here's the question, "Do we like what we see?" I don't know why, but there seems to be a strange metamorphosis that takes place at night: A woman goes to bed looking like Eva Longoria, but when she wakes up in the morning, she looks like the Wicked Witch of the East. Similarly, a man goes to bed looking like Brad Pitt, but when he wakes up in the morning, he looks more like Shrek.

So when we awaken and we look into the mirror, what do we do? We start making adjustments based on what we see. That is what the Word of God is to be for the believer. The Word is a mirror that reflects to us who we are, and we are to make adjustments based on what it reflects to us. We don't react to the facts of our circumstances, but to the truth of His Word.

The question becomes, "Why is that so difficult for us to believe and do?" It is because, according to psychologists, our personal belief system is made up of five areas: (1) social environment, (2) authority figures, (3) self-image, (4) repetitious information, and (5) our experiences.[9] Often the fact of these elements of our personal belief system don't correlate to what the Word says about us. Let me give you some examples:

1. *Social Environment*—This means we have a tendency to be a reflection of what that environment tells us we are. People who grew up in poverty-inflicted environments have a tendency to think that may be their lot in life. They may have had a parent who said something like this, "Do you think money grows on trees? Do you think there's a money tree in the backyard?" That parent is communicating lack or poverty. "Some people are the *have's* and some people are the *have not's*. We're the *have not's*."

I often demonstrate this in my meetings by this little demonstration. I take out a massive, oversized pair of costume blue sunglasses. I usually make a reference to making a fashion statement. Then I pull out a white note card, and I ask an audience member, "What color is this card?" He or she usually looks at me funny and says, "White!"

I usually make a funny look back and indignantly say something like, "Oh, really. I say it's blue" (looking through my blue lenses).

I move to the next participant, and I ask the same question again. Again, the person says, "White!" I may go through a series of people who all respond white, while I dispute their evaluation by declaring, "It's blue."

Here's the point. The card is white, but if I see it as blue, it's blue to me. I may even ultimately say it's white to fit in with everyone else, but the truth of the matter is, it's still blue in my belief system.

Similarly, someone may stand up in church and declare that God wants to prosper us. He or she may even validate it with Scripture. Those who have a poverty mindset join the crowd in nodding their heads in agreement, but what they hear out of their personal belief system is, "Do you think there's a money tree in the backyard?" Often they want the Word to be true, but their personal belief system keeps them from being fully persuaded to apply any of the principles and actions to prosper.

2. *Authority Figures*—We have a tendency to believe what the most important people in our lives tell us to believe as true. A very important person in my life told me (in words and actions) that I would never amount to anything! I thought to myself, *If this person loves me, and this is what this person sees, it must be true.* The result was, for years, I lived a self-sabotaging lifestyle. Every time I got ready to break through to a new level, I would do something to sabotage my progress or opportunity. Why? Because I believed I was never going to amount to

anything. I really believed it until I learned to look into a new mirror.

3. *Self-image*—Many psychologists believe we will never rise above the image we have of ourselves in our hearts. If we want to change an area of our lives, we have to see ourselves in our hearts differently.

4. *Repetitious Information*—This is something we hear over and over again until we assume it is true, whether it is or not (it's a pretense). I once heard a speaker quote Adolf Hitler as saying, "If you tell a lie often enough, long enough, people will believe it."

Some time ago, I watched some debates in a presidential primary. The members of a political party openly "bashed" a sitting president. Some of the allegations seemed to have no basis of truth. Because the president had no access to the foray to defend himself, his poll numbers plummeted. Repetitious display of "fact" (right or wrong) swayed the beliefs of the public.

This is also a dominant principle for advertisers. Marketers suggest an interested hearer for their product doesn't usually make a purchase until they've seen an ad at least three times. Ads are a combination of information and imagination. Principles often don't change a person; images of that principle do. Repeated exposure to "truth" is convincing and can move people to an end. That's why people who are told over and over again (through various means) that they aren't valuable, act accordingly.

5. *Experience*—We have a tendency to believe that our experiences communicate truth to and about us.

Repeated negative experiences can immobilize people moving toward success. Proverbs 13:12 tells us, *"Hope deferred makes the heart sick...."* Hope unrealized can cripple people's pursuit of their destiny.

Howard Gardner is a leading educator from Harvard University. He did a 20 year study on the same group of individuals. Here are his amazing findings:

1. Age 4—100 percent of participants tested out as geniuses.

2. Age 20—10 percent of all participants tested out as geniuses.

3. Age 24—2 percent tested out as geniuses.[10]

What this says to me is, God puts genius into all of us, but we let life's experiences "beat it" out of us. *Organic Christianity* seeks to restore God's genius by helping us become fully persuaded of our identity in Him. This brings us to an incredibly important principle: We become fully persuaded of truth by renewing our minds to truth.

FULLY PERSUADED

Organic Christianity is more about renewing our minds to who we already are than trying to become who we aren't. Remember, we've already been given everything we need for life and godliness (see 2 Pet. 1:3). We've already been blessed with every spiritual blessing in the heavenly realm (see Eph. 1:3). We already have in us everything to do exceedingly, abundantly beyond what we could ask or think (see Eph. 3:20). We are complete in Him (see Col. 2:10).

The problem is, we're not fully persuaded of who God is, what He has already done, and who He has made us to be. How then do we become fully persuaded?

This revelation is perhaps the most important thing we can understand for our lives outside of salvation. The key to being fully persuaded of God's truth for us is to renew our minds to who we truly are. Romans 12:2 gives us this quintessential truth:

> *Be not conformed to this world: but be ye transformed*
> *by the renewing of your mind, that ye may prove what is*
> *that good, and acceptable, and perfect, will of God* (KJV).

Here are four incredible, essential principles that will enable us to become persuaded of the truth:

1. Be not conformed to this world.

2. Be transformed.

3. Renew your mind.

4. Prove the perfect will of God.

I've written an entire book on this topic (*The Greatest Secret*), and it is not my intent to replicate its content. I want to give you the essential guidelines and some new information that will take you from where you are to where you want to be.

Sometime back, when God started to reveal to me a coming Reformation or Reclamation, I sensed that God was moving His Church from a reasonable facsimile to the fullness of the expression of His Kingdom. I inquired of the Lord, "How will this come into being?" He almost immediately took me to Joshua 1:8,

Do not let this Book of the Law depart from your mouth; but meditate on it day and night, so that you may be careful to do everything written in it, Then you will be prosperous and you will be successful.

He said to me:

+ Incubation (meditating on God's Word)

+ Revelation (the result of meditation)

+ Impartation (bestowing or intertwining revelation in our lives)

= Manifestation (the invisible Kingdom becoming visible in our world).

In other words, meditating on God's Word brings good success. I define *success* as "progression toward a worthwhile goal that has meaning to us and meaning to God, culminating in a desired end." Good success is success without the divorce, without a dismembered family, without the loss of health, without emotional breakdown.

Then God took me to Proverbs. *"For as he thinks in his heart, so is he..."* (Prov. 23:7 NKJV). *"Keep your heart with all diligence, for out of it spring the issues of life"* (Prov. 4:23 NKJV). This term *issues* in Proverbs 4:23 is the Hebrew term for boundaries. The boundaries of my life are determined by what is in my heart. Success, real success, is determined from the inside-out, not the outside-in. Meditation allows us to focus on something until we are fully persuaded of truth (or a lie for that matter), until it is imbedded in our conscious and subconscious minds. It becomes a part of the makeup of our being until it is our nature to act accordingly.

This is done both in the positive and negative. Worry is simply meditating on the negative or evil. The result is fear. When we meditate on truth, the result is faith. This is what Romans 12:2 is all about.

FOUR KEYS TO BECOMING FULLY PERSUADED

Key #1: Be Not Conformed

The first principle is to not be conformed to this world or this world's system. The term *conformed* comes from two words. The prefix *con-* means "with or together with."[11] *Form* means "a way or pattern of doing something."[12] Paul is communicating that we must not be with or together with the way or pattern of the world's system. Why is that important? It is because we can't access God's system (Kingdom) from the world's system. Paul's first principle echoes a warning: All we can ever produce is what is natural to that system. Paul wanted to show the limitation of the world's system of truth and how to tap into God's Kingdom.

The world's system operates the opposite of God's Kingdom. The world's system does have productivity, but we cannot access God's Kingdom from it. The world's system can produce success, but not good success. God grants prosperity, but adds no sorrow to it (see Prov. 10:22).

Let me give an example. Matthew 3:2 states, *"Repent, for the kingdom of Heaven is near."* Usually when that verse is preached, people say, "That's right, have godly sorrow for wrongdoing so someday you can go to Heaven." I would never minimize that revelation, but there's much more to this verse. This verse is saying *repent*, which literally means "to think differently or to change our thinking."[13] In other words, Jesus is saying we can't access the Kingdom thinking the way we're thinking now.

It is crucial for us to understand the full implications of what the Kingdom of Heaven means in its entirety. The Kingdom of Heaven is the abode of God and the rule and reign of God. It is also the location and resources of God. The Kingdom of God is the governance or system for how to access the Kingdom of Heaven or God's provision.[14] The declaration of this passage is to change our minds (or thinking) so we can access the resources that God longs to put at our disposal. It is essential that we are operating in the right system—God's Kingdom—which is always based on His truth.

God's system operates exactly the opposite of the world's system. In God's system, if we want to receive, we have to give. If we want to increase, we have to decrease. If we want to become the greatest, we have to become the least. If we want to live, we must die (to self). It is essential to be fully persuaded of God's system if we want to fully access the fullness of the Kingdom.

Assuredly, the devil wants to muddle this perception. Most believers, if asked who public enemy number one is, would respond, the devil! However, satan has already been defeated (see Col. 2:14-15). Satan's victory comes through the realm of the flesh (see Gal. 5:19-21). According to Romans 8:5-6, the flesh is a mindset that dictates our actions. It's the root of our bad decision-making. According to John 6:63, *"The flesh profits nothing"* (NKJV). It doesn't take much of a businessperson to figure out not to invest in something that has no return.

Paul further amplifies on this by noting that the flesh is the opposite of operating in the spirit (see Gal. 5:16). He says such operations end up *"...so that you do not do the things that you wish"* (Gal. 5:17 NKJV). We want to access God's system, but we can't because we're in the world's system. In essence, the flesh is humanity's efforts to do God's will. It is people trying to meet a need their own way. The result is lust instead of love. They postpone (by drugs, alcohol, excessive entertainment, and so forth) instead of appropriating peace.

They become angry instead of trusting God. Those who live like this will not inherit the manifestation of the Kingdom of God and will not have the joy of God flowing over them.[15]

Key #2: Be Transformed

This term *transform* used in Romans 12:2 is another fascinating word. It likewise comes from two words. The prefix *trans-* means "over, above and beyond," and *form* is "a way or pattern of doing something." This term gives us the idea that there is another pattern that is so far above and beyond conforming that it has no real comparison. The way we cross over to God's system of provision is by being transformed by His truth.

The term is the Greek word *metamorphose,* which is where we get our English word *metamorphosis. Metamorphosis,* at its root, means "to be radically transformed." When we think of *metamorphosis,* we most often think of a caterpillar becoming a butterfly. A few hours after it has emerged from its chrysalis, it stretches its wings and leaves the limitations of its former life behind. In essence, it becomes what it already is. It really is amazing, however, how something so infantile crawling on the ground can emerge as something of such exquisite beauty. This is the kind of total transformation God seeks to establish in our lives. Once we are transformed by His truth, we no longer resemble our former selves. We leave one level of living behind and step into the abundant living God has for us.

Someone might come to you and say, "I've seen your life. It doesn't look like much." Your response should be, "I'm being transformed." Similarly, others might think the same thing about your ministry, spouse, church, or finances. Maybe they say, "I know your husband. He doesn't look like much." Look at them, smile, and say, "Yes, he is being transformed."

Let me illustrate to you what I mean. When my son Jonathan was 11 years old, a relative gave him a gift card to Toys "R" Us®.

Although he had already spent most of its value, the card still had $7.12 left on it. As you might imagine, "It was burning a hole in Jon's pocket." Jonathan spent the next few days coaxing his dad to go shopping. After some persuading, I agreed to take him to the toy store. As soon as we "hit" the store, Jonathan made a beeline to the gaming area of the store, where all the systems and electronic games that start at a "billion dollars" and up are located. I remind you he had $7.12 left on his gift card. After about an hour and a half of examining every game and system, I finally convinced him to look at something more commensurate to the value of his card. We ventured over to the action figure area of the store. He finally settled on a "Transformer." If you've never seen them, they are action figures that are human or robotic in form, but when you move a few parts, they transform into something totally different. By moving a few parts, a human turns into something altogether different, like a car, truck, tank, bazooka, or something. This is the exact idea of what Paul is communicating in Romans 12:2. If you don't conform to the world's system, but instead are transformed, you'll be changed into a different person who doesn't resemble your former self. That is why the Bible calls you a new creation or a new species of being (see 2 Cor. 5:17).

Please note this, there is a major and massive difference between being "changed" and being "transformed." On the surface, they may appear to be the same or similar in concept. Beneath the surface, they are radically different. The word *change* means "to cause to go from one state to another, to alter, to make different, to quit one thing and to start another, or to substitute."[16] *Transform,* on the other hand, suggests "to alter in form or appearance, a metamorphosis, to conform to the will of God, a release of divine nature, an alteration of the heart, to change the inner nature, to change one's mind or to exchange."[17]

As we can see, change comes from the outside-in, transformation comes from the inside-out. Transformation is an inward effortless alteration. *Organic Christianity* is far more about transformation than change. Change can actually retard transformation. In the Church, we've been more about behavioral modification than transformation. No wonder so many believers wonder whether their "change" has lasting ramifications. True transformation through the power of Christ comes from within us. The real question becomes, *How?*

Key #3: Renewing the Mind

The third principle of Romans 12:2 is renewing the mind. Transformation is the result of renewing the mind. The term *renew* is another fascinating word. It means "to renovate or to restore to its original state."[18] If we renovate something, we take old things out and put new things in. Recently, we renovated our Bible school auditoriums and offices. We took out old tiles, carpeting, chairs, platforms, sound systems, monitors, televisions, and so forth, and replaced them with new ones. We got rid of the old and replaced them with the new.

The same thing holds true of our lives. If we don't like the output (manifestation), we must change the input. We understand this in computer language: "garbage in, garbage out." We often use the quote, but most of the time in the Church, if we don't like the output, we try to work on the output more intensely. We can never change output until we change the input.

How, then, do we renew our minds? How do we create new dominant thoughts? The key is, once new dominant thoughts get into our hearts, they *will* effect new manifestations. Proverbs 23:7, says it this way, *"As he thinks in his heart, so is he..."* (NKJV). The term *think* here means "doorkeeper or gatekeeper." In other words, our thinking (dominant thoughts) is a gatekeeper to our hearts. What gets in our hearts is what we're going to do. This verse doesn't mean maybe, probably, or possibly. What dominant thoughts get into our hearts are exactly what we will manifest. We will do whatever is in our hearts.

Proverbs 4:23 amplifies this, *"Keep* [guard] *your heart with all diligence, for out of it spring the issues of life"* (NKJV). The New International Version says, *"Above all else, guard your heart...."* This indicates that there is nothing more important or higher than this.

Listen, born-again, Spirit-filled believer—*"Above all else...."* Sit up and pay attention. This is the highest priority for a believer: Guard your heart, for out of it come the issues of life. Again, the term *issues* means "boundaries, limitations, or stagnations."[19] Your boundaries in life are determined by what is in your heart. Boundaries are not primarily from your background, education, or race (by themselves). Boundaries are not the result of what your momma said, what your daddy did, or what your peers projected. Your boundaries are about what dominant thoughts you let into your heart.

The issue comes down to the fact that too often in the Church we say things though we don't really know what they mean. We say things like, "You have to believe in your heart," or, "You have to do it from your heart." Really!? What does that mean, and how do I do that?

Hebrews 4:12 reveals a key that unlocks this door:

> *For the word of God is living and active. Sharper than any double-edged sword, it penetrates* [dividing asunder] *even to dividing soul and spirit, joints and marrow; it judges the thoughts and attitudes of the heart.*

This is primarily a passage about the efficacy of the Word of God, but if we look carefully, it also gives us a biblical definition of the heart. The purpose of this two-edged sword is to penetrate or divide asunder the aspects of the heart. The term *divide asunder* means "to separate for the purpose of distinction." The question is, What is it distinguishing in the heart? What is the heart?

Here in this passage the writer of Hebrews tells us what the heart is. There are two aspects of the heart that the Word is to penetrate and separate: soul and spirit. The job of the heart is to mediate the soul and spirit. When these two elements of the heart line up, nothing is impossible for God in our lives. The limitations and boundaries are broken.

Your human spirit is the place where God dwells (see Rom. 8:10,16). It is the place where God speaks to us. The soul is our mind, will, emotions, and imagination.[20] Our spirits are a new creation and are perfect (see Heb. 12:23). The soul, however, must be renewed with God's truth. This is the key to allowing the truth to permeate our beings and to promote accessing the Kingdom of God. Therefore, the job of our hearts is to line up the soul with the spirit, with God's truth. When these two forces are in agreement, then the energy and the power of God are released in people. The Word then divides and discerns the thoughts and intents of the heart. Thoughts precede actions, and intents (moral understanding or conscience) precede thoughts. God made us to operate out of our spirits, but we are often sabotaged by a soul not aligned with the intent.

Take a look at the following figure:

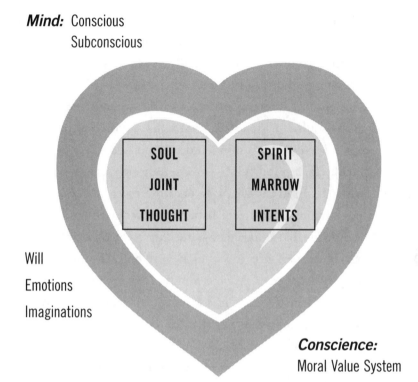

Mind: Conscious
Subconscious

SOUL
JOINT
THOUGHT

SPIRIT
MARROW
INTENTS

Will
Emotions
Imaginations

Conscience:
Moral Value System

The problem is most people operate out of their souls rather than their spirits. Often an event or circumstance creates a dominant belief that enters people's hearts (personal belief system) and limits the boundaries of their lives. Operating out of the soul suggests that our dominant thoughts come out of our imagination, emotions, will, and mind:

Imaginations—Most research indicates we will never rise above the image we have of ourselves in our hearts. If we want to change an area of our lives, we must first change the image of ourselves in that area first.

Emotions—According to research, emotions travel 80,000 times faster than a thought.[21] That is why we often are affected more by emotions than principles. In turn, our emotions affect our wills and our minds, and our minds affect our actions. If we don't line up our lives with Kingdom truths, it's possible for our unrenewed minds to wreak havoc in our lives. (Of course, the opposite is true as well. If renewed truth encounters us emotionally, it too affects our minds, wills, and emotions. The result is positive change.)

In understanding how this principle works, we must next understand that the soul is made up also with the mind. The mind also has two parts; the conscious mind and the subconscious mind. The job of the conscious mind (CM) is to determine truth. The job of the subconscious mind (SCM) is to take the truth and to make it come to pass. Its job is to create habits, comfort zones, and consistency. The SCM is like a huge data bank that records every thought, idea, emotion, or experience. It will make sure our words and actions stay aligned with what our CM determines as being true. It creates an automatic response system, and it is where our personal belief system (PBS) exists. Psychologists suggest that 90 to 95 percent of our daily decisions come out of our SCM.

The repercussions and effects of this understanding are obvious. As long as your SCM tells the CM truth that is healthy and productive, this is an incredible system. If, however, through experiences or improper training, the CM has adopted beliefs that are contrary to the Word of God, it will produce wrong responses and actions that limit us and prevent us from our full potential. We can miss God's abundant life because of unrenewed thinking about who we really are in reference to organic Christianity.

Let me give two examples of how these two aspects of the mind work. If I taught you how to drive a car, you must first learn to drive on the conscious level. Everything, most likely, would be very mechanical. You would slowly learn all the mechanics—the steering wheel, brake, accelerator, clutch, speedometer, and so forth. Once it becomes a learned procedure (habit), by going from the conscious level to the subconscious level, you lose the discomfort of the rote mechanical process. In fact, many people can drive while listening to the radio and having a conversation on a cell phone all at the same time. I don't recommend it, but you can do it. Why? The SCM has created a habit and a comfort zone. You can perform the task without even thinking about it.

In most areas of your life the subconscious mind creates habits, personal belief systems, and comfort zones that create decisions that are programmed. The job of the SCM is to produce consistency. So it strives to keep you in that comfort zone, so much so that if you update with new programming, it will work to keep you there, even if it has to sabotage you.

It is what psychologists call a "set point"—a mind-set or a self-limiting belief. It is much like the automatic pilot on an airplane. If you set out to a destination and set the automatic pilot at 30,000 feet, its job is to maintain that altitude. If I grabbed the controls and pulled up the controls to ascend to 35,000 feet or I descended to 20,000 feet, once I release the controls it would return to 30,000 feet.

This is exactly how the SCM works. Its job is to create habits that keep you consistent. If those beliefs are productive and beneficial, that becomes a real benefit. However, if your habits and beliefs are contrary to the truth, they can be unproductive or, worse, destructive. They place ceilings or limitations (an automatic pilot) in your life. Your SCM must be renewed to the truth to break set points that keep you from expressing the fullness of organic Christianity.

This is the reason you see some startling results in culture. Research shows 80 percent of lottery winners, though they win millions of dollars, are back at their original income level in a relatively short period of time. Similarly, 95 percent of people who lose weight on diets return to their original weight.[22] Your SCM will work to keep you in the comfort zone of your self-image established by the CM. Your thinking at the subconscious level can create comfort zones that can affect your destiny.

Key #4: Prove

Before I get eminently practical with this process of mind renewal, let's examine the fourth principle of Romans 12:2, *"Prove what is that good and acceptable and perfect will of God"* (NKJV). This term *prove* means "to establish as genuine, approve, validate, discern, to recognize revelation or by implication to manifest."[23] This is talking about manifesting the will of God in our lives.

Once we are no longer conformed to this world's system (breaking free from its limitations), but instead are transformed to a higher way of thinking (by renewing our minds and establishing our hearts), we will be able to recognize, validate, and manifest God's will for our lives. It's time to think differently and live life as God intended.

Renewed thinking and a transformed heart result in recognition of Heaven's resources and open doors to God's Kingdom. During a meeting I had with Oral Roberts some years ago, he told me that miracles are coming to us regularly. People either receive them or they pass by them. It's really a matter of whether people recognize them or not.

In our brains there is something that causes us to filter out unimportant information and focus on meaningful facts or opportunities. It is called a Reticular Activating System (RAS). There are three aspects to RAS:

1. *Positive focusing*—One example of positive focusing is when a party is taking place in a noisy room and down the hallway comes the faint cry of a baby. No one hears the baby except the mother. Why? Because she is focused on her baby.

2. *Negative filtering*—An example of this is people who live near the airport. We might think to

ourselves, *How can a person sleep with planes flying overhead every few minutes?* Those who live there have no trouble because they have filtered out the noise from their thinking.

3. *Individual perception*—This occurs when two people see the same accident, but have two totally differing accounts. Why? They each had a different vantage point or perception of what happened.

RAS[24] causes us to filter out unimportant information and focus on what we've told our SCM is important for the moment. It immediately transmits vital information to the CM. It causes us to recognize things we might otherwise miss.

Here's the gist of Romans 12:2. When we are not conformed to the world's system but are transformed by the renewing of our minds, we will begin to recognize people, ideas, and resources according to our most dominant thoughts. If we can transform our PBS to the truth of God's Word, God's Kingdom will be opened to us.

TRANSFORMING YOUR PERSONAL BELIEF SYSTEM

How is this done practically? It is done by meditating on God's Word. This is not some New Age mumbo jumbo. For there to be any counterfeit, there must first be an original. New Age and transcendental meditation are simply aberrations of the originals. Examine this passage to validate the truth:

My son, pay attention [KJV: "attend to"] to what I say [KJV: "unto my sayings"]: listen closely to my words. Do not let them out of your sight. keep them within your heart; for they are life to those who find them and health to a man's whole body. Above all else, guard your heart, for it [your heart] *is the wellspring of life* (Proverbs 4:20-23).

Here are some incredible keys:

1. *Pay attention to God's words and concepts.* Literally this means "to attend, to meditate, to wait upon or imagine God's Word."[25] If you don't see it, you can't receive it. For instance, if you see giving or tithing as depletion, you will never do it. You must see life through faith that is focused on truth. You have to see the truth of how increase works. (See my website for the *Barrier Buster Manual* and biblical meditation CDs for Scriptures in this area.)

2. *Don't let them out of your sight.* In other words, life is filled with circumstances and experiences seeking to cause you to lose focus on the truth. Repetition is the key to reinforcing truth. According to psychologists, it takes 21 days to create a new habit. Repetition over 21 days helps overcome false focus in your SCM.

3. *Keep it in your heart.* Renew the soul chamber of your heart to the truth that is in your spirit. Let your conscious mind assimilate ultimate truth, and through repetition, allow it to get into your SCM and set up an automatic response system that will change your present self-limiting beliefs.

4. *This process creates life, health, and boundary-breaking in your life.* It makes you fresh, alive, and strong. It positions you to access God's Kingdom.

John 8:31-32 ties us back to this process, making us free, *"...If ye continue in My word, then are ye My disciples indeed; and ye shall know the truth, and the truth shall make you free"* (KJV).

Please notice in this verse that the truth does not set you free. It is the truth you *know* that sets you free. Again, this word *know* is not intellectual knowledge. This term means "intimate, experiential knowledge." This is knowledge that has been internalized or become revelation. This is knowledge that makes you intimate with the Savior. The result is freedom from things that limit everything that has been granted to you for life and godliness (see 2 Pet. 1:3).

Let's amplify further as to how this happens. Psalm 1:1-3 states,

> *Blessed is the man who does not walk in the counsel of the wicked or stand in the way of sinners or sit in the seat of mockers. But his delight is in the law of the Lord, and on his law he meditates day and night. He is like a tree planted by streams of water, which yields its fruit in season and whose leaf does not wither. Whatever he does prospers.*

The psalmist notes four keys to going from where you are to where you want to be:

1. *Don't walk in the counsel of the wicked.* This means don't walk with those who cultivate the world's system because it can only produce what that system can produce. That system collides with the Kingdom of God.

2. *Don't walk in the way of sinners.* What is the way of sinners? It is the operation of the flesh (doing God's will your way) and unbelief. Such action profits nothing, is contrary to God, and means that the things you want to do you cannot do (see John 6:63; Rom. 7; Gal. 5:16-17).

3. *Do not sit in the seat of mockers.* Mocking what? Mocking the truth of God's Word. All such activity short-circuits your personal belief system and the manifestation of the Kingdom. Mockery repeatedly listened to (in all its forms, media, authority figures, peers, and so forth) brings contempt or, at best, confusion to the truth.

4. *Delight yourself in the law of the Lord.* Instead, he continues, *"His delight is in the law of the Lord."* This term, *delight,* means "to have a high degree of satisfaction, to desire that which is precious or valuable pursuit."[26] I once had a college professor who told me it means, "You can't get enough of." It's like a football junkie on New Year's Day with four large screen televisions going with a different game on each set. It's like a woman in a mall with a sale. She shops until she drops.

Then the psalmist says to eliminate the negative and accentuate the positives. *Delight yourself in the law of the Lord.* What is the law of the Lord? Certainly it's God's Word. A law, however, is a principle that tells you how a thing works best. You pursue such principles by meditating on them day and night. The term *meditate* means "to utter, murmur, ponder, stretch, see beyond, muse, or imagine."[27]

So this term means to mutter or utter. If we take an honest look at our lives, we often mutter and utter many days. "I can't believe what she did to me. Can you believe it? I was minding my own business when all of a sudden…" Get the picture? If we're going to mutter, we might as well do it according to the truth.

The term also means "to ponder or muse." As you dwell on God's truth, it causes you to see beyond, to stretch beyond where you are in your circumstance. The word also means "to imagine." The word *imagine* means "to think without limitation." It enables you to see yourself according to the truth (in the positive sense). It creates a new "image" on the inside of you. Your SCM then works to make this image come to pass. It remedies your present situations. Biblical meditation is a way to intentionally increase the manifestation of your faith.

Before you worry that this is New Age or transcendental meditation, let me assure you it is not. Remember, satan is not a creator. All he can do is mimic or pervert truth. Don't let his deception rob you of the missing ingredient to transforming your personal belief system. It is the Bible that encourages meditation—continual musing on God's Word, which is inspired by the Holy Spirit (see 2 Tim. 3:16).

The psalmist says a person should meditate *"day and night."* What does that mean? Quite simply, start your day and end your day in biblical meditation. When you start your day looking into the perfect law of freedom (see James 1:22-24), you will begin to see yourself according to real truth, which the enemy will try to contest all day long. When you end your day meditating on God's Word, it will reinforce the same truth the enemy sought to steal from you all day long. Another reason to end your day in biblical meditation is that your SCM never turns off. As you feed truth the last thing of the day, it dwells on it all night long. That's why it sometimes when you go to bed thinking about a situation the next morning you wake up with a solution. In essence, meditation is focusing on something to the point it never leaves your conscious thinking. It begins to create an inner influence in you.

THE RESULTS

Now look at the amazing results this process provides:

1. *You are like the tree planted by streams of water.* Like the vine and the branches described in John 15, you are connected to the ultimate source in life. You are connected to the King and His Kingdom.

2. *You yield fruit.* Again, just like John 15, you bear fruit (15:8). Fruit is the manifestation of its source. Apple trees produce apples. Orange trees produce oranges. A believer produces what he believes for from the King's Kingdom.

3. *Your leaves do not wither.* You do not dry up in times of drought around you.

4. *Whatever you do prospers.* You are favored, rendered successful, advancing in growth or wealth, gaining the things properly desired, making successful progress, and using your ability to use God's ability to meet any need.

This is precisely the picture reinforced in Joshua 1:8:

> *Do not let this Book of the Law depart from your mouth; meditate on it day and night, so that you may be careful to do everything written in it. Then you will be prosperous and successful* [KJV: *"good success"*].

What an incredible revelation. Here are the applications to the process:

1. *Confession*—The confession of your lips must be added to your imagination. Confession is simply speaking truth instead of fact. I confess or profess God's Word, not simply my circumstances. This is a massively important principle to affect your personal belief system. Psychologists call this "self-talk." There has been some incredibly important research done in this area. Psychological research has found something called psycholinguistics. I was introduced to this concept via a teaching tape from Lou Tice of the Pacific Institute. There he reveals this stunning research. He states that if you simply confess something, it gets into your personal belief system about 10 percent. If you confess with imagination (meditation), it gets into your personal belief system 55 percent. If you confess a thing with imagination and emotion, it gets into your personal belief system 100 percent.[28]

    Most of us in our lives speak facts instead of truth. We speak our bank account instead of God's provision. We speak our physical state instead of God's health and healing, and so forth. It's time to stop confessing our struggles and start confessing the truth. One may be a reality in the physical; the other is a reality (by grace) in the spiritual. We must come to understand that what is in the spiritual is greater than what is in the physical. What God has done by grace, we receive by faith. Once our confession reinforces to our PBS the truth of the Spirit, we become fully persuaded of its efficacy.

We confess a thing in personal (I) present tense (am). Some might think *If it's not a reality, how can it be present tense?* It is present tense in the Kingdom of God by grace (see 2 Pet. 1:3; Eph. 1:3). And we confess a thing positive. It is essential our confession is positive. The SCM does not recognize negatives.[29]

2. *Consistency (Repetition)*—Joshua's exhortation to meditate *"day and night"* is a call to repetition. Research indicates that it takes 21 days to change a habit or a belief.[30] Some researchers suggest it is 30 days, some 60 days, others suggest 90 days. I believe it is in reference to what Sigmund Freud called the "Pain/Pleasure Principle." You make decisions toward what you consider pleasure and away from pain. For instance, if pornography is pleasure and God keeping you from it is pain, it is almost impossible to stop the habit. However, if you realize that God's blessing is pleasure and pornography is keeping you from that blessing, meditation can rapidly bring change to your personal belief system.

3. *Conation (Application)*—*Conation* is a psychology word that means "to pursue a thing, or make an effort."[31] At its root it means "you can't stop me unless you kill me." There will come a time when meditation results in personification. You are motivated from the inside-out. It is essential to note here that this is the third definition of *grace*. It is a

divine influence upon the heart.[32] When truth is intertwined in your personal belief system, grace is imparted that influences you from the inside-out. It is a natural outlet of your life to operate out of godliness and truth. It is natural to see beyond and operate out of the Kingdom of God. It becomes natural to be led by the Spirit.

WHAT IS YOUR INTENTION?

A few years ago I met with a life coach who was a productivity expert primarily in the secular arena. During lunch, I asked him what the real key that he taught corporations for success was. He said, "That is simple; it is: I + M = R."

With a profound look on my face I responded, "What?"

He said, "Ron, it's a formula that stands for Intention + Mechanism = Results."

After pondering the formula, I replied, "Is that anything like Faith + Corresponding Action = Results."

He said, "Exactly!" He then probed further, "What percentage do you think in this formula is intention and what percentage is mechanism?"

His probe took me off guard. I wanted to sound intelligent, and I knew it was probably 50/50 or 80/20; 80/20 sounded more intelligent so I went with it.

His response further caught me off guard. He said, "You're absolutely wrong! The correct answer is 100 percent intention, 0 percent mechanism."

"Wait a minute," I protested. "How can you have a formula where one of the pieces is 0 percent?"

"It's easy," he said. "Once your intention is set, you will always find a mechanism."

It actually took me several hours to grasp what he said. *Intention* is "a firmly fixed or directed attitude." It is a determination of an end. It is a determined end.[33] If all intention is firmly fixed, you will find a mechanism or means to make it happen. In reference to truth, when you are fully persuaded, grace will find a mechanism to provide a supply for faith to bring results. Biblical meditation is what sets your intention.

In examining all the definitions of meditation, I discovered a five-fold process of biblical meditation. (For a full explanation of these, refer to my book, *The Greatest Secret*.)

1. *Still Stage*—Psalm 46:10 says, *"Be still, and know that I am God...."* The term *still* used here is the Hebrew word for "still, cease, draw towards, relax, or desist."[34] The root of this term is *rapha*, the Hebrew term meaning "to heal, cure, repair, pardon, or comfort."[35] Psychologists call this alpha state. It's that state between being asleep and awake. This is the state where your SCM is most influenced. It is a state of high receptivity.

2. *Imagination Stage* (see Ps. 1:2-3)—This is your meditation or when you see yourself according to the truth. Here is where you create new dominant images in your thinking. This is the place where the conscious mind chooses the new truth of the Scripture, and through repetition, this truth goes into your personal belief system in your SCM. It is here that confession, imagination, and emotion change your beliefs.

3. *Strategy Stage* (see Josh. 1:8)—Based on the truth I see, what action or application do you want me to take.

4   *Action Stage*—This is the place where you do something *everyday* toward your highest priority.

5.   *Thanksgiving Stage*—According to Philippians 4:6-7, thanksgiving guards what is in your heart and mind. Remember, you don't thank people for what they're going to do, but what they've already done. This is the recognition of the supply of God's Kingdom done by grace in the finished work of Christ.

This is the process of becoming fully persuaded. It is simply daily consistency that is often lacking in most believers' lives. This is the discovery that set Janine free in her life. I met Janine at a service in our church that I was conducting. She had the worst case of fibromyalgia I'd ever seen. Fibromyalgia is a disease that is characterized by long-term body-wide pain and tender points in joints, muscles, tendons, and other soft tissue. In worse-case scenarios, it causes fatigue and can in some cases be crippling. In Janine's case, she hadn't really gotten out of bed for several years. Some friends brought her to our service for prayer. We prayed, and she seemed to get some immediate help, but she still left having to be aided by friends.

I gave Janine a set of biblical meditation CDs on healing and righteousness. I instructed her to meditate with them day and night, but especially at night. I didn't see Janine again until about six months later. I looked out in my Bible college class and there she sat. She explained to me she took those CDs and did as she was instructed. The result was a steady and continual transformation over the next months. She finally said, "I felt so good I decided to enroll full-time in Bible school. So here I am." It is an absolutely incredible story.

It is time to become fully persuaded because the truth does set you free, free from sickness, free from sin, free from boundaries, free from limitations, free to step into your destiny.

Let's take a moment to summarize what we've seen up to this point...the manifestation model. Grace is the unmerited favor of Christ's finished work. It is the supply of God. Righteousness is right standing with the Father as a gift I receive by faith. This qualifies me to receive from His Kingdom where grace has provided every provision I need for my destiny. This, in turn, gives me confidence. Now I can renew my mind to the truth of God's Word. My natural response is to believe and follow that truth (and the author of that truth). Now, you are ready to respond in faith. Get ready to understand faith in a new level. It's time to take the ethereal mystery out of faith and to gain a new, pragmatic understanding. Let's go...

• •

ORGANIC THOUGHTS

1. Does your philosophy dictate your theology, or does your theology dictate your philosophy?

2. Are you free as a believer? Free to love God and be loved by Him? Free to receive from His Kingdom? Free to know truth?

3. Has there been control in your life that has robbed you of the best in life?

4. Do you find yourself fully persuaded with God's truth?

5. Are there some facts in your life that are bigger than the truth? Are there strongholds, arguments, or pretenses that need to be broken in your life?

6. Is the Word of God a mirror in your life?

7. Are there things in the five elements of your PBS that are setting themselves up against the knowledge of God?

8. Are you committed to meditating on God's Word in order to be fully persuaded of His truth?

9. The way to break barriers is to create new dominant thoughts. The keys are: (1) Identify self-limiting thoughts or weaknesses. (2) Find the antidote. (It is the opposite of your weakness; for instance, the antidote to fear is love. The antidote to poverty is prosperity. The antidote to sickness is healing.) (3) Gain revelation. (Meditate on truth until it makes you fully persuaded.) (4) Use repetition. (It takes 30 days to create a new habit.) (5) Rethink. (The end is a new perspective.)

10. Does the understanding of biblical confession help you to know how to become fully persuaded? Make sure you confess it, imagine it, and feel the emotions of it.

11. Are there things you can set your intention to?

12. In meditation, use the five steps to guide you into productivity.

Chapter 6

• • • • • • • • • • • • • • • • • •

THE LAW OF FAITH

I found myself surrounded by a multitude of people at the altar following a service I had just conducted. But I was focused on a single voice. She pleaded, "Will you pray for my father? He has Parkinson's disease." I had noticed this man trembling during the service in his seat. In fact, he had to hold on to the seat in front of him to stabilize himself. Without hesitation I said, "Of course I will. God is about to change the course of your life." Sheepishly she looked at me and replied, "How can you be so sure?" With no false humility I stated, "It is because my faith is not in my faith, it is in God's grace. It is in His unmerited, free, finished work."

At that point, I saw her father's head slant toward me. As we prayed, all trembling immediately ceased, to a chorus of crying in the background. Somehow today, faith has become about faith in our faith rather than faith in His grace...

You might think that's just a bunch of theological jargon, but I suggest to you it is foundational to organic Christianity. The former focuses our attention on ourselves, the latter upon God. Unwittingly, if we are not careful, we can make faith about a work we perform.

Somehow, we have taken faith and made it something we do to move God. Organic Christianity suggests that God has already moved 2,000 years ago. We are not trying to get God to do what He has already done, but we receive what He already did 2,000 years ago by grace through faith (see Eph. 2:8-9). This is the essence of Ephesians 1:3, *"Praise be to the God and Father of our Lord Jesus Christ, who has blessed us in the heavenly realms with every spiritual blessing in Christ."*

This extraordinary verse reveals so much to us about God's blessings on believers. It answers four essential questions concerning how God blesses us:

1. *When?* Here Paul uses the past tense participle *"has blessed."* This points to the prospering or blessing of believers in eternity past. God's blessing is in the eternal past. It is something that is accomplished.

2. *With what? "Every spiritual blessing!"* In the eternal past, God provided every spiritual enrichment you will ever need. I've already explained this phrase *"spiritual blessing,"* which literally means "supernatural endowment."[1] God has granted a preternatural provision or bounty in the eternal past.

3. *Where? "...in the heavenly realms."* This is simply a Pauline phrase for the Kingdom of Heaven. Simply put, in the eternal past, God put every supernatural provision for life and godliness in the Kingdom of Heaven.

4. *How? "...in Christ."* In the finished work of Jesus Christ (see John 19:30), God enacted all the supernatural provision you will ever need, unmerited by

you (grace), and placed it in His Kingdom for you to receive by faith. Since these benefits have already been bestowed on believers, they should not ask for them, but receive them by faith.[2]

It is similar to what God did for Joshua. God had already promised the land to him in Joshua 1. Therefore, Joshua didn't need to ask God for it, but enter into the enjoyment of its provision. That doesn't mean there aren't obstacles in the way; it means you can be assured that God will lead you through them to the full manifestation of His provision. This is what Paul is getting at in Second Corinthians 1:20-21: *"For no matter how many promises God has made, they are 'Yes' in Christ. And so through Him the 'Amen' is spoken by us to the glory of God. Now it is God who makes both us and you stand firm in Christ...."* Here Paul tells us that the 7,700 promises of God are yes in the finished work of Christ. We are thus to live "through Him." Christ's promises are completed by grace and we are to live through Him or to rest in the finished work of Christ. Thus, we are to *"stand firm"* in them. This concept of "stand firm" carries the idea of a guarantee of a transaction or a promise.[3] We can "rest" in the finished work of Christ by grace and receive it through faith.

A HISTORY LESSON

There has been much that has been shared in the Body of Christ about faith over the last 30 years. I'm not here to negate that, but simply to offer a broader perspective. You may even think this thought process is simply a matter of vernacular, and maybe it is, but it is the intent of organic Christianity to take what has become the ethereal, impractical nature out of faith. *Do I have enough faith? How much faith is enough? How do I get enough faith to see the Kingdom of God manifested and make it practical?* Such emphasis focuses attention on us instead of on God.

THE DEFINITION OF FAITH

Quite simply, faith is believing the truth and acting on it. It is taking God at His Word. Once we are fully persuaded of the truth, it is only natural to trust God's nature and act accordingly. Grace is God's unmerited provision, His unearned and undeserved favor. Faith is our response that appropriates what God has already provided.

Faith simply means "to trust in, rely on, adhere to, persuaded, convinced, conviction of truth or trust."[4] That's why it is essential to renew our minds to the truth, not only to the conscious mind, but also in the subconscious mind, where our personal belief system exists. Research shows why this is important:

- The conscious mind (CM) controls 2 to 6 percent of what we actually do.

- The subconscious mind (SCM) controls 94 to 98 percent of the decisions we make.

- Impulses travel at 120 mph in the CM.

- Impulses travel at 100,000 mph in the SCM (or 800 times faster than the CM).

- The CM processes 2,000 bits of information per second.

- The SCM processes 4,000,000,000 (4 billion) bits of information per second.

- The CM loses real focus every 6 to 10 seconds.[5]

Remember, beliefs are not necessarily truth. Beliefs are nothing more than specific neural patterns we have created in our brains that are so ingrained in us that they create an automatic response. These beliefs are not the way necessarily because they are truth, but because we have accepted them as truth. For instance, by the time teenagers are 17 years old, they have, on average, heard 150,000 times the words, "No, you can't." They've heard, "Yes, you can," about 5,000 times.[5] That's 30 times more "You can't," than "You can." Often this unwittingly creates a powerful belief of "I can't." That's why development of faith is essential for believers.

Faith, then, is becoming fully persuaded in such a way that we tap into the creative power of God (His grace), whereby people can transform circumstances and situations in the natural realm. In essence, faith is trusting in the character of God. The key to organic Christianity is not to focus on our faith, but to focus (meditate) on the finished work of Christ. Don't ask, "Do I have enough faith?" Instead, focus on the finished work of Christ (grace).

Let's examine this idea in the law of faith in Romans 3:27, *"Where is boasting then? It is excluded. By what law? of works? Nay: but by the law of faith"* (KJV). As a Bible college director, I'm often asked things like, "What do I need to do to receive the blessings of God?" It is usually followed up with assertions like, "I've been praying, reading my Bible, tithing, and going to church. But still I'm not seeing my breakthrough."

These questions and explanations are the root of the issue. Their response is indicative of trying to move God by performance. Unwittingly they've turned faith into a work to move God, which in essence is not faith at all. The assumption is, when I do enough good things, it will influence God to act on my behalf. This presumption ignores God's injunction to recognize grace that is received by faith. This kind of thinking ignores justification by faith. When we realize the only way to tap into God's blessing is by grace, there is no boasting at all about what we've done. Boasting based on achievement is ruled out.

Paul further notes in this passage, doing works to move God cannot justify us before God. *"We maintain that a man is justified by faith apart from observing the law"* (Rom. 3:28). Now notice Paul uses the phrase *"the law of faith"* (Rom. 3:27b KJV). Faith is governed by law. The word *law* used here, in Greek, means "principle."[7] It is not a reference to old covenant law. A law, in this sense, is a principle that tells us how a thing works best. Thus, faith is governed by principle, just like electricity in this world. The law of electricity was here since creation. Yet, it took a bald guy with a kite and a key to discover it and then to learn how to use it. Similarly, we can't really deny faith; we must discover what the laws of faith are and learn how to operate in them.

In essence, Jesus hasn't saved, blessed, prospered, healed, or delivered anyone in 2,000 years.[8] What God did 2,000 years ago now becomes a reality when mixed with faith (see Heb. 4:2). Faith appropriates or receives the gift grace has provided. Faith doesn't move God; He has already moved. Faith is the means to receive grace.

The writer of Hebrews (quite possibly Paul) reinforces this idea in the great "faith" chapter. Hebrews 11:1 states, *"Now faith is the substance of things hoped for, the evidence of things not seen"* (KJV).

In this unsurpassed passage on faith, the writer reveals four keys (or laws) to accessing the Kingdom of Heaven through the law of faith:

Key #1: "Substance"—The term *substance* used here means "tangible, substantiate, reality, title deed, inventory, or to be substantive."[9] In other words, faith is something tangible or real. It is a title deed. If I have a title deed to land in Florida, I may never see that land, but I can be confident I own that existing land because I have credible documentation.

Notice this term also means "inventory." *Inventory* is "a detailed listing of things in one's possessions."[10] The Word of God contains approximately 7,700 promises that are our possessions by grace. This inventory creates an expectation in us. Expectation promotes a corresponding action to appropriate what is ours. Faith then substantiates God's Kingdom. *Substantiate* means "to establish evidence, prove, verify, assurance, to give substantial firm, to make real."[11]

Key #2: "Of things"—The term *things* in Greek is the word *pragma*. This word means "a thing already done."[12] There is an inventory with my name written on it of what God has already appropriated for me, by grace. Wow!

Key #3: "Hoped for"—Obviously *hoped* means "anticipated or expected (anxious anticipation, earnest expectation)."[13] There is in Scripture what I call "the law of expectation." The law of expectation says, "That which you believe in your heart with expectation becomes self-fulfilling prophecy" (see my book *The Greatest Secret* for full explanation). Many psychologists suggest that 85 percent of our actions are based on our expectations. What we do or don't do is based on our expectations. Faith is an inventory of things already done (by grace) that creates an earnest expectation in us, which results in a corresponding action.

Key #4: "Evidence"—In a court of law a lawyer produces evidence before a jury. Evidence is data on which a conclusion is based. We all understand evidence today. We can watch detective shows like *CSI* (Crime Scene Investigations) to make us aware of the importance of evidence. A person may say to me, "I've never been in your house." Yet, when I examine my living room, I find that person's fingerprints on my coffee table. Even though I've never seen that person in my house, I know that person has been there based on the evidence. Evidence causes us to believe or even to reevaluate what we thought to be true previously. This evidence of Hebrews 11:1 points to the fact of what God has already done for us. Thus, our faith is in His grace (what He has already done), not in our faith (our performance of the law). Faith provides the evidence of the works.

I see people who torture themselves over this issue. I didn't have enough faith. I didn't pray enough or fast enough or perform the law enough to bring results. Trying to move God is not faith at all; it's living under the law (our performance of it).

Hebrews 11:3 adds to this thought: *"By faith we understand that the universe was formed at God's command, so that what is seen was not made out of what was visible."* It is essential to note that it does not say these things were made from things that don't exist, but from things from the invisible realm. If I were to give you a tour of Heaven, there would be rooms there with your name on them. In them would be every provision for life that you will need to fulfill your destiny (see 2 Pet. 1:3). They are present by grace, unmerited by you, to receive by faith. Now, it's time to become fully persuaded of the truth.

There is a key principle that is revealed here: *The parent force of the seen realm is the unseen realm.* Faith is not, "Fake it until you can make it." The physical realm is dominated by the spiritual realm. The seen realm is dominated by the unseen realm. When what you see in the spiritual is more real than what you see in the natural world, the spiritual realm will dominate the natural realm.

The clearest example of this in Scripture is Second Kings 6. In this passage, the king of Syria is at war with Israel. Every time he sets a trap for Israel, God speaks to the prophet Elisha, who warns Israel, and they continually avert "the best laid plans of mice and men." Not understanding the spiritual dynamics of these events, the king of Syria can only assume he is being betrayed by a spy in his camp.

Finally, the king manages to surround Elisha and his servant at Dothan. The servant arises the next morning to discover the dilemma. In panic, he races into the prophet and exclaims *"We're surrounded."*

Unmoved, Elisha responds in Second Kings 6:16, *"Don't be afraid....Those who are with us are more than those who are with them."*

You can almost see the stunned look on his servant's face. Obviously the product of a higher education math program, the servant sets out to do some addition. He pokes his head out the door and begins counting: ...50, 100, 200, 300, and 500. He looks back in at Elisha and counts...1, 2. He must have thought, *I don't know where you got your education, but your math leaves something to be desired.*

Then, this unforgettable scene unfolds.

> *Elisha prayed, "O Lord, open his eyes so he may see."*
> *Then the Lord opened the servant's eyes, and he looked*
> *and saw the hills full of horses and chariots of fire*
> [angelic hosts] *all around Elisha* (2 Kings 6:17).

God's forces then struck the enemy with blindness and ultimately delivered them over to Israel's troops in Samaria. Similarly, the issue for most of us is, we only see in the physical realm. The chariots of fire didn't just arrive when Elisha's servant's eyes were opened. God's provision was already present in the unseen realm.

THE GOD-KIND OF FAITH

Mark 11:22-25 is a classic passage in understanding the laws that govern faith. In this passage Jesus curses a fig tree and uses it as a lesson to train His disciples about faith. In 11:22 it states, *"Have faith in God..."*

Many scholars believe this verse is better translated from the Greek in the subjective genetive, which means it should say: *"Have the faith of God"*[14] or the God-kind of faith. The idea here is that this is not simply about what we can generate, but what God deposits in us. Most questions about faith gather around the concept, "How do I get enough faith?" The fact is, we receive supernatural faith at salvation. In Romans 12:3 (KJV), Paul tells us that we receive *the* measure of faith. In other words, Pastor so and so doesn't receive one level of faith and the congregation member a much less measure. We all receive the measure of faith. This is what Peter tells us in Second Peter 1:1, *"...to them who received like precious faith..."* (KJV). The Greek term for "like precious" means "equal in value."[14] In other words, the same faith that was resident in Peter when he raised Dorcas from the dead (see Acts 9:36-43) is the same quality of faith existent in us.

Similarly, in Galatians 2:20 Paul tells us, *"I am crucified with Christ..."* (KJV). Paul advocates dying to self, but note how he says such death takes place. We die to self by experiencing what Jesus did at Calvary. We reckon ourselves dead by what happened in Christ's death (see Rom. 6: 11). He continues, *"...nevertheless I live, yet not I, but Christ liveth in me..."* (KJV). Notice the Christian life is not primarily living for God, but God living through us (see 1 John 4:9). He finishes the verse by saying, *"...and the life which I now live in the flesh I live by the faith of the Son of God, who loved me and gave Himself for me"* (KJV). Paul again suggests we are to live by the faith of the Son of God.[15] Again in Ephesians 2:8-9, he emphasizes this fact, *"For we are saved by grace, through faith—and this not of ourselves, it is a gift from God—not of works, lest any man should boast."*

It can be said that the same quantity and quality of faith that Jesus has is at work within us. Because Christians have not understood this, they have spent their time asking God for faith or for more faith. It would be much like if I gave you a Bible and then you turned around and asked me for my Bible.[16] I would probably stand stunned in silence, trying to figure out what you were trying to get me to do.

Philemon 6 reiterates this thought, *"That the communication of thy faith may become effectual by the acknowledging of every good thing which is in you in Christ Jesus"* (KJV). Paul is not indicating that

Philemon needs something more, but that he needs to recognize what he already has. The word *acknowledge* means "to admit, recognize, to state what one has rescued or report receipt of."[18] You can only acknowledge what you already have.[19]

If you've examined the endnotes, you'll realize I am acknowledging the theological debate over whether Mark 11:22 and Galatians 2:20 should be translated, "Have faith *in* God" or "Have the faith *of* God." I personally lean more to the latter than the former for the reason laid out in the endnotes. This eliminates the issue of, "Do I have enough faith?" Obviously, I already possess the God-kind of faith in me. It's not a matter of getting more or of better quality. It is a matter of renewing my mind to what I already have in Christ. However, for the sake of argument (which I really have no desire to do, but someone will raise the issue), let's say this passage is better translated "Have faith in God." Go back to the definition of *faith:* "trust in, rely on, adhere to."

In essence, faith is trusting in the character of God. One of my definitions of *character* is "doing the right thing, regardless of the cost to you." Mark 11:22—*"Have faith in God..."*—is communicating that we need to trust God's character, that He will do the right thing no matter what. Since I am fully persuaded, by renewing my mind, it is only natural to act in accordance to His Word. That is the essence of faith. It's not so much about quantity; it's more about conviction.

Confusion comes in for a lot of people because the Bible talks about no faith, little faith, and great faith. There are many Scriptures that talk about degrees of faith (see Matt. 6:30; 8:10,26; 14:31; 16:8; 2 Cor. 10:15). Those references, however, are not so much about how much faith we have, but how much faith we manifest. That's why in Luke 17:5, when the disciples ask the Lord to *"increase our faith,"* His somewhat obscure answer is that they should use what they already have (see Luke 17:5-10).

I tell you the truth, if anyone says to this mountain, "Go throw yourself into the sea," and does not doubt in his heart but believes what he says will happen, it will be done for him (Mark 11:22-23).

It is here that Jesus illumines two key laws for faith: confession and not doubting.

1. *Confession* (say)—We must learn to confess truth and not circumstances. In Mark's vernacular, it is time to stop telling God about our mountain and start telling our mountain about our God. When we realize what God has done by grace, we must learn to speak those truths over our circumstances. Life doesn't dictate to us; we dictate to life. I've literally had people tell me that it would be hypocritical to confess something that is not true. They reiterate that to say that my needs are met (spiritually, physically, mentally, and so forth) is hypocritical. The fact is, they are true by grace (see Eph. 1:3). They are true in the unseen (see Heb. 11:3). So, instead of saying, "I can't..." it is, *"I can do all things through Christ who strengthens me"* (Phil. 4:13 NKJV). Our background may tell us, "You can't," but God has provided everything we need for life and godliness (see 2 Pet. 1:3). So, we can say, "I can." We don't have to say, "I don't have the finances"; instead, it is *"My God shall supply all your need according to His riches in glory by Christ Jesus"* (Phil. 4:19 KJV). We don't say, "No one is with us." But, instead we say, *"If God be for us, who can be against me"* (Rom. 8:31). I don't simply reiterate a doctor's report; I declare, "By His

stripes I have been healed" (see 1 Pet. 2:24). Does confession change our circumstances? No! Our confession influences our hearts (see Rom. 10:9-10). "*...Out of the overflow of the heart the mouth speaks*" (Matt. 12:34). Heart convictions affect the subconscious mind. What's in our subconscious mind seeks to find a way to make what we say come to pass. It establishes new beliefs. What we believe causes us to focus on God's grace (unmerited favor of His finished work). We simply receive, by faith, God's grace, so we *say to our mountain, move* (see Mark 11:23).

2. *Doubt in our hearts*—Then Jesus adds this important clause, "*does not doubt in his heart.*" The Greek term for "doubt" is *diakrino*. It means "to judge between two things or to be in conflict with yourself."[20] The issue is not that we don't have enough faith; the issue is that our faith is negated by our unbelief. What I call the Law of Belief says, "What we believe in our hearts with confidence becomes our reality." The Law of Correspondence states, "Our outside world corresponds directly to our inward world."

I have often demonstrated this in meetings with this example: I get a large trash barrel that has two handles. I tie a rope to both handles. Then, I get two volunteers. One volunteer is "faith," the other is "unbelief." I ask each of them to grab a rope and to pull in the opposite direction. Often times I'll have a guy be "unbelief" and a gal be "faith." So often, "unbelief" out pulls "faith." I'll then stop them and remove "unbelief." When "faith" begins pulling, she moves the barrel with ease. The issue is not our lack of faith, but our unbelief that negates our faith.

Some might think, *That's an interesting illustration, but is it biblical?* Look at Mark 9:24. This is the story of the demon-possessed boy whom the disciples could not heal (he had symptoms of epilepsy). The dad is explaining the symptoms to Jesus, *"It has often thrown him into fire or water to kill him. But if You can do anything, take pity on us and help us* (Mark 9:22)." You can almost hear the indignation in Jesus' voice as He responds, *"If You can?"* It is almost like the scene in *Father of the Bride 2.* Steve Martin's character is the husband of a pregnant wife whose daughter is pregnant at the same time. He is exhausted from trying to take care of both women (the daughter's husband is out of the country on business). About the time both women are due, there's a series of false alarms about delivery, and as a result, he doesn't sleep for a couple of weeks. A friend disperses him a heavy-duty sleep aid, and you guessed it, about the time he "crashes," both moms are ready to deliver. The next turn of events makes for a hilarious excursion to the hospital as he is falling asleep and the friend who gave him the sleeping pills, but doesn't drive, is now driving everyone to the hospital. Ultimately he gets both women in a wheelchair to their proper location. Meanwhile, George (Steve Martin's character) slumps into the nearest wheelchair dozing off from the overdose of sleep aid. Unwittingly, he has sat in the wheel chair of a person who is to have a proctology exam. A nurse comes by and haphazardly wheels him into the exam. Some moments later he emerges from the room hitching his pants and exclaiming, "Do *I know* you?!!!" It's a very funny moment.

Similarly, Jesus is asking, do you know Me? *"If I can?"* Obviously Jesus is not insecure; He is addressing the father's unbelief. Jesus continues, *"...Everything is possible for him who believes (verse 23)."*

The dad responds, *"...I do believe, help me overcome my unbelief* (verse 24)." The point is not his lack of faith, but that his belief is negated by his unbelief. Similarly, in Luke 8, Jesus is dealing with a man named Jairus, whose daughter has died, as he is in the process of trying to contact Jesus to pray for her. Those around him say, "Don't bother Jesus. Your daughter is dead." Overhearing the situation, Jesus says, *"Don't be afraid; just believe, and she will be healed"* (Luke 8:50). In other words, believe only—believe without the unbelief.

Doubt and unbelief are the real culprits to halting the laws of faith. The five elements of our personal belief system, which we discussed earlier, (social environment, authority figures, self-image, repetitious information, and experiences) are a reflection of circumstances that cause people to lose sight of God's provision of grace. What we focus on longest becomes strongest. These elements can cause us to lose sight of being fully persuaded. Proverbs 13:12 says it like this, *"Hope deferred makes the heart sick...."* When radical expectation of good (joy) is put off, it makes the heart sick. Remember, Proverbs 4:23 says, *"Keep your heart with all diligence, for out of it spring the issues of life"* (NKJV). This is the law of belief: "What we believe *in* our hearts with confidence becomes our reality." We can't trust in, rely on, or adhere to what we have doubt and fear over. Crisis poses a challenge to faith. This is what Jesus is addressing with His disciples in Mark 11:23:

> *I tell you the truth* [obviously, He is negating something that is false], *if anyone says* [confession] *to this mountain, "Go throw yourself into the sea," and does not doubt in his heart but believes* [uses the laws of faith] *that what he says* [confesses] *will happen, it will be done for him.*

The issue is not so much the quantity or quality of faith as much as it is unbelief from our circumstances and the five elements of our personal belief system that negate it. When what we see *in* the unseen

(Kingdom of Heaven or grace) dominates what we see in the seen, the unseen will dominate the seen.

Now comes the pivotal verse: *"Therefore I tell you, whatever you ask for in prayer, believe that you have received it, and it will be yours"* (Mark 11:24). At first glance this verse seems to be mumbo jumbo. How do we believe we receive? This, however, is an essential concept. We believe, or have faith, in what grace has already done, and we manifest from the spiritual to the physical. Faith appropriates what cannot be seen (see Rom. 4:17; Heb. 11:1). This process may be in an instant or over a process of time. *Shall* indicates that what we possess in the present will manifest sometime in the future. By faith we believe that He is answering before there is physical evidence. So, we live by faith, not by sight (see 2 Cor. 5:7). The whole process can be abdicated or aborted by doubt. However, once we understand our faith is in grace, we will see an explosion of the Kingdom's blessings.

Let me help you understand this process. Some years back I went to the doctor for a routine physical. During the examination, the doctor, a friend of mine, said, "You need to come back for a follow-up visit." So about a week later, I came back for the follow-up exam. It was one of those really fun routines like going to Disney World, where they ran a tube up my nose, through my throat into my lungs, to take a biopsy. I returned a week later for the prognosis. My friend looked at me and stated seriously, "I've got good news and bad news. Which do you want first?"

Reflecting on the demeanor of his tone, I said, "Let's start with the bad news and end with the good news."

My doctor gave me my diagnosis, "Ron, you have a potentially terminal disease."

I thought I had misunderstood him, and I said, "What?" He reiterated the bad news. I then asked, "What is the good news?"

My friend kindly said, "In your case, it is only deadly about 25 percent of the time."

That wasn't exactly the good news I was looking for in my life. Suddenly, I was faced with my own mortality and a potentially terminal and very rare lung disease. I can't begin to describe the emotions that raced through me in a moment like that. Finally, in a moment of faith, I stopped the echoing voices of doom. I declared internally, "I serve a healing God. I have prayed for many others who have been healed."

The doctor prescribed treatment for a disease that he admitted they didn't know the origin of or how to treat. Usually they give chemotherapy or doses of steroids. Eventually I voted for neither (I am not recommending my route for anybody; I'm just telling you my story). The next Sunday I was at my church, and my pastor announced that if people needed healing, they should stand to their feet. I stood, and he instructed those around us to lay hands on us and pray the prayer of faith. People did as they were instructed, but there was no manifestation that day, that month, or that year. It was at that time God began instructing me about faith, and I began to believe God had given me what I needed.

I began to speak to my mountain (disease) about my God rather than to God about my mountain. I confessed God's Word, and I saw myself according to the truth of His Word. I felt the emotions as if it were a completed fact. I confessed God's Word present tense and positive every day. I majored on God's finished work of Ephesians 1:3. I meditated on God's Word until my soul and spirit lined up. I eliminated the doubt that sought to prohibit my faith. Sometime later, when I had to get some insurance funding, I had another exam. This doctor looked at my history and ran a thorough battery of tests. The report was the disease was burned out and non-progressive. My doctor is a Christian, so I asked, "Is that anything like healed?" He said, "It really is!" I've gone through two incidences like that where God delivered me from possible devastating results.

It launches my faith to understand that it is faith in His grace, not faith in my faith. My focus is God, not me. It settles me to know He has given me the faith I need. I know people who argue that degrees of faith (no faith, little faith, great faith) indicate growth in faith, not just in manifestation. That particular thought is simply a matter of vernacular that says the same thing. I'm perfectly OK with that. If that is what best helps people, that's great! My goal is not to be right as much as it is to be helpful. For me, it helps me to know I have what I need, and I need to cultivate it. The essence of faith is simply trusting the nature of God. The more intimate with Him I become, the easier it is. I trust in, rely on, and adhere to what I am fully persuaded of in His Word.

How do I cultivate faith? Romans 10:17 explains how, *"So then faith comes by hearing, and hearing by the word of God"* (NKJV). Often I hear people say things like this about this verse. "Faith comes by hearing and hearing and hearing and hearing God's Word." Quite frankly, I know many people who hear over and over again without it igniting any manifestation of faith. The Greek reads precisely like this, "Faith comes from hearing and hearing through the Word of Christ." Faith "comes from or originates"[21] from hearing. The term *hearing* implies more than listening. It gives the idea of understanding.[22] Faith comes from or comes forth from understanding, comprehension, or revelation of the Word. The term for "Word" here means "utterance or spoken word."[23] Who's doing the speaking? It is the Word of Christ. Faith is cultivated by the revelation of Christ speaking His Word alive to us. The result is that faith comes forth from us. Jesus is the author and finisher of *our* faith (see Heb. 12:2). He is the initiator and culmination of the faith existent in us. As we hear the revelation of the truth of His Word, we become fully persuaded of it. It is only natural to respond according to God's character.

God gives us His finished work by grace. God gives us the deposit of *the* measure of faith. Our job is simply to cultivate it by allowing the Holy Spirit to make the Word come alive in us (usually through study and meditation). It then becomes natural to respond accordingly. That's faith!

THE SET-UP

One day, as I was meditating on this, I began to cry because I realized I had been set up—set up to succeed. God, by His grace, unmerited by me, provided everything I would need for life and godliness (see 2 Pet. 1:3). I simply had to access His gift by faith. God deposits the faith in my life (see Rom. 12:3). I simply have to cultivate it by His truth. So I wouldn't botch it, He provided the truth in His Word. Since He has a lifetime of exhibited integrity, it's only natural I respond by trusting in, relying on, and adhering to God's character.

If that is not enough, He also provides the grace or empowerment to live it. This is not a discussion about theology; this is an invitation to live the fully manifested Christian life. This is a call to exhibit the Christian life. Remember, actions speak louder than words. This is not about theological banter, but an ability to live the life. Let's examine the next progression: grace, God's ability or empowerment.

ORGANIC THOUGHTS

1.   How does your understanding of Ephesians 1:3 change the way you pursue God?

2.   Beliefs and truth are not necessarily the same thing. Truth is the beginning of faith.

3.   How does the understanding of faith in His grace, as opposed to faith in your faith, affect

you? Have you unwittingly tried to move God by your performance?

4. What do you feel about the phrase, "In essence God hasn't saved, blessed, prospered, or healed anyone in 2,000 years"?

5. How do you view the laws of faith in Hebrews 11:1?

6. How do you feel about recognizing that you already possess the measure of faith (see Rom. 12:3)?

7. Do you understand that the real issue is not your lack of faith, but your doubt negating your faith?

8. How do you believe you receive in Mark 11:24?

9. Faith is essentially trust in God's character.

Chapter 7

• •

LIVING OUT LOUD

Virtually everyone knows the phrase: "Actions speak louder than words." The basic idea behind this clause is that actions speak louder than words as a determinant of behavior and character. People can say anything, but when what they say is contrary to what they do, it is easier to judge what they believe by what is done than by what is said. Our lives should be louder than words. The key is to live our lives out loud! The discourse of organic Christianity is not about correct theological dialogue, but about the Kingdom of God erupting in our lives. It's about getting what we say we believe to manifest. It is living out loud! The whole concept of organic Christianity is not just to understand the original intent of the Gospel, but also to manifest this life we call abundant (see John 10:10).

The life of the Gospel was made to be extraordinary. Extraordinary living surpasses the norm. It breaks away from the status quo.[1] It is a life that is exceptional, remarkable, amazing, unimaginable—well, abundant. Isn't this what the world discovered about the early Christian believers? This is the revelation of the Book of Acts. Acts 4:12-14 records it like this,

"Salvation is found in no one else, for there is no other name under heaven given to men by which we must be saved." [By the way, this ends the debate about Jesus being the only way to God.] *When they saw the courage of Peter and John and realized that they were unschooled, ordinary men, they were astonished and they took note that these men had been with Jesus. But since they could see the man who had been healed standing there with them, there was nothing they could say.*

In other words, they saw ordinary men doing extraordinary things. Normal, regular, common people performed extraordinary actions. The distinguishing feature was, they *"had been with Jesus."* They had an intimacy with the Son of God. Jesus takes the common and makes them uncommon. He transforms what is normal into what is remarkable.

What was the event that was so earth shattering and amazing? Acts 3 records the event: There was a crippled man from birth who was daily carried to gates outside the temple to beg. One day he saw Peter and John and begged them for money. Peter responds with the infamous exhortation in Acts 3:6, *"...Silver or gold I do not have, but what I have I give you. In the name of Jesus Christ of Nazareth, walk."* They didn't have silver or gold upon them, but they had something to give. You can't give something unless you have something.

What they had was the name of Jesus! The name of Jesus was not an addendum to a prayer, "In Jesus' name, amen!" This phrase in Greek means "in connection to the revelation of Jesus."[2] The name stresses a vital connection to the person. It is a legal authority to act on behalf of that person with access to all his or her resources. When my girlfriend, Judy Johnson, became my wife, she took my name and she became Judy McIntosh. She now has access to everything my name has access to. As believers, we take on Jesus' name and become Christians. When we operate in connection to the revelation of Jesus, we can access the provision of all of His resources (see Eph. 1:3).

The disciples didn't have access to silver and gold (see Acts 3:6), but they gave the beggar what they had, a vital connection to the Son of God and His resources of Heaven. Extraordinary! They were ordinary people with the extraordinary ability to manifest remarkable accomplishments.

That is why the statement in Acts 4 is so significant. The chief priests and the temple guard came to Peter and John and demanded they cease speaking and acting in Jesus' name. They seized them and jailed them. The next day the chief priests inquired, *"By what power or what name did you do this?"* (Acts 4:7). Then Peter retorts,

> *If we are being called into account today for an act of kindness shown to a cripple and are asked how he was healed, then know this, you and all the people of Israel: It is by the name of Jesus Christ of Nazareth, whom you crucified...that this man stands before you healed* (Acts 4:9-10).

At this point we would assume all the religious leaders would rejoice over the astounding miracle of this crippled man. Like most transitions of the spirit, when philosophy trumps theology, people often seek to discredit our attempt to share the organic Gospel to preserve their religion.

This is what makes Acts 4:12-14 such an amazing passage of Scripture. Now listen to it again,

> *"Salvation is found in no one else, for there is no other name under heaven given to men by which we must be saved." When they saw the courage of Peter and John and realized that they were unschooled, ordinary men, they were astonished and they took note that these men*

had been with Jesus. But since they could see the man
who had been healed standing there with them, there
was nothing they could say.

Extraordinary! It's hard for religion to dismantle the extraordinary!

This is not an isolated event. In Acts 10, Peter, a disciple of Jesus, and Cornelius, a centurion in the Italian regiment, have separate visions preparing them for a momentous occurrence. When they meet, Cornelius bows in reverence (literally "worship").[3] In Acts 10:26, Peter makes him get up and says, *"...I am only a man myself."* Peter was so extraordinary that Cornelius considered him a god. In Lystra, in Acts 14, Paul heals a man crippled in his feet from birth who had never walked, in the name of Jesus. The crowd cries out, *"... The gods have come down to us in human form!"* (Acts 14:11). In verse 15, Paul responds, *"Men, why are you doing this? We too are only men, human like you...."* When Paul was bitten by a venomous and deadly snake, but was unaffected because of his faith, the inhabitants again proclaimed him a god (see Acts 28:6). It was said of these early disciples, *"...These who have turned the world upside down have come here too"* (Acts 17:6 NKJV). Wow! Extraordinary! Their lives were living out loud—and everybody noticed.

Organic Christianity is not about simply rediscovering the original intent of the Gospel; it's about living out loud. It's about living with distinguishing marks that separate us from the world's system until people sit up and take notice of the distinction. They may think, *I know this person. This person is just like me. What makes him remarkable? Oh! He's been with Jesus!*

What is this "ability" that brought the extraordinary to the ordinary? Certainly the Book of Acts is about the person of the Holy Spirit, but there is also a remarkable missing ingredient. The missing ingredient was and is God's grace! Following the events of Acts 4, the chapter comes to a culmination with this: *"With great power the apostles continued to testify to the resurrection of the Lord Jesus, and much grace was upon them all"* (Acts 4:33).

The extraordinary was done because they had great power and much grace was upon them.

This is the theme of the Book of Acts. Ten times it speaks of the ordinary becoming the extraordinary as a result of grace. Look at Acts 6:8, *"Now Stephen, a man full of God's grace and power, did great wonders and miraculous signs among the people."* When Barnabas arrived in Antioch, Acts 11:23 tells us, *"When he arrived and saw the evidence of the grace of God...."* He obviously saw cause and effect. Paul and Barnabas encouraged new converts to continue in the grace of God (see Acts 13:43). Acts 14:3 continues this thought,

> *Paul and Barnabas spent considerable time there* [Iconium], *speaking boldly for the Lord who confirmed the message of His grace by enabling them to do miraculous signs and wonders.*

Paul and Barnabas came back to Antioch, where they were committed to the grace of God (see Acts 14:26). The council at Jerusalem recognized it was through grace that people are saved (see Acts 15:11). Similarly, the sustaining power of God for believers is grace (see Acts 15:40; 18:27). In Acts 20:24 is Paul's amazing summation of his entire ministry,

> *However, I consider my life worth nothing to me, if only I finish the race and complete the task the Lord Jesus has given me—the task of testifying to the gospel of God's grace.*

Then eight verses later he adds, *"Now I commit you to God and to the word of His grace, which can build you up and give you an inheritance all among those who are sanctified* [who belong to God].

The way we go from ordinary to extraordinary is the Gospel or the Word of His grace. The way we are sustained in our lives, the way we receive our inheritance, is through the extraordinary, remarkable, exceptional grace of God. The way we become heirs of this world is God's grace (see Rom. 4:13). That brings us to the last progression of the manifestation model—grace. Some may be thinking, *But that was the first progression.* This is what Peter calls the manifold grace of God (see 1 Pet. 4:10). The term *manifold* means "many forms of, varied forms or pages, multivarious."[4]

Grace is "unmerited favor." God did something for us that we can never earn. Now, that only tells us that it is free. A second definition of *grace* is "the finished work of God" (see John 19:30; 2 Pet. 1:3). Unmerited by us, God has provided every spiritual blessing (supernatural endowment) we need for life (see 2 Pet. 1:2-3; Eph. 1:3; John 19:30). Once we meditate on that grace, it becomes "a divine influence upon our hearts." The last definition of *grace* is "empowerment or ability."[5] *Grace* is the ability to live out the Christian life and to experience His Kingdom. I like to say it like this: *Grace* is my ability to use God's ability to meet any need.

One time someone asked me, is the Christian life hard? I said, "No, it's impossible!" Apart from God, we can't live it or receive its blessings. With Him, nothing is impossible, and it becomes easy (see Matt. 11:28-30). Perhaps the biggest frustration among serious believers is the inability to get what they believe to manifest. So many believers struggle with the inability to change. Most Christians stay the same for a lifetime.[6] Grace is God's ability in us to conquer life. Life doesn't dictate to us; we dictate to life. This is the essence of Romans 5:17:

> *...how much more will those who receive God's abundant provision of grace and of the gift of righteousness reign in life through the one man, Jesus Christ.*

The essence of the Christian life is the freedom to control our destiny through grace and righteousness. The keys to establishing success and God's Kingdom are grace and righteousness. Notice this important key! Grace and righteousness cause us to rule "through" Jesus Christ. Again, it is more important to live *through* Him than *for* Him (see 1 John 4:9).

SINNER SAVED BY GRACE?

How does this work? First, we receive the abundance of grace. God has provided everything we need for life and godliness, unmerited by us (see 2 Pet. 1). The fact that He also made us righteous by faith means we are qualified to receive His provision by faith. As we act in faith, grace empowers us with God's ability to conquer life's circumstances to establish His Kingdom to us and through us. This is the *exchanged* life more than the *changed* life.

The Christian life is really about renewing our minds as to who we already are. Most believers think we are sinners saved by grace. Nothing could be further from the truth. We are complete in Him (see Col. 2:9-10), and we must renew our minds and our hearts to our true identity. We are not sinners saved by grace; we are the righteousness of God in Christ Jesus, operating in grace.

Right behavior is of little value if inwardly we crave to act another way.[7] Ultimately, we will act out what is in our hearts. This is why Paul continues in Romans 5:20-21,

> *The law was added so that the trespass might increase. But where sin increased, grace increased all the more, so that, just as sin reigned in death, so also grace might reign through righteousness to bring eternal life through Jesus Christ our Lord.*

"The law was added" to God's original intent of grace (see Gal. 3:17). Why was it added? *"So that the trespass might increase."* The law was added to show we couldn't keep it so we would see our need for a Savior. Sin had already defeated us, and we didn't know it. The purpose of the law was to define sin so we would know what was defeating us. In the transitions in covenants, *"Grace increased all the more."* There is more grace than sin and temptation. However much that sin increased, grace increased more.

The term *sin* used here is the Greek word, *hamartia*. The term *sin* or *sins* is used in Romans 49 times. The word *hamartia* is used 47 times. The other two terms, *hamartano* and *hamartema,* are used just once. Here is why this is extraordinarily important. According to Greek scholar William Barclay, *hamartia* is a noun. A noun is a person, place, or thing, not an act (which is a verb). It simply means "missing the target, the failure of a plan or purpose."[8] *Hamartia* does not describe a definite act of sin; it describes the state or intent of sin from which the act of sin comes.[9] It is sin universal. It is a power that has people in its grasp. It means "to be in the control of or subjection to its power."[10]

The purpose of the law was to define sin. The law created sin. This is a positive thing; if we lack an understanding of sin, it could destroy us, and we wouldn't know why. Law defines sin, but it cannot cure it. When we focus on it, it causes us to be attracted to it. Grace destroyed the tendency or propensity to sin. Our individual sins are an expression of that condition in our hearts.[11] It is the sin nature or tendency that grace destroys.

Some may be thinking, *If the tendency to sin has been broken, no one informed me, because I still feel the pull, baby.* That's because many haven't renewed their minds to their new creation realities (see 2 Cor. 5:17). They are still dealing with their personal belief systems from before their salvation experience. God made us new in our spirits, but we must renew our minds to who we have become. God not only dealt with the act of sin, but the intention of sin. He eradicated the inclination to sin. Then He empowered us or gave us the ability to conquer sin. Remember, all pain in life is the result of sin (ours, Adam's, or someone else's). Grace is not freedom to sin, but freedom from sin.

Paul continues on about this remarkable revelation in Romans 6: *"What shall we say, then? Shall we go on sinning so that grace may increase? By no means! We died to sin; how can we live in it any longer?"* Paul spoke with such fervor on grace's unmerited favor that there is always someone who feels like it is a license to sin. Paul says that's just plain idiocy. He is building to an incredible climactic argument in verses 14 and 15.

However, he continues on in verse 2, Paul had so convincingly proven salvation and righteousness by grace that there was no real theological argument left. The only real argument left was and is practical. People feel, *If we don't relate to God by how we perform, then why resist sin?* Paul says there are two answers to this:

1. We are dead to sin (see Rom. 6:5-6).

2. It gives satan access to our lives (see Rom. 6:15-16).

Sin is deadly and in every respect should be resisted, but God in His magnificent insight changed the motivation to live free from sin.[12] We don't resist sin to be accepted by God; we live out separated lives in order to not give the devil access to our lives. Wow!

Paul helps us to understand what this means in Romans 6:6, *"For we know that our old self was crucified with Him so that the body of sin might be done away with, that we should no longer be slaves to sin."* The "old self" or the *"old man"* (KJV) is our sin nature. Being dead to sin doesn't mean we are incapable of sinning; it means the propensity and proclivity (inclination) toward sin—or the sin nature—has been eradicated when we were born again. The old self that was inclined toward sin is now dead. We no longer have a sin nature. Therefore, we are no longer slaves to sin. Therefore, Paul continues, *"In the same way, count yourselves dead to sin but alive to God in Christ Jesus"* (Rom. 6:11). The term *reckon* or *count yourselves* is an accounting term meaning "to take an inventory or to assess a condition that already exists."[13] It conveys the idea that since being dead to sin already exists, we are no longer subject to sin's dictates. We are free to act accordingly. Once we recognize this, it frees us from the grip of sin.

Most believers think that because they still feel an urge to sin, the old self or propensity to sin is still existent. That's not what this passage indicates. The reason the urge still exists is because we've not renewed our minds or reckoned ourselves to our new covenant reality.

Before I get practical with this, let me finish Paul's thought. As a result of all this, he concludes, *"For sin shall not be your master, because you are not under law, but under grace"* (Rom. 6:14). This statement is an absolute shock to most people. The Church has felt that the way to overcome sin was law, not grace. Here Paul says we conquer sin through grace, not law. Law can only define sin; it has no power to deliver us. Grace is the power to conquer sin and to live in freedom. How? This is the culmination of the manifestation model for the Kingdom of God to erupt to and through our lives. Grace is unmerited favor we can never earn by performance. It accesses every benefit of the Kingdom. Since we are righteous not based on our performance but on what Jesus did, and we receive it by faith, we are qualified to receive from Him. We renew our minds to new covenant, new creation realities as to "who we are in Christ," and grace becomes a divine influence on our hearts. Accordingly, we become intimate with God, and it is natural to believe Him and receive from Him. He then releases an empowerment to act accordingly.

The reason that sin has a grip on too large a portion of the Church is that they are living under law, not grace. Law was intended to lead us to grace (see Rom. 5:20-21; Gal. 3:24-25). Law defined the problem; grace was the solution. The problem is most Christians are new covenant believers living under the old covenant (see Heb. 8:6-13). Since we live under the law, we define our problem, but we never truly conquer it. The law's job is to produce guilt, condemnation, and death (see Rom. 3:19; 4:15; 5:20; 7:5; 2 Cor. 3:7; Gal. 2:16; 3:3,10,19,21; Heb. 7:18-19). Grace is the empowerment to conquer sin.

The problem is most Christians are still unwittingly living under the law. So they wake up in the morning and say, "I'm not going to sin today." (By the way, this is so defensive in its posture.) Maybe it's, "I'm not going to look at that pornography," or "I won't lust." The problem is, law simply defines sin. The result is, they become sin-conscious. Their focus is on themselves. The problem with such an improper focus is, they, in and of themselves, are inadequate to deal with it. We don't want to become self-conscious, but God-conscious and righteousness-conscious (see Rom. 3:19-22). The result is a generation of spiritually schizophrenic believers and a youth culture with only 4 percent Bible-based believers.

The massive objection comes from the next verse, *"What then? Shall we sin because we are not under law but under grace?..."* (Rom. 6:15). It seems we always come full circle back to this question (see Rom. 6:1,15; 1 Cor. 15:34; Gal. 5:1,13). There seems to be an innate fear in so many people that grace and freedom will lead to the act of sin. There is little doubt if we preach grace there are people who will try to use it to justify some aspect of sin. That's why Paul brings this argument to a climax in verse 16, *"Don't you know that when you offer yourselves to someone to obey him as slaves, you are slaves to the one whom you obey...."* In other words, the one we obey is the one we submit to. By obeying the devil, we give him access to our lives. If this is not rectified, we become slaves to sin (see Rom. 6:16b). This allows the devil to produce death in us (see Rom. 7:13).

In essence, Paul is dealing with the motive and means of a believer. Why do I obey God? Is it to get out of trouble with Him? Is it to enhance my public persona or to improve my self-worth? Are my efforts to relieve my guilt of past or present mistakes? Are my motives to avoid the possibility of negative consequences? Second, how do I go about my obedience? Am I depending on my own ability or the ability of God? If my trust is in me, I am in legalism to that same degree. If I am depending upon God, then I am in grace.

There was a movie some years ago called *Hollow Man.* Although I never saw the movie, I saw the trailer for it, and it caught my attention. The premise of the movie is that a group of scientists discover a formula that, when injected, causes people to become invisible. The lead scientist, played by Kevin Bacon, injects himself with the serum and he becomes invisible. Once he becomes invisible, he does despicable things, because no one can see him. The question arises, was it the invisibility that was evil? No! The invisibility only revealed what was in his heart! Similarly, grace reveals what is in people's hearts. It is what is in our hearts that manifests itself in our lives.

Righteousness (being right with God) and holiness (being separated from the world's system) don't cause God to love us more. He loves us in this moment the most He possibly can. Our lack of holiness does not cause Him to love us less. However, our holiness can cause us to be sensitive to the moves of God, and the lack of holiness can cause us to lack sensitivity to God. Our lack of holiness won't change God's attitude toward us, but it will change our attitude toward God. It won't cause God to love us less, but it will cause us to love God less. The way our hearts go is the way we go (see Prov. 23:7).

GRACE: THE POWER TO CONQUER LIFE

The law proved people cannot live this life by human effort. This is the essence of the two covenants. Under the old covenant, *"The law was given through Moses"* (John 1:17a). God interrupted and added to His promise in order to define sin because it had defeated us and we didn't know it (see Gal. 3:22). Thus, in the new covenant, *"Grace and truth came through Jesus Christ"* (John 1:17b). Grace and truth—the Word (see John 17:17)—were given to fulfill what the law was and what the law could only point out, but was powerless to do. This is why Paul states to Titus,

> *For the grace of God that brings salvation has appeared to all men. It* [grace] *teaches us to say "No" to ungodliness and worldly passions, and to live self-controlled, upright and godly lives in this present age* (Titus 2:11-12).

It is grace that teaches us to conquer sin. How? Once we realize God has provided for us everything we need for life and godliness (see 2 Pet. 1:3), by grace unmerited by us, there is no need to seek to meet our needs by the flesh (doing God's will our way). We understand we are already blessed (past tense) with every spiritual (supernatural) blessing and empowerment in the Kingdom of Heaven (see Eph. 1:3). Since I'm in right standing with the Father by faith, I am qualified to receive it (see Col. 1:12). Thus, I renew my mind to the truth. Understanding what I have and who God is, it is only natural to put my faith in Him. The result is I not only access God's provision, but His empowerment as well. It is my ability to use God's ability to meet any need. Grace is God's ability to conquer sin and life.

This is the essence of what Paul is saying in Hebrews 4:16: *"Let us therefore come boldly to the throne of grace, that we may obtain mercy and find grace to help in time of need"* (NKJV). What is my time of need? It is when I sense I'm about to make a mistake, when I make a misstep, or when I am seeking something I'm missing. Paul notes, in that moment, that I'm to come boldly. *Wait a minute! How can I come boldly if I've just made a mistake?* It is because I come in God's righteousness. Where is it I come? I come to the throne of grace. I don't come to the throne of judgment. What do I find there? I find mercy. *Mercy* is God not giving me what I deserve. *Mercy* is God's ability to forgive. I also find grace. *Grace* is God giving me what I don't deserve. *Grace* is the ability to conquer.

In fact, James says, *"He gives us more grace..."* (James 4:6). He gives more grace than temptation or allurement to do things in my own strength. He adds, *"God opposes the proud but gives grace to the humble"* (James 4:6b). Humility, in essence, is submitting to the view and opinion of God. God resists or abstains from people who try to do things on their own. In essence, He is saying, "You want to try this on your own? OK, good luck with that! However, if you submit to the view and opinion of My Kingdom, I grant more power to conquer than the power that seeks to conquer you."

The thing that often makes sin powerful in our lives is the way we view it. For most people, sin is pleasure that God is keeping them from. But God is not a sadistic father trying to keep us from enjoying life. Quite the contrary; God realizes that all pain is the result of sin. If I truly understand I'm a new creation, then sin has no power over me. In fact, if we understand that sin is a distinctive and painful force, we won't give into it.[14] God is not seeking to punish us; He is looking to protect us.

When we try to operate by human effort or by keeping a standard of the law, we frustrate or neutralize the grace of God (see Gal. 2:21; 3:3). Paul later reinforces this by saying, *"...you have fallen away from grace."* This phrase, *"fallen away from grace"* does not indicate in any way the loss of salvation, as many people try to indicate. Listen to the whole verse: *"You who are trying to be justified by law have been alienated from Christ; you have fallen away from grace"* (Gal. 5:4). What an incredible verse. He says that those who seek to be right with God through the law are alienated or, as the American Standard Version states, *"severed"* from Christ. He says that they have fallen away from grace. They are alienated from the empowerment of God to conquer their circumstances.

This is what he is trying to communicate to us in his example of Second Corinthians 12:7-9,

> *To keep me from becoming conceited because of these surpassingly great revelations, there was given me a thorn in my flesh, a messenger of Satan, to torment me. Three times I pleaded with the Lord to take it away from me. But He said to me, "My grace is sufficient for you, for My power is made perfect in weakness." Therefore I will boast all the more gladly about my weaknesses, so that Christ's power may rest on me.*

Most times these verses are interpreted to mean that satan is throwing havoc on Paul and grace is allowing him to "gut it out." Nothing could be further from the truth. Let's dissect this verse and find its organic meaning. The phrase *"to keep me from becoming conceited"* or *"and lest I should be exalted"* (KJV) often leads people to believe that God is the author of this *"thorn in the flesh* (KJV)." However, the opening of this verse literally reads, "to lift over for advantage" or "to raise up over a thing."[15] This is not God dealing with Paul for pride, but satan trying to keep Paul's revelation from being exalted or recognized for advantage. This passage makes it clear that the *"thorn in the flesh"* (KJV) was a messenger sent from satan. It is not sickness, as some people would indicate, or some physical malady sent by God to humble him. The term *messenger* in Greek is the term for "angel."[16] This was an angel from satan or, in other words, a demon sent to persecute or distract Paul in order that his "great revelations" not be lifted up for the Kingdom's advantage.

God's response is, *"My grace is sufficient."* Again, most people view this as God saying, "You can make it through this." Grace is spiritual supply or empowerment. In other words, God is saying "Wake up! You have unmerited access to the supply of My power to overcome."

The problem is, we think it is more important to be strong for the Lord instead of strong in the Lord. Any time we feel a state of lack, inability, or sin, we need the grace of God. Grace is God's ability to come through for us. This is what Paul was trying to reinforce once again in Hebrews 4:16. We come to God's throne of grace not in our own performance, but in righteousness to obtain His ability on our behalf. Grace becomes a divine influence on our hearts that strengthens and enables us.

WE CAN'T FIGHT ON TWO FRONTS SIMULTANEOUSLY

Once a son of a military man told me this wartime principle: "You can't fight on two fronts at the same time. If you divide your efforts, it will weaken both fronts, and you will be subject to defeat." The application for believers is this, if the whole emphasis is warring on the inside, there is little time to war on the outside. If our whole emphasis is on conquering sin, there is little time to conquer the world with the Kingdom.

This is the amazing story of the Book of Acts. They received great power and much grace to manifest God's Kingdom in life. Peter heals the lame man at the Gate Beautiful (see Acts 3). The apostles performed many miracles, signs, and wonders (see Acts 5:12). Stephen (a non-apostle, by the way) did many great wonders and miraculous signs among the people (see Acts 6:8). Philip performed miraculous signs in such a prolific way that the entire city of Samaria was captivated by the Gospel (see Acts 8:4-8). Sorcerers such as Simon were astonished by the great signs and wonders wrought by Philip (see Acts 8:9-13). Virtually unknown believers such as Ananias impacted their greatest enemies, like Saul of Tarsus, with the Gospel (see Acts 9:1-16). People deadened to God were awakened by Peter (see Acts 10:1-26). Men like Peter were miraculously delivered from the grips of prison and their enemies (see Acts 12). Paul saw the lame man from birth healed at Lystra (see Acts 14:8-15). Paul and Silas were miraculously delivered from prison and launched a church at Philippi (see Acts 16:16-40). The apostles cast out demons who were afflicting people (see Acts 19). The believers were given courage to overcome persecution of the enemy, stoning, imprisonments, shipwrecks, hardships, and dangers of all kinds. Most of them were ordinary people who did extraordinary things! How? By great power and much grace (see Acts 4:33).

In all honesty I stumbled into this revelation while looking at the passage in Acts 20:24, about how Paul was committed to the task of testifying to the Gospel of grace. I followed one connecting verse to another until I realized there were ten references to how grace is a dominant theme in the Book of Acts. I knew the power of the Holy Spirit was a dominant theme in Acts, but it is the dual nature of great power and much grace that was upon them that translated ordinary men to do extraordinary things. It was the combination of God's power and God's grace (ability) through His disciples that turned the world upside down (see Acts 17:6). Somehow, we have drifted away to rules and regulations that have left a generation in fear of making a mistake that they might "set God off." The result is a generation that doesn't realize that it is the goodness of God that leads people to repentance (see Rom. 2:4).

DON'T CRY OVER SPILLED MILK

One of my favorite stories is about a famous scientist who was responsible for several very important medical breakthroughs. When he was being interviewed by a newspaper reporter, he was asked how he was able to produce so much more than most people.

He responded by saying it all came from a lesson his mother taught him when he was two years old. He had tried to take a bottle of milk out of the refrigerator. In his effort, he lost his grip and spilled the entire contents on the kitchen floor. His mother, instead of scolding him, said, "What a wonderful mess you've made! I've rarely seen such a huge puddle of milk. Well, the damage is done. Would you like to get down and play in the milk before we clean it up?"

In fact, that is what he did. After a few minutes his mother continued, "You know whenever you make a mess like this, eventually you have to clean it up. So, how would you like to do that? We could use a towel, sponge, or mop. Which one do you prefer?"

After they were done cleaning up the milk, she said, "What we have here is a failed experiment to carry a big bottle with two tiny hands. Let's go out to the backyard and practice. See if you can figure a way to carry it without dropping it." And they did!

The scientist knew from that moment forward he didn't have to be afraid of making mistakes. Instead, he learned that mistakes were opportunities for learning something new—which ultimately made him the scientist he became.[17]

Life is filled with missteps along the way. That doesn't mean that God's mad at us. I am in no way suggesting God is not just or there are no consequences for sin. However, our missteps should cause us to run toward God, not away from Him. Instead of anger, He comes to us with the goodness of the Lord that leads to repentance (see Rom. 2:4). In repentance, I change my thinking to do things His way. My faith releases God's grace on my behalf.

In light of this, let's examine the role of the Holy Spirit. Primarily, He is a comforter. John 14:26 says, *"But the Comforter, which is the Holy Ghost, whom the Father will send in My name..."* (KJV). (See also John 15:26.) John continues this thought,

> *Nevertheless I tell you the truth; It is expedient for you that I go away: for if I go not away, the Comforter will not come unto you; but if I [Jesus] depart, I will send Him unto you* (John 16:7 KJV).

Jesus knew His leaving was important so that the role of the Holy Spirit would be enacted in our lives. The word *comforter* is the Greek term *parakletos*. The word means "counselor, intercessor (one who pleads one's case), one called along-side to help, advocate, comforter."[18] There is little doubt the main job of the Holy Spirit is to comfort, not condemn. His job is to guide us into all truth (see John 16:13). It is to guide us into His counsel, direction, and leading. His job is to comfort the afflicted, not to afflict the comfortable.

Some might think, *Wait a minute, what about the next verse? "When He comes, He will convict the world of guilt in regard to sin and righteousness and judgment"* (John 16:8). The job of the counselor is to convict of sin. In the context of this passage the Holy Spirit is convicting the "world" of sin. The term "convict" here means to present, to expose facts or to convince of truth.[19] The Spirit works in the hearts and minds of the unsaved to show them the truth of who God is. The "grace world" is quick to point out that the job of the Holy Spirit is to convict the "world" of sin, not the believer. I do believe it is more important to convict people of righteousness than sin. Once a person knows who He is, sin loses its appeal.

Some grace teachers believe that since our "sins are forgiven past, present, and future" there is no need for repentance. This phrase simply means that Christ would have to die all over again at each indiscretion. The idea is that the sin of believers doesn't have to have repentance. Personally, I don't have a problem with the idea that the Holy Spirit guides us into all truth, whether it is truth verified in the Word or verifying my lack of understanding of it. If I'm heading in the wrong direction a U-turn is not only important, but also essential.

This issue has to do with the question of whether or not every sin has to be confessed in order for people to be justified or righteous. Quite frankly, that is impossible, as we discussed previously. Romans 14:23 tells us that whatever is not faith is sin. Sin is not simply, "You don't smoke, drink, spit, or chew or go out with the girls or guys who do." There are sins of omission as well as sins of commission. Failing to have "a quiet time" after God told me to could be an act of a lack of faith—which I never remembered to repent for. A man's anger at his wife for forgetting to pick up his laundry falls into a similar category. James 4:17 notes, *"Anyone, then, who knows the good he ought to do and doesn't do it, sins."*

However, that doesn't mean we don't need to repent. If the spirit of truth leads us into the truth of a shortcoming in our lives, we need to change our thinking to Kingdom thinking. There are 14 references and 16 verses having to do with believers repenting (see Rom. 2:4; 2 Cor. 7:9-10; 1 Cor. 12:21; 2 Tim. 2:25; Heb. 12:17; Rev. 2:5,16,21-22; 3:13; 4:20-21; 10:9; 16:11; 23:19). Second Corinthians 12:21 illuminates this clearly, *"I am afraid that when I come again my God will humble me before you, and I will be grieved over many who have sinned earlier and have not repented of the impurity, sexual sin and debauchery in which they have indulged."* Our sin does affect our relationship to the Kingdom and our relationship to ourselves (see 1 John 3:19-22).

This aspect of the function of the Holy Spirit is done in the context of the rest of the verse,

> *...and righteousness and judgment: in regard to sin, because men do not believe in Me; in regard to righteousness, because I am going to the Father, where you can see Me no longer; and in regard to judgement, because the prince of this world now stands condemned* (John 16:8-11).

He notes three things here in this passage:

1. The Holy Spirit convicts us of the sin of not believing in Jesus. The Holy Spirit is not trying to "nail" us every time we mess up. He shows us where we lack

faith to lead us back into trusting God. Obviously, our wrongdoing is an indication of our wrong believing. He wants us to refocus on the Father to be full of power and to have great grace upon us (see Rom. 4:8; Heb. 10:10,14).

2. The Holy Spirit convicts of righteousness. *Righteousness* in its most base form means, "As it should be."[20] Jesus came to give us life as it should be—abundant and complete. It means I'm in right standing with the Father based on Jesus' finished work, and I receive it by faith. Once I understand that God has provided everything I need in life by grace unmerited by me (see Eph. 1:2-3; 2 Pet. 1:1-3) and I know I am right with God and qualified to receive it, then there's no need to act in the flesh (see 1 Cor. 15:34). Righteousness is a state of being that, when understood, prompts right action. The Holy Spirit doesn't want us sin-conscious, but righteousness-conscious.

3. The Holy Spirit convicts of judgment. This is not referring to the Holy Spirit revealing that people are going to hell if they don't repent. He adds, "... *because the prince of this world is judged* (KJV). The Holy Spirit is assuring us that satan is judged and stripped of all his authority over us. "...*This is the victory...even our faith*" (1 John 5:4).

Our sin is not rooted in our sin nature (see Rom. 6:1-6), for we no longer have such a nature (see Rom. 6:6). Sin is rooted in our personal belief system (see Heb. 4:12). *Sin* is simply "missing the mark."[21]

The real issue is, What is in our hearts? No matter what we believe doctrinally, if there's a disconnect with our hearts, it affects how we see the Kingdom and how we see ourselves. People whose hearts are established in the Gospel will have little to do with the allurement of sin or temptation. *Sin* is "missing the mark and so not to share in the prize."[22]

THE BIGGEST PROBLEM IN THE BODY OF CHRIST

The biggest problem in the Body of Christ is we are a new covenant people living under an old covenant. As long as we make people live under law, instead of grace, we retard the manifestation of the fullness of God. We are sentencing people to live under the definition of the problem rather than the solution. This is why so many people are surviving, instead of thriving. The ordinary becomes a thief of the extraordinary.

This is what the author of Hebrews is trying to communicate in Hebrews 8:6-13:

> *But the ministry Jesus has received is as superior to theirs as the covenant of which He is mediator is superior to the old one, and it is founded on better promises. For if there had been nothing wrong with that first covenant, no place would have been sought for another...."The time is coming declares the Lord, when I will make a new covenant with the house of Israel and with the house of Judah. It will not be like the first covenant I made with their forefathers....This is the covenant I will make with the house of Israel. After that time, declares the Lord. I will put My laws in their minds and write them on their hearts. I will*

be their God, and they will be My people. No longer will a man teach his neighbor, or a man his brother, saying, 'Know the Lord,' because they will all know Me, from the least of them to the greatest. For I will forgive their wickedness and will remember their sins no more." By calling this covenant "new," He has made the first one obsolete; and what is obsolete and aging will soon disappear.

Living under the law—where legalistic performance is required in order to be right with God—is obsolete. The word *obsolete* simply means "no longer in use, disused, outmoded, no longer current, indistinct or imperfect as compared to the new."[23] My mother-in-law grew up as a secretary typing on a manual typewriter. It had the small keys, the large ribbon, and the keys that were hard to press. The electric typewriter made it obsolete. The electric gave way to the IBM "Selectric" typewriter. Ultimately, that gave way to personal computers. The first personal computers were so large they could hardly fit on a desk. Today the evolution of computers has grown until my cell phone has more information capacity than those early large computers.

What the author of Hebrews is saying is that living under the law instead of under grace is like going back to a manual typewriter instead of using a laptop computer. It has left the Church as a reasonable facsimile of the real thing. God has made us to live the extraordinary, but we've settled for the ordinary.

• •

ORGANIC THOUGHTS

1.   Are you living out loud?

2. Do you see the possibilities of extraordinary living?

3. Did you notice that the key to going from ordinary to extraordinary is intimacy with God?

4. How does the principle of "the name" of Jesus affect your thinking as a believer?

5. Does the Church carry a distinctiveness that separates it from the world?

6. Notice that it is the combination of the power of the Holy Spirit and God's grace that makes the ordinary, extraordinary.

7. Have you seen God's grace as God's ability before?

8. What is the true purpose of the law?

9. Have you reckoned yourself dead to sin?

10. Have you, at times, been a new covenant believer living under the old covenant? Do you see how grace overcomes sin and positions you to receive God's Kingdom?

11. Do you understand how living under the law puts your focus only on you (and on sin)?

12. What is your motive in serving God? Is it to get out of trouble or to get to know Him? Are you relying on your ability or upon God's ability?

13. Does the manifestation model make sense to you?

14. How do you view sin? Is sin pleasure, or is it a source of pain?

15. Do you see how grace is the key to the extraordinary?

16. How does the Holy Spirit convicting you of righteousness lead to victory?

Chapter 8

· · · · · · · · · · · · · · · ·

GIVING BIRTH TO THE NEW REFORMATION

I was casually walking into a luncheon when unexpectedly I had a "blast from my past." In the luncheon was a couple I hadn't seen in years. It didn't take long to figure out they had been "through the ringer" of life. Within minutes, they began rehearsing doctor's visits, a financial crisis, and family problems. Their faces revealed that they had lost all the vitality of life and the vitality of their faith. They had unwittingly resigned themselves to suffering and loss. My responsibilities kept me from having an in-depth conversation with this disillusioned couple, so I shared a few passing thoughts in an attempt to help them. What "hit me" in this encounter, however, was the fact that organic Christianity is not about theological accuracy; it is about people's destinies (by the way, the conversation is now ongoing). Most people are preoccupied with life's situations and circumstances and they have lost sight of their own destiny.

In the words of Jerry Lee Lewis (please pay attention; I don't quote him very often), "There's a whole lot of shakin' going on."

The economy is shaking. The job market is shaking. World stability in light of terrorism is shaking. That's exactly what the writer of Hebrews said,

> *At that time His voice shook the earth, but now He has promised, "Once more I will shake not only the earth but also the heavens." The words "once more" indicate the removing of what can be shaken—that is, created things—so that what cannot be shaken may remain. Therefore, since we are receiving a kingdom that cannot be shaken, let us be thankful, and so worship God acceptably with reverence and awe* (Hebrews 12:26-28).

The writer of Hebrews is indicating there is "a whole lot of shakin' going on." Shaking is an attempt of the enemy to distract us from stepping into our destiny. However, there is an important notation in this passage:

> *The words "once more" indicate the removing of what can be shaken—that is, created things—so that what cannot be shaken may remain. Therefore, since we are receiving a kingdom that cannot be shaken...* (Hebrews 12:27).

Paul (if indeed he is the writer of Hebrews) is indicating that everything else around us may be shaken, but its purpose is to reveal what cannot be shaken—God's Kingdom. Without a doubt, God's Kingdom is His rule and reign in our lives. It is also the location and resources for our destiny. In other words, when we realize what God provided by grace, unmerited by us, in His Kingdom, we are unshaken. According to Romans 14:17, the Kingdom of God is righteousness, peace, and joy in the Holy Spirit. The Kingdom of God is encapsulated in our understanding that our right standing with the Father is not based on what we've done, but what Jesus did, and we receive that by faith. The result is it brings peace to our lives (see Isa. 32:17).

I am not moved by my circumstances. The consequence of not being moved by my circumstances is that it positions me for joy in my life. *Joy,* in essence, is "radical anticipation of good."[1] Such joy results in confidence in God's grace, supply, and provision in my life.

Let me give you an example. Some years back, my wife, Judy, and I took a ministry trip to Mexico. We found ourselves in a remote, inaccessible, poverty-laden city. When our host missionary picked us up at the airport, he loaded our luggage into an SUV and we headed a long way out there. During our conversation, we passed some towns and villages. Our host would comment, "There is a town of 20,000 people and no Gospel message." Similarly, there would be a town of 10,000 or 50,000 people that had heard no Gospel message. We finally arrived at our town. It had none of the conveniences we take for granted every day in America. There was no accessible drinking water, no hot and cold running water, no air-conditioning, and so forth. The church we were ministering in was nothing more than three unfinished walls with a canopy draped over it that leaked like a sieve when it rained. We ministered every night for a week. Every night the crowd grew. There were a number of miracles that took place, and the word spread around town. In fact, the host pastor estimated to us that 90 percent of those we prayed for received an instantaneous touch from God.

As we came to the final days of our stay, the host missionary asked me if I would share on marital fidelity. It seemed like an odd request so I asked him, "Why?" He told me it was because the men in this area didn't feel like they were men unless they had two or three women on "the sly"—even in the Church. I realized I wasn't there to do "my thing," so I prepared to share on the topic. That night as I got ready to minister, one of the local pastors who had overheard the pastor's request for me to preach on marital fidelity asked me if I intended to comply. I responded, "Yes, I am!" Without any hesitation, he replied, "I don't care how you teach this or how much Scripture you use, the men in this area will not receive it."

So, on that encouraging note, I set out to minister. I began by saying things like, "Women should be esteemed—women should be elevated—women should be lifted up." As I was proclaiming the virtues of women, I noticed a man on the front row vehemently shaking his head, "No!" I thought to myself, *This guy is not going to intimidate me!* I leaped off the platform, and my interpreter leaped off with me. I increased my intensity in expression, and the man seemed to correspondingly shake his head, *no,* accordingly. Ultimately, I went on with the service, and there were some wonderful results.

After the service was over, I was standing behind the platform and some of my American team was gathered around me. One of the gals from the team looked at me and said, "Did you see that man openly defy you in the service tonight?" I responded, "You mean the guy shaking his head, no, at me?" She nodded in affirmation.

Now the host missionary was overhearing the conversation and asked, "Who was it?" I looked around the platform, and I pointed out the man some distance away. He chuckled and pointed out, "Oh, Ron, that's Julio. He has a nervous condition. His head always goes back and forth like that." We all laughed over the event. When I returned to the privacy of our bungalow, I felt like I heard the Holy Spirit say, "Things are not always as they seem!"

What was true of that humorous situation is true in your life—things are not always as they seem. It may seem hopeless. It may appear there's no way around the doctor's report. It may seem there's more month than money. It might look like hope is gone out of your family. Here is a word from God for you, "Things are not always as they seem!" That doesn't mean every individual situation works out just the way you want, but God is going to end things in victory. Don't lose sight of your destiny!

Living an extraordinary, exceptional, remarkable, unimaginable, amazing life doesn't mean it's free from bad circumstances. It means that God's incredible grace has given you the supply to all you need by faith—and such faith releases His remarkable ability on your behalf. Extraordinary living isn't always spectacular. It's not just you emptying every hospital by faith. It also has to do with everyday life. It's the...

- Courage of a woman who overcomes her fear of crowds to share a miraculous answer to prayer and encourage many people in a congregation.

- Discipline of a man who gets up an hour earlier to run the block in an attempt to restore his health.

- Vision of a teacher who attempts to draw out an inattentive student to discover that student's gifts in life.

- Perseverance of a college student who overcomes an overwhelming set of tests and doesn't quit.

- Love of a parent who loves a rebellious child into the child's destiny.

- Ability (grace) of God to conquer sin and life.

- Character enacted in all of life. It is what I call the Law of Correspondence: Our outside world corresponds in direct proportion to our inward world.

What is *character?* It is the aggregate qualities or characteristics that make up who we are. Character (good character) is doing the right thing, not the easy thing. Character is the will to do right, regardless of the cost to us. Character is who we are when no one is looking. Character doesn't come from reading a book about it, but making right decisions when tempted to do wrong things. And, such lifestyle comes out of grace. Look at Romans 5:1-5:

> *Therefore, since we have been justified through faith, we have peace with God through our Lord Jesus Christ, through whom we have gained access by faith into the grace in which we now stand. And we rejoice in the hope of the glory of God. Not only so, but we also rejoice in our sufferings [KJV: "tribulations"], because we know that suffering produces perseverance; perseverance, character; and character, hope. And hope does not disappoint us....*

The passage begins with the word *therefore.* Every time we see *therefore* we must ask ourselves, "What is it there for?" This term means "consequently, or for the reason of, in view of, or accordingly."[2] Paul had just conclusively proven justification or righteousness by faith so that Judaizers would not add to the organic message of the Gospel. Being right with God was faith alone, not faith + the law (see Rom. 3:19-22; 4:2-8;13-25).

He says, since this is true, we have peace *with* God. In other words, the war with God is over. God is not mad at us. Peace comes from God to my life when I relate to God by faith, not by performance.

My peace with God allows me to gain access by faith into His grace. The term *access* means "permission, or ability to enter."[3] *Access* means "admission"; it is like an admission ticket. I can't get into an event without a ticket. If I want to go to the Super Bowl, I need a ticket. If I want to go to the movies, I have to have a ticket for admission. Once we realize we are right with God by faith, it brings peace to us with God. We overcome spiritual schizophrenia. I realize not only that God *can*, but He *will* for my life. That frees me to believe Him or to have faith. That faith is not in my faith, but in His grace. My faith is not in the law (God's demand for defining my shortcomings), but in His grace (supply, provision, ability). Faith is now admission into the fullness of God.

Stay with Paul's progression; it's amazing. This access into God's grace causes us to rejoice in the hope of His glory (see Rom. 5:2). This term *glory* can mean "the view and opinion of God."[4] Anyone can rejoice in good times, but I can rejoice in tribulation as well because of the view and opinion of God. His view and opinion is the result of His grace (see Rom. 5:2-3). That rejoicing produces *perseverance*. The idea behind this word is more than just not quitting. It gives the idea of "I turn neither to the right nor the left, but I stay on the path God has got marked out for me." Such perseverance develops character. This term *character* means "approved as a result of overcoming in testing."[5] It gives you the idea of the "mettle" or temper of a veteran as opposed to a raw recruit."[6]

This is important because this is the mettle necessary for the New Reformation. One expert has said that in the next five years we'll either have revival or anarchy.[7] Personally, I vote for a revival or Reformation. This is a call to a Reformation or at least a Reclamation (reclaiming the Gospel at its organic roots—nothing added to it). Like with Luther in 1517, it's a Reformation that will consist of:

- *Sola Scriptura* (Scripture alone)

- *Sola Christus* (Christ alone)

- *Sola gratia* (grace alone)

- *Sola fide* (faith alone)

- *Sola de gloria* (the glory of God alone)

Again, this Reclamation will be a movement of:

- A people, not just a person (not just celebrities on television or book covers, but a people who know who He is and who they are)

- A people who know God intimately (not about Him, but know Him)

- A people who know their identity (know who God is, what He has already done, and who He has made them to be)—a call to grace

- A people of faith (not faith in our faith, but faith in God's grace)

- A people who understand God's Kingdom (a Kingdom that reflects the supply of His grace)

Why is this essential? Isaiah 43:18-19 says it like this:

> *Forget the former things; do not dwell on the past. See, I am doing a new thing! Now it springs up; do you not perceive it? I am making a way in the desert and streams in the wasteland.*

Isaiah says God can be doing a new thing and people don't perceive it (new to us, not to God). He suggests there are two things that, if people fail to do them, can cause people to miss it:

1.   *Forget the former things*—We all have a tendency to want to dwell where we are comfortable, where we are familiar. Virtually every new move of God is resisted by those who were a part of the last move of God (not by those who experienced nothing, but by those who experienced something). We have a tendency to want to go back to the former thing. If we stress the old thing, we miss the new thing.

2.   *Don't dwell on the past*—Our past does not determine our future. If we let the five elements of our personal belief system determine our identity (self-image), it often discourages us from stepping into our destiny. If we see ourselves in lack, as never having enough or as never amounting to anything, our RAS (reticular activating system) encourages us to stay in our comfort zone.

In this passage, Isaiah asks a poignant question, *"Do you not perceive it?"* This word *perceive* is the Hebrew term *yawdah.* It means "to know at the most personal level, to grasp, to recognize, discern, or to be impressed by."[8] That's why First Chronicles 12:32 tells us the sons of Issachar discerned the times and seasons and knew what Israel should do. In many ways, God's will for this year is the same as it was for last year—or any year. It is to fully manifest the Kingdom of God *to* us and *through* us. However, organic Christianity demands that we perceive a reclamation of anything that has been diluted.

People resist change because they resist change because they resist change. Those who pioneer the change are often misunderstood. People know things are not being fully manifested, but often they opt for a little insanity—doing the same thing over and over again, yet expecting a different result. Tough times often produce new results. Isaiah says it like this, "...*This day is a day of distress, and rebuke and disgrace, as when children come to the point of birth and there is no strength to deliver them*" (Isa. 37:3). He points out that there's a child in the birth canal, but there's no strength to bring the child into the world. He says there are three things to keep us from manifesting what's in the birth canal: distress, rebuke, and disgrace.

Distress can keep us from giving birth to our destiny. The word *distress* comes from two words, *di-*, which means "double, two-fold, or two,"[9] and *stress,* which means "adversity, anguish, intense pain."[10] It is a double stress. Do we live in a time of intense pain? The term *rebuke* gives us the idea of "reasoning being challenged, to chastise, a refuting of fact."[11] In a time of postmodernism, situation ethics, relativism, and progressivism, the reasoning of the Church is being challenged at every level. The last hindrance is *disgrace.* Interestingly, this is a compound word with a prefix *dis-,* which means "opposite of, to deprive of or absence of,"[12] and *grace. Disgrace* is the opposite of grace. It means "to despise, condemn, scorn, or reject."[13]

Well, I have a word from God for you. It's time to get through what you're going through and be what you want to see. If you want to see something you've never seen before, you have to do something you've never done before. I have good news and bad news for you. First, the bad news:

- One to three million teenagers run away from home every year in the land of the free and the home of the brave.[14]

- The third leading cause of death in teenagers is suicide.[15]

- The leading cause of death in children under five is parental abuse.[16]

- The divorce rate in America is over 50 percent.[17]

We're dealing with eating disorders, drugs, terrorism, and an economy gone south. Now that's the bad news!

Here's the good news! The devil is mentally retarded! Why? Because he thinks he is creating fatalism, but instead he is establishing divine dissatisfaction. There's a group of people who are being raised up who are fulfilled, but not satisfied. They won't settle for anything less than the full manifestation of the Kingdom of God.

A few years ago, I was ministering in north Houston. A friend of mine was ministering at Lakewood Church, where the Osteens pastor. I went down to Houston a day early to visit my friend. I arrived at Lakewood early to enjoy some fellowship with my friend. That night, my friend was preaching away when he said, "There's a move of God in the birth canal. God is about to give birth to something extraordinary!"

When he said that, I got Holy Ghost doo dads all up and down my arms. I knew what he was saying was true. I stayed for some polite fellowship afterward, but I was distracted by the word that was interacting with my spirit. On my way back to the resort area where I was staying in north Houston, I felt impressed to look at this passage in Isaiah. I wasn't even sure what it was. It read, *"This day is a day of distress and rebuke and disgrace, as when children come to the point of birth and there is no strength to deliver them"* (Isa. 37:3). It hit me that there was something

God wanted to manifest, but distress, rebuke, and disgrace were holding it back.

I thought to myself, *If distress, rebuke, and disgrace are holding it back, how do we overcome them?* I felt led to look at Romans 8:11,

> *And if the Spirit of Him who raised Jesus from the dead is living in you, He who raised Christ from the dead will also give life* [KJV: *"quicken"*] *to your mortal bodies....*

This term *quicken* is the word for "to make alive, revitalize, to bring forth" (by implication, "to give birth to"). Wow!

The same Spirit that raised Christ from the dead is living in us! This power is the ability to bring forth or to give birth to what is in the birth canal. My next thought was, *How do I tap into this resurrection power?* I turned to Hebrews 12:1:

> *Therefore, since we are surrounded by such a great cloud of witnesses* [it helps me to know the great saints who have gone on before us are cheering us on], *let us throw off everything that hinders and the sin that so easily entangles, and let us run with perseverance* [there's that word from Romans 5 again] *the race marked out for us.*

In pursuit of our destiny from God, we have to overcome any number of obstacles that seek to hinder us. We must overcome fear, lack, low self-esteem and self-worth, past environments, negative reflections of past authority figures, feelings of, "I'm not good enough," and various temptation in order to not be dissuaded from our destiny and the best life has to offer.

The writer of Hebrews presses on, *"Let us fix our eyes on Jesus...."* This is not on Christian celebrities, not on people who have disappointed us, not on authors of books, but upon the One who never disappoints. We don't let circumstances dim the truth. Our eyes are fixed on Jesus: *"Let us fix our eyes on Jesus, the author and perfecter* [KJV: *"finisher"] of our faith..."* (Heb. 12:2). Jesus is the initiator and culminator of our faith—not faith in our faith, but faith in Him and His grace.

The writer progresses on in verse 2, *"...who for the joy set before Him endured the cross, scorning its shame, and sat down at the right hand of the throne of God"* (Heb. 12:2). There it was—the way I get resurrection power to overcome distress, rebuke, and disgrace is the same way Jesus got through the cross to resurrection power. It was *"the joy set before Him."* It is, again, the joy set before us.

Listen to these Scriptures:

> *...the joy of the Lord is your strength* [no joy, no strength] (Nehemiah 8:10).

> *...in Your presence is fullness of joy...* (Psalm 16:11 NKJV).

> *...weeping may endure for a night, but joy comes in the morning* (Psalm 30:5 NKJV).

> *Those who sow in tears will reap with songs of joy* (Psalm 126:5).

> *Rejoice always, pray without ceasing, in everything give thanks; for this is the will of God in Christ Jesus for you. Do not quench the Spirit.* (1 Thessalonians 5:16-19 NKJV).

Wow! Here in this passage there are the four steps of joy to bring what's in the birth canal into manifestation:

1. Be Joyful Always

What is the author of this passage saying? Evidently there's a way to tap into joy (it's a grace) when we need it. This is precisely what James tries to address, *"My brethren, count it all joy when you fall into various trials"* [NIV: *"face trials of many kinds"*] (James 1:2 NKJV). How many of us want to say, "Why? Why do I have joy in trials and temptations? That's the time I usually have the least joy." It is because of what it produces through us and to us. Here's something that is essential to understand. There is no victory without a battle. One presupposes the other.

James pushes forward, *"Because you know that the testing of your faith develops perseverance"* (James 1:3). There's that word again. How many of us have ever prayed for patience (perseverance)? How many of us will never do it again? About the time we ask for it, there's a reason to use it. Perseverance is that quality that says, "I will stray neither to the right nor left, but I will stay on the path of my destiny that God has mapped out for me." Now please note this. James does not say the testing of our faith produces perseverance. Some might say, "That's exactly what verse 3 says." It's not the testing of our faith that produces perseverance; it is joy in the midst of our trial that produces perseverance.

James, again, presses forward, *"Perseverance must finish its work so that you may be mature and complete, not lacking anything"* (James 1:4). Everyone wants to be lacking in nothing, but not everyone is willing to gain joy to persevere through the difficulty and persecution in order to see destiny manifested. Patience is not passive waiting. Patience is sustained faith.

Note that there is a testing of our faith. Whatever is revelation to us will be tested. I head a Bible college as part of my duties. We never have class that we don't have testing. Why do we give tests? To see if the student knows the answers. Why are there tests in life? To see if we know the answers. Some might say, "I know all about love. In fact, the Gospel in one word is *love*." They may even join Dionne Warwick and sing, "What the world needs now, is love, sweet love; it's the only thing that there's just too little of...." However, we don't know if we really know how to love until something or someone unlovable comes along. Some might say, "I understand prosperity. It is just *'Give, and it will be given to you...'*" (Luke 6:38). That's lovely, but do you still believe that when your income begins drying up? I've been there, done that, and got the t-shirt. I believe it.

James culminates this thought in verses 5-8,

> *If any of you lacks wisdom, he should ask God, who gives generously to all* [part of Ephesians 1:3] *without finding fault* [righteousness and grace], *and it will be given to him* (James 1:5).

God responds to faith righteousness, not works righteousness.

> *But when he asks he must believe and not doubt, because he who doubts is like a wave of the sea, blown and tossed by the wind. That man should not think he will receive anything from the Lord; he is a double-minded man, unstable in all he does* (James 1:6-8).

This is the devil's main tool to create cognitive dissonance or double-mindedness against the knowledge of God (see 2 Cor. 10:3-6). This creates spiritual schizophrenic believers. However, joy in testing produces perseverance to overcome distress, rebuke, and disgrace to give birth to the destiny that is in the birth canal.

Jesus continued this thought process, *"I tell you the truth you will weep and mourn while the world rejoices. You will grieve, but your grief will turn to joy"* (John 16:20). There will be times of sorrow and grief, but those of us who know the Lord can tap into joy. Jesus continued,

> *A woman giving birth to a child* [here's our goal] *has pain because her time has come; but when her baby is born she forgets the anguish because of her joy that a child is born into the world* (John 16:21).

The wrong time to ask a woman if she wants another baby is when she is having the current one. The pain of the moment could be quite distracting. However, every element of pain is forgotten, because of the joy she has when her child is born into the world. There can be pain, distraction, and distortion along the way to manifesting our destiny (and God's). Joy is the sustaining, compelling force in our life to give birth to the new move of God.

Jesus explained this, *"So with you: Now is your time of grief, but I will see you again and you will rejoice, and no one will take away your joy"* (John 16:22). Here, Jesus is referring to His resurrection (contextually, to His disciples, but there is something for all of us). No person can take away our joy. No one takes our joy. We have to give it up. Joy is our strength to give birth to our destiny.

> *I tell you the truth, My Father will give you whatever you ask in My name. Until now you have not asked for anything in My name. Ask and you will receive, and your joy will be complete* (John 16:23-24).

What an incredible revelation. We can pray in Jesus' name, and He will put the necessary grace and resources in our hands. Remember, using the name of Jesus is to have connection to and the revelation of Jesus. It is the power of attorney to access anything Jesus has access to in His life. The result is our joy is complete. There is a joy that takes us through and a joy that fulfills.

Jesus culminates this chapter and this revelation in John 16:33,

> *I have told you these things, so that in Me you may have peace. In this world you will have trouble [KJV: "tribulation"]. But take heart [KJV: "be of good cheer"]! I have overcome the world.*

Jesus is saying, "I'm telling you this ahead of time, so that when 'stuff happens' you won't be discouraged." Jesus notes that in this world we will have tribulation. Sometimes I'll ask a crowd, "How many of you are in this world?" Inevitably, there is someone who doesn't raise a hand. To which my response is usually something like, "There are aliens in the crowd. I've slipped into Roswell, New Mexico, and I didn't realize it." We're all in this world, and as a result, we will experience tribulation. Jesus says, "Don't be uptight. I've been there, done that, and got the t-shirt. I've overcome this world, so you can as well. So, 'Be of good cheer.'" The idea of this term *good cheer* is "to encourage, to have courage or hope, comfort, joy, be of good spirit, or to shout."[18]

To me, it's much like the old laundry commercial for a product called Shout®. In the commercial, a little boy comes running across the screen and he falls down and messes up his pants. The announcer's voice says, "What are you going to do about it?" Then, the mother says, "I'm going to Shout® it out!" Then a little girl scampers across the screen in her little party dress. She too falls down and messes up the dress. Again, the announcer's voice says, "What are you going to do about it?" Again, the mother confidently spouts, "I'm going to Shout® it out!"

It is precisely the same thing with our lives. The bottom falls out, the finances dry up, the doctor's report comes back negative, the child momentarily goes berserk. The devil challenges, "What are you going to do about it?" Your response should be, "I'm going to shout it out!" Why? A shout is often used in Scripture as an act of praise (see Ps. 47:1). Praise creates the presence of God (see Ps. 22:3). In His presence there is fullness of joy (see Ps. 16:11). The joy of the Lord is our strength (see Neh. 8:10). Strength is the ability to give birth to what is in the birth canal.

2. *Pray Without Ceasing*

The second injunction to help us bring to birth what's in the birth canal is, *"Pray without ceasing"* (1 Thess. 5:17 NKJV). We have to pray and not give up. Our lives are based on convictions, not reflections. People who live by reflection reflect their circumstances or other people's opinions around them. People of convictions live convinced of God's grace and supply. These people are unmoved by circumstances or people's opinions. They persevere (see Heb. 6:12).

Twice in my life I've been diagnosed with potentially terminal diseases. I can remember the emotional drain in hearing the doctor's diagnosis. I have vivid memories of the transition of thought to understanding the provision of God's grace and provision. I can see in my mind the peace and finally the joy of walking through one of life's tribulations. On one occasion, the process went on for over three years before a new doctor's report revealed an unequivocal breakthrough and healing. We have to pray and not give up!

3. *In Everything Give Thanks*

First Thessalonians goes on to say, *"In everything give thanks..."* (1 Thess. 5:18 NKJV), which is our third tool of joy. What is the difference between thanksgiving and joy? Thanksgiving is the manifestation of joy. It is joy enacted. We don't thank people for what they're going to do, but for something that's already done. Thanksgiving is a spiritual force.

Let me show you this principle in the Book of Jonah. Everybody knows the story of Jonah and the whale or the big fish. God comes to Jonah and tells him He needs him to be His evangelist to

Nineveh. Jonah hated the Ninevites and decided to take a "fishing expedition" to Tarshish instead. Little did he realize he was about to catch a big one. On the journey, a storm raises its ugly head. In fear for their lives, the crew casts lots to see if someone on board is responsible for the pending catastrophe (old covenant). Can you imagine their surprise when the lots fell to the evangelist of God? As the storm intensifies, Jonah relates, "Throw me overboard and everything will be OK." They throw Jonah overboard, and he is swallowed by Moby Dick. He spends three days in the belly of the big fish. That changes his perspective. Basically, he has two options. Option #1 is to wait for the fish to swallow some wood and some other people, build for himself a pulpit, and begin a church. Finally, he can declare "We've got a whale of a church" (I want to apologize ahead of time for such a lame remark). The second option is to repent! Jonah chose the latter.

In Jonah 2 it records,

> *From inside the fish Jonah prayed to the Lord his God. He said: "In my distress* [there's that word again from Isaiah 37:3] *I called to the Lord, and He answered me....But I with a song of thanksgiving, will sacrifice to You. What I have vowed I will make good. Salvation comes from the Lord." And the Lord commanded the fish, and it vomited Jonah onto dry land* (Jonah 2:1;9-10).

Please get the picture here. Jonah is in the belly of the fish for three days. During this time, the gastric juices of the fish probably bleached his skin white. Maybe it took off a portion of the hair from his head. He probably had seaweed draped over his body. Suddenly, the big fish appears on the shores of Nineveh. There were probably a couple of old Ninevite retirees fishing on the dock—maybe drinking a little Jack Daniels®. Suddenly, a big fish appears—and—burp!! Out comes this regurgitated figure of an evangelist crying, "Repent!" What are they going to do? They're going to repent, baby!

That's what happened to the entire city. All of Nineveh experienced a move of God. Even the animals repented (see Jon. 3:7). When a cat repents, that's a move of God.

Please, don't let my trite attempt at humor cloud this dynamic principle. The joy of the Lord is necessary in difficult times to overcome distress, rebuke, and disgrace to give us strength to give birth to our destiny and God's.

4. Do Not Quench the Spirit's Fire

Finally, First Thessalonians 5:19 says, *"Do not quench the Spirit"* (NKJV). The New International Version puts it, *"Do not put out the Spirit's fire."* Why is it important to end with this injunction from Paul? It is because modern Judaizers, Gnostics, and Antinomians will try to maintain status quo. I respect everyone's desire to be right. However, when things don't work as they should, I go back to see if we have the organic Gospel—nothing added to it. It's time to experience the fullness of the Kingdom. So don't quench the Spirit. It's time to regain a reclamation of the Gospel at its base roots. It's time to use the manifestation model to bring us to the fullness of grace through faith to experience God's Kingdom.

• •

ORGANIC THOUGHTS

1. Does the shaking in the world affect your perception? Remember things are not always as they seem.

2. Are you ready to not only experience freedom in your life, but also to help others reclaim the fullness of the Gospel?

3. Have you allowed former things or your past to rob you of your future?

4. Are you ready for a New Reformation?

Chapter 9

FREEDOM!

Nearly everyone knows the story of the Scottish freedom fighter William Wallace because of the movie, *Braveheart*. He is the man who procured Scotland's liberty from English oppression in the early 1300s. Scotland had been under the oppression of English monarchs for years. When Wallace returns to his home in Scotland as a young man, his only intent was to live in peace with the love of his life. His marriage is interrupted by the murder of his wife by English noble colonists. His need for revenge grows into a quest for Scottish freedom from tyranny.

The Scottish nobility is more interested in protecting their holdings than fighting for true freedom. They gather their people for compromise at Sterling, where Wallace shows up with a band of warriors, with blue war paint on their faces, ready for battle. Ignoring Scottish nobles, Wallace appeals to the hearts of the Scottish people. He echoes a resounding speech, "Sons of Scotland...you have come to fight as free men and free men you are." His countrymen begin to gain a hint of their true identity. He evokes a legitimate pride in who they are, as he reminds them that living in fear is not living at all. One day we will all die. Then comes this recognizable and searing rhetoric, "And dying in your beds, many years from now, would you be willing to trade all the days from this day to that, to come back here and tell your enemies that they may take our lives, but they'll never take our freedom!"

I love the unfolding of the scene in the movie, because his childhood friend and second in command looks at him and says, "Fine speech. Now what do we do?" The new covenant isn't about making speeches that win arguments; it is about positioning people to experience freedom and intimacy with God that brings the manifestation of the Kingdom!

What is Wallace's response? He says, "I'm going to pick a fight." Wallace's speech and action inspires Scotland to win the battle of Sterling and to begin Scotland's liberation. Wallace follows his obsession (his conviction) and defeats England time and time again. He is on the brink of securing Scotland's liberation when he is deceived and lured into his capture. He is falsely tried, condemned to die, and imprisoned. Awaiting his fate, the future English queen, who is motivated by his passion, tries to entice him to take a potion to ease the pain from his pending public torture. Then he proclaims a gripping statement, "All men die, but not all men truly live." It brings me full circle back to my introduction where Irenaeus states, "The glory of God is man fully alive." Grace is about the Church and His people being fully alive. It's not about good people fulfilling their religious duties. It's about living through God and God living through us, in fullness.

The film ends with a gruesome scene of Wallace being tortured in an attempt to get him to recant of "rebellion" to England. In the courtyard of Westminster Hall in England in the midst of public torture, Wallace is given one last chance to recant of his "treason." The English magistrate quiets the crowd, so Wallace's last words could be heard. In a last gasp, he excoriates at the top of his lungs,

"Freedom!!!" Wow! Where is such conviction of passion in the Church today, people who are willing to put their lives and reputations on the line for true freedom?

The Book of Galatians is Paul's militant legacy to grace and freedom. He forcefully and effectively denounces the Judaizers' message of legalism for God's organic message of grace. He concludes his argument with the Christian declaration of independence and our emancipation of proclamation, *"It is for freedom that Christ has set us free..."* (Gal. 5:1). The questions are freedom from what and freedom for what? Galatians 4:21-31 tells us it is freedom from the law in order to be right with God. In this passage Paul summarizes Genesis 16, 17, and 21. It is the story of Abraham's two sons Isaac and Ishmael. Sarah, his wife, is barren and commends Abraham's legacy to her maidservant, Hagar. Sarah would, in turn, raise the child as her own, as was the custom in that day.

Abraham did as she wished (of course he did) and Hagar gave birth to Ishmael. However, God made it clear that this was not the child He had promised to Abraham (see Gen. 20). So when Abraham was 100 years old and Sarah was 90, Sarah had a child supernaturally, named Isaac.

Paul is interpreting the significance of these events. Ishmael was the product of the flesh, or self-effort, just as people who trust in the law for self-justification. In contrast, Isaac's birth was supernatural. Since Abraham and Sarah were both past the age of childbearing, his birth was miraculous. Likewise, salvation by grace is a miracle; it's not of self-effort (or the flesh). Paul is suggesting legalism binds, not frees.

It is in this context Paul calls believers to freedom that exceeds what religion can offer. This is a freedom that exceeds the boundaries of human control, freedom to love and be loved, a freedom to experience the fullness of God's Kingdom, without condemnation. These verses truly are our declaration of independence.

Paul was saying our destiny is not wrapped up in a set of rules and regulations, but we are empowered to experience it by God's Spirit and His love (see Gal. 5:16). Instead of the fear of punishment of breaking the law, Christians are motivated by the love of God.

Once again this raises the question of the fear of God. Scripturally, the Bible speaks about two kinds of "the fear of the Lord." One is the abject fear and terror of an unrepentant sinner before the justice of God. You see this in Isaiah 2:10, 19, and 21 and in Revelation 6:15-17. However, a Christian under grace need not fear the wrath of God. Again, First John 4:18-19 says it clearly, *"There is no fear in love. But perfect love drives out fear, because fear has to do with punishment. The one who fears is not made perfect in love. We love because He first loved us."*

The meaning of "the fear of the Lord" for a believer is reverent awe.[1] Psalm 33:8 captures this thought clearly: *"Let all the earth fear the Lord: let all the inhabitants of the world stand in awe of Him* (KJV)." One of the ideas of this term "awe" is to be inspired. The idea is comparable to wonder, respect, or reverence. It is the concept to respect above all else.[2] I'm in such wonder and awe of God that I can't imagine doing anything other than what He says. A person in awe is fully persuaded that God's prescribed lifestyle can't possibly be matched. For instance, lust can never be a substitute for true love. This leaves the person with the logical conclusion of obedience. This is how Abraham was willing to sacrifice his only son on Mount Moriah (see Gen. 22:12). It is this kind of "fear of the Lord" that prompts God to share His most intimate secrets. In Psalm 25:14, David reveals, *"The Lord confides in those who fear Him."* In the New Covenant Jesus tells us, *"Whoever has My commandments and obeys them, He is the one who loves Me. He who loves will be loved by My Father and I too will love him and show* [reveal or disclose][3] *Myself to him"* (John 14:21). Loving God causes me to keep His commandments and to see His full manifestation. Psalm 103:17a notes, *"But from everlasting to everlasting the Lord's love is with those who fear Him."* True intimacy is found in those who've discovered this "awe." This kind of "fear of the Lord" is an invitation to honor, respect, and esteem. To the person who discovers it, God reveals His greatest secrets.

Legalism and fear lead by guilt and anticipation of punishment. Such fear leaves believers with an opaque and distant relationship to the God of the universe. You may understand the Book (the Bible), but you never truly know the author (God). This is the state of much of the Church today. True awe and reverence respects God in such a way as to understand that He offers an incomparable lifestyle, one like no other. Kingdom living is the most fulfilling life a person can experience. After all, God really is smarter than I am. While the fear of the Lord is the beginning of knowledge (see Prov. 1:7), the culmination of knowledge is the love of God (see John 14:21).

Obviously, there is an ongoing issue of people who think freedom is an excuse to do something not in keeping with God's character. Thus, once again, I refer to Paul's conclusion in Galatians 5:13, *"...do not use your freedom to indulge the* [flesh]...." It is not freedom to sin, but freedom from sin. Sin always comes with a price (see Gal. 5:15). Paul is seeking to change the motive of believers' actions. We don't act to be accepted; we do so because we are accepted by God. Now Paul turns his attention to freedom...for what? It is freedom to live by the Spirit (see Gal. 5:16).

NEW COVENANT THEOLOGY

One day as I walked through the café of our Bible college, I saw one of our second-year students sitting alone, working on his computer. As I walked by, he sought to gain my attention. He collected himself, trying to ask his question just the right way. He stumbled around for a while, while speaking on the state of the Church. He finally concluded with a question, "Pastor Ron, why isn't the Church a closer mirror and representation of the early Church?"

My first thought was that is more like a seminar, not a five minute answer. After pondering for a second, I replied, "Our biggest problem is we are a new covenant church operating under old covenant principles." He gave me a stunned look, and we had what amounted to an illuminating conversation.

All this talk about law and grace is simply to bring us to a comprehension of new covenant theology and operation. We are not to live under condemnation, but motivation. We were not made to live under the magnification of our shortcomings, but the application of the Kingdom's potential. We were not made to live under demand of the law, but the supply of grace. Law is a demand that is an obligation. Grace is a supply that is a motivation. Law focuses on inadequacy; grace focuses on God's adequacy for our lives. Grace frees us to live by the Spirit.

This, then, becomes Paul's dominant conclusion: we are free to be sensitive to the Spirit's promptings. This is why he transitions in verse 16 with, "*So...*", or in reflection of all this law and grace talk, "*...I say, live by the Spirit and you will not gratify the desires of the* [flesh—"sinful nature" is an erroneous translation[4]]. *For the* [flesh—again, not "sinful nature"] *desires what is contrary to the Spirit and the Spirit what is contrary to the* [flesh]..." (Gal. 5:16-17). What the law was powerless to do, the Spirit, through grace, easily grants.

Grace frees you to live by the Spirit. He adds the idea that you can't live by the Spirit and walk in the flesh at the same time (see Gal 5:16). He continues, "*They are in conflict with each other, so that you do not do what you want*" (Gal. 5:17b). There are things you want to do, but you cannot do because you are in the wrong system (covenant). You can't access God's system from the world's system (flesh). All you can produce is according to what system you are in. Similarly, you can't access the freedom supply from the slavery of demand. He brings the conversation to a culmination by suggesting, *"But if you are led by the Spirit, you are not under law"* (Gal. 5:18). Godly living is not predicated by the rules, but the leading of the Spirit. Just as justification is not possible by works, so the manifestation of the Spirit cannot be achieved by human effort. The product of being led by the Spirit is about being fully persuaded of the truth, until the natural response is faith and sensitivity to an intimate relationship to the King of the Kingdom. The Galatians only knew self-effort. Paul is showing them transformation (rather than change) from their heart.

Being led by the Spirit is the opposite of self-effort, self-dependence, and trying to obey the rules. Galatian Christians had been duped into thinking Christianity was all about the rules and it sapped the life out of them. The Spirit and the law are opposites; they are opposed to each other. It's not trying to be right with God by trying to keep the law.

Just in case you are not sure how to distinguish being led by the Spirit or the work of the flesh, Paul decides to clearly delineate them. First he lists the works of the flesh: *sexual immorality* (including fornication, prostitution, homosexuality, and pornography), *impurity* (moral uncleanness in thought, word, or deed), *debauchery* (extra-marital affairs, promiscuity, etc.), *idolatry* (sorcery, witchcraft, drugs), *hatred* (enmity between groups, prejudice), *jealousy* (of unnatural kinds), *fits of rage* (outbursts of anger), *selfish ambition* (self-aggrandizing attitude to get ahead at another's expense), *dissensions and factions* (hurtful and harmful division).⁵

Now does that sound like an invitation for Spirit-led believers, under grace, to act accordingly? I think not. Then, he adds this punctuating comment, *"...I warn you, as I did before, that those who live like this will not inherit the kingdom of God"* (Gal 5:21).

Legalists, or those whose philosophy is control, immediately suggest that this is right. If you have sin (or at least habitual sin), you can't go to Heaven. The phrase *"the kingdom of God"* used here means, "will not enjoy having God's rule over them."[6] Greek scholar R.C.H. Lenski notes the phrase "shall not inherit" (the Kingdom of God) means to mind all that he has said in regards to the epistle of Galatians (see Gal. 3:15), regarding inheritance (see Gal. 3:18), including minor heirs (see Gal. 4:1), full grown sons (see Gal. 4:7), and with the inheritance of Isaac (see Gal. 4:21,30). All of this reveals that Paul does not mean they shall not enter Heaven. His Kingdom, used here, is inherited in this life—His government.[7]

The acts of the flesh mentioned here are in contrast to being led by the Spirit. Paul points out that the fruit (or manifestation) of the Spirit brings nine graces (see Gal. 5:22-23). Note that the term "fruit" used here is singular. These are nine attributes of one characteristic: *love* (agape, the God kind of love), *joy* (radical anticipation of good), *peace* (to be unaffected by your circumstances), *patience* (to persevere), *kindness* (moral integrity, wholeness, benevolence toward one another), *goodness* (beneficence), *faithfulness* (fidelity), *gentleness* (humility), and *self-control* (self-mastery).

He adds this insight, *"against such things there is no law."* The law is not against such virtue. In other words, the law is unable to produce these qualities. It is God's grace, by the Spirit, that produces such an awesome lifestyle that accesses the Kingdom of God.

Paul concludes his masterful treatise with these words, *"Those who belong to Christ Jesus* [believers], *have crucified the sinful nature* [flesh] *with its passion and desires"* (Gal 5:24). They no longer need to respond to the flesh. Christ dealt with this nature (see Rom. 6:6) at Calvary. Please note, this passage is written in the aorist or past tense, suggesting this is something that has already taken place. This does not refer to what many claim is dying to self. Paul is issuing a call to identify with everything the finished work of Christ has provided (grace). Therefore, we reckon ourselves dead to sin and alive to Christ (see Rom. 6:4,9,11). Thus, you can recognize what's in you (the finished work of Christ), to get it to you and through you.

We began in Chapter One by stating that organic Christianity is more about living *through* Him, than *for* Him. The latter's emphasis is about you; the former is all about Him. This is what Paul is intimating, that the new covenant theology is living by the Spirit.

To live by the Spirit means to conduct our actions according to the revelation of God's Word and Kingdom quickened by the Holy Spirit. In other words, we live *through* Him. This means we operate in the revelation of what the finished work of Jesus Christ has provided for you, through grace. Grace, in the finished work of Christ, has provided us with every spiritual blessing in the heavenly realm (see Eph. 1:3). Therefore, I don't need to entertain the flesh, because everything I need is in the Kingdom (see Matt. 6:33). I need to learn to live "through Him."

This is what Paul is trying to say in Ephesians 2:18, *"For through Him* [Christ] *we both* [Jew and Gentile] *have access to the Father by one Spirit."* Through Christ (His finished work and righteousness), we have access to the King and His Kingdom. Though we live in this world, we are citizens of another world (we are in the world, but we are not of it). Therefore, we are not subjugated to the circumstances of our lives. God's plan was not just to get us into Heaven, but to get Heaven into us. We have access for Heaven to come to earth (see Matt. 6:10; Ps. 115:16). When we obey Kingdom principles, Heaven is authorized and initiated to influence and interfere in earth's affairs (see Gen. 1:26). Similarly, Paul says, *"No, in all these things we are more than conquerors through Him* [Christ], *who loved us"* (Rom. 8:37). The idea in Greek is we continuously live conquering life's situations, one victory after another through Christ's finished work.[8]

Phillipians 4:13 amplifies further, *"I can do everything* [KJV, "all things"] *through Him* [Christ] *who gives me strength."* This is not a self-motivational verse. This is not an "I'll pull myself up by my bootstraps" kind of verse. I can do all things through the understanding of the finished work of Christ by grace. It is this understanding in the Christian life that is our access to grace (provision or supply).

This thought is further amplified in Ephesians 2:8-10, by showing the object of grace through faith, *"For it is by grace you have been saved, through faith—and this not from yourselves, it is the gift from God—not by works, so that no one can boast. For we are God's workmanship, created in Christ Jesus to do good works, which God prepared in advance for us to do."* It should be obvious by now we don't work to be right with God, but neither should we miss the objective of grace. It prepares us to do something. Grace empowers us to fulfill our destiny.

Second Corinthians 12:9a shows us how this works, *"...My grace is sufficient for you, for My power is made perfect in weakness"* Grace is empowerment through Christ. Grace is my ability to use God's ability to meet any need. It is an ability to go beyond our natural ability. Thus, when we try to live our destiny on our own ability, we create frustration and limitation. God always makes His plan for our lives beyond the scope of our natural ability. We must learn to live through Him, so He can live through us.

The word *through* means to go in one side and out the other, from end to end, by way or means of.[9] Our lives were never meant to be limited to our self-effort, but by way or means of what His finished work has produced. Once we learn to rely on and access His finished work, He empowers us to manifest our destiny. Grace (unmerited favor, by the finished work of Christ), gives way to righteousness (right standing with God—which when coupled with grace causes us to reign in life (see Rom. 5:17), gives way to truth (when we are fully persuaded of it, by renewing our minds to His Word), gives way to faith (because we are intimate with Him it is natural to believe and obey Him), gives way to grace (the ability of God through our lives), to manifest His Kingdom. Living through Him causes Him to live through you. It is grace for grace (see John 1:16).

THROUGH HIM, THROUGH YOU

Here is the conclusion of the new covenant and *Organic Christianity*. Once we understand "through Him," it allows Him to live through us. New covenant Christianity is not about religion.

Perhaps my biggest apprehension is that as "good" as religion is, it entirely misses the point. People (good people) are so involved with their Bible studies, prayer meetings, good works, and outreaches they miss the life behind it. They are so busy working for God, they miss working with (and through) God. Their faith is so much about getting eternal life (Heaven), they miss the "life" of eternal life. Eternal life really is not about living forever; everyone lives forever, it just depends on where. Eternal life is about intimacy with God (see John 17:3). It is that intimacy that makes life extraordinary (see Acts 3:1–4:12).

The Christian life is far less about forgiveness of sins than intimacy with God. Sometimes our preoccupation with sin causes us to be myopic (see 2 Pet. 1:9) in perspective, until we miss the essence of our faith. Our faith is not about how many rules and regulations we keep (compared to someone else) until we imitate the best of us. It's about the recognition that we live through Him (see 1 John 4:9), by recognizing what the finished work of Christ means to us. This is what I mean when I say we don't live as much for Him as through Him. This is what the *"much grace"* of the Book of Acts taught the believers who *"turned the world upside down"* (Acts 17:6 KJV). Christianity is not so much about giving my life to God as it is about Him *becoming* my life. It's not about Him becoming a part of my life; He *is* my life. That's why Paul says, *"For to me to live is Christ..."* (Phil. 1:21). This is what Paul was trying to communicate in Galatians 2:20-21, *"I have been crucified with Christ and I no longer live, but Christ lives in me. The life I live in the body, I live by faith in the Son of God who loved me and gave Himself for me. I do not set aside [negate] the grace of God, for if righteousness could be gained through the law, Christ died for nothing!"*

The Christian life is about Him living through us. The real question is, how does this work? He lives and I don't? What does that mean? Is it all Him and none of me? The fact is, His life is hidden in us. Look at Colossians 3:3-4, *"For you died [in Christ], and your life is now hidden with Christ in God. When Christ, who is your life...."* Christianity is not about Christ being a part of my life—He is my life! Like a submerged jug in water, the water is in the jug and the jug is in the water. Likewise, we are in Christ and Christ is in us. He uses our personality, our gifts, and our experiences to live out of us. We recognize and operate out of the revelation of His finished work that grace has provided for us.

Paul subtly maps this out for us in Galatians 2:20, *"I have been crucified with Christ...."* If you are not careful you miss the essence of this phrase. This is about trusting, not trying. Being crucified with Christ isn't about the classic doctrine of dying to self. Notice, *"I have been crucified"*, is past tense, *"...crucified with Christ."* This is not an invitation to die to self; this is an invitation to appropriate the finished work of the crucifixion (see John 19:30). Thus, we are to "reckon ourselves dead to sin and alive to Christ" (see Rom. 6:11). Our old man is dead (see Rom. 6:6); now we are free to truly live. Since we are a "brand new species of being" (see 2 Cor. 5:17), God is now free to manifest His life to and through us. Suddenly, I become the real me, free from the shackles of my past.

How? "By faith in the Son of God." Because faith doesn't believe God will, but believes God has (already done it), it totally changes my perspective. I believe He has given me new life (see 2 Cor. 5:17). I believe He has given me everything I need for life and godliness (see 2 Pet. 1:3), by grace unmerited by me (see Eph. 1:2-3). I believe

His Word (truth) is trustworthy, and it is natural to trust the one I'm intimate with and who loves me unconditionally. I believe I'm right and clean before Him in this very moment (see 2 Cor. 5:21). I believe He is not a God who *will*, but a God who *has* (see Eph. 2:8-9). I believe He is releasing His power in me to do what I never could do on my own.

The result is, "***I do not*** [negate or] *frustrate the grace of God: for if righteousness come by the law, then Christ is dead in vain*" (Gal. 2:21 KJV) by substituting this exchanged life for a set of rules and regulations. That's why Paul reiterates that right standing with God (righteousness) does not come through the law. Christianity is not about doctrine. Doctrine only helps me to understand the process of His life living through me. This is the essence of living out the manifestation model.

The church world has, past and present, said, "This is too good to be true! This is too simple." So they've substituted, unwittingly, legalism for the life of God. This is not about principles being an end in themselves—they lead us to Him. This is about having life (zoe: the God-kind of life) and life to the full (see John 10:10). This is about our God expressing Himself (showing up and showing off) in and through us. I'm in Christ and He is in me. The result is more than a breakthrough; it is about a breakout. Breakthrough is momentary in nature; a breakout has momentum that is perpetual in nature. This is far better than anything religion can muster.

If we are not careful, we'll only exchange one doctrine for another. We throw around similar nomenclature and vernacular and we may miss the radical difference. We are in danger of what Paul said in Galatians 1: our Gospel "*is really no gospel at all*" (Gal. 1:6). This is a call for a new covenant people to stop living in the old covenant. It is a call to what is organic in nature to God's intent.

Paul's effort in Galatians is to that very interest. Paul uses this book to contrast rules with intimacy with God. He contrasts regulations with life (see Gal. 1:6-10; 2:11-21; 3:1-24; comparing Gal. 4:1-28 with 5:1-13). He culminates his argument by calling believers to freedom (see Gal. 5:1,13). How does he conclude? By calling us out of law to walking in the Spirit, *"So I say, live by the Spirit...."* We are no longer to live from the outside-in (the immaturity, or beginning of knowledge, of fear and rules) but from the inside-out.

He continues, *"...and not gratify the desires of the* [flesh]." We don't deny the flesh so we can walk in the spirit; we walk in the spirit so we can conquer the flesh. In so doing we keep in step with God's Spirit (see Gal. 5:25). This is the organic intent of God. It is this Spirit who reveals the finished work of Christ and the folly of the flesh (see Gal. 5:24), so the life of God is free and flows through us.

What is organic is better for you than you can imagine! People think that by adding to it, they've made it better. However, all they've really done is made it synthetic. The real is amazing. My prayer is that substitutes no longer rob us of the real. Let's do amazing!

ENDNOTES

INTRODUCTION

1.   Irenaeus, *Against Heresies* 85 AD. Crossroadsinitiative.com/library-article/149-man-fully-alive-is-the-glory-of-God.

CHAPTER 1

1.   George Barna, quoted on the Navigators website, www.navigators.org/us/staff/scalabrin/items/domestic%20 missionaries20greatly%20needed.

2.   Joseph Prince, *Unmerited Favor* (Lake Mary, FL: Charisma House, 2010), x.

3.   Joseph H. Thayer, *Thayer's Greek-English Lexicon of the New Testament* (Grand Rapids, MI: Baker Book House, 1977), #1097.

4.   James Strong, *The New Strong's Exhaustive Concordance, Greek Dictionary of the New Testament* (Nashville, TN: Thomas Nelson Publishers, 1990), #4152.

5.   Thayer, #2129.

6.   Andrew Wommack, *Discover the Keys to Staying Full of God* (Tulsa, OK: Harrison House, 2008), 1.

7.   Strong, #2937.

8.   http://www.biblestudytools.com/dictionaries/bakers-evangelical-dictionary/judaizers.html; accessed December 7, 2011.

9.   *Webster's New World Dictionary*, College Edition (The World Publishing Company, 1957), s.v. "Pervert."

10. Thayer, #243.

11. Andrew Wommack, "Grace: The Power of the Gospel," *Andrew Wommack Ministries*; http://www.awmi.net/extra/article/grace_power; accessed May 10, 2011.

12. Wommack, *Discover the Keys to Staying Full of God*, 1.

13. *Ibid.*

14. *Webster's New World Dictionary*, s.v. "Cursed."; Strong, #4982.

15. Strong, #1344.

16. Strong, #1344.

17. *Webster's New World Dictionary*, 1365.

18. Strong, #4152.

19. Thayer, #2129.

CHAPTER 2

1.   Ron Luce—quoted this statistic in his message at Word Explosion, 2010, at Victory Christian Center, Tulsa, OK, August 16-17, 2010.

2.   Ron McIntosh, "Reaching a Generation," Victory Fellowship of Ministries article (February 2009).

3. Andrew Farley, *The Naked Gospel* (Grand Rapids, MI: Zondervan, 2009), 1.

4. *Webster's New World Dictionary*, s.v. "Productivity."

5. Mark Victor Hansen and Robert G. Allen, *One Minute Millionaire* (New York: Harmony Books, 2002), 18.

6. Andy Andrews, *The Traveler's Gift* (Nashville, TN: Thomas Nelson Publishers, 2002), 154.

7. *Ibid.*, 155.

8. *Ibid.*, 157.

9. Strong, #5484.

10. John Bevere gave this statistic in his message at Word Explosion, 2010, at Victory Christian Center, Tulsa, OK, August 20-21, 2010.

11. Strong, #5485.

12. Thayer, #5485.

13. *Webster's New World Dictionary*, s.v. "Righteousness."

14. Strong, #114.

15. Joyce Meyer, *The Grace of God* (Tulsa, OK: Harrison House Publishers, 1995), 14.

16. *Webster's New World Dictionary*, s.v. "Abolish." See also the King James Version.

17. *Webster's New World Dictionary*, s.v. "Fulfill"; Strong, #4138.

18. Chuck Swindoll, *The Grace Awakening* (Nashville, TN: Thomas Nelson Publishers, 2003), 2.

19. Andrew Wommack, *Andrew Wommack Bible Commentary*, Romans 5:20; http://www.awmi.net/bible/rom_05_20; accessed May 10, 2011.

20. *Andrew Wommack Bible Commentary*, Romans 4:3; http://www.awmi.net/bible/rom_04_03; accessed May 10, 2011.

21. *Andrew Wommack Bible Commentary*, Romans 4:4; http://www.awmi.net/bible/rom_04_04; accessed May 10, 2011.

22. *Ibid.*

23. *Webster's New World Dictionary*, s.v. "Heir."

CHAPTER 3

1. *Webster's New World Dictionary*, s.v. "Importance."

2. *Ibid.*, s.v. "Significance."

3. Strong, #5485.

4. *Andrew Wommack Bible Commentary*, Ephesians 2:15; http://www.awmi.net/bible/eph_02_15; accessed May 11, 2011.

5. *Webster's New World Dictionary*, s.v. "Abolish."

6. *Andrew Wommack Bible Commentary*, Galatians 2:19; http://www.awmi.net/bible/gal_02_19; accessed May 11, 2011.

7. Stephen Scott, *Mentored by a Millionaire* (Hoboken, NJ: John Willy & Sons, Inc., 2004), 4.

8. Brian Tracey, *Create Your Own Future* (Hobuken, NJ: John Willy & Son, Inc., 2002), 241.

9. Strong, #4052.

10. John Bevere, *Extraordinary* (Colorado Springs, CO: Waterbrook Press, 2009), 62.

11. Martin Luther, "Spirit and Letter," *Christian Classics Ethereal Library;* http://www.ccel.org/ccel/luther/sermons.v.vii.html; accessed May 11, 2011.

12. Martin Luther, "Christ Supersedes Moses," *Christian Classics Ethereal Library;* http://www.ccel.org/ccel/luther/sermons.v.viii.html; accessed May 11, 2011.

13. "Romans 1:16-17 Commentary," *Precept Austin;* http://preceptaustin.org/romans_116-19.htm; accessed May 11, 2011.

14. *Ibid.*

15. Strong, #4982.

16. Ron McIntosh, *The Greatest Secret* (Lakeland, FL: White Stone Books, 2007), 10.

17. Strong, #2127, 2128, 2129.

18. Thayer, #2128.

19. Strong, #4152.

20. *Ibid.*, #3341.

21. *Ibid.*, #3340.

22. This takes 21 days, according to Maxwell Maltz's study in *Psycho-Cybernetics* (New York, New York : Pocket Books, 1989). See my book, *The Greatest Secret,* for full understanding. Also, our *Barrier Busters Manual* will teach you how to break barriers and conquer sin. It is available on our Website: http://www.rmmimpact.com.

23. Strong, *Hebrew and Chaldee Dictionary,* #8444.

24. *Ibid,* #8176.

CHAPTER 3½

1. Albert Barnes, *Barnes' Notes on the Old and New Testaments* (Grand Rapids, MI: Baker House Books, 1983), 388.

2. Strong, *Hebrew and Chaldee Dictionary,* #3374. Most people view this as reverence, not dread.

3. *Andrew Wommack Bible Commentary,* John 14:21; http://www.awmi.net/bible/joh_14_21; accessed May 11, 2011.

4. Andrew Wommack, "God's Kind of Love," *Andrew Wommack Ministries;* http://www.awmi.net/extra/article/gods_love; accessed May 11, 2011.

5. R.C.H. Lenski, *St. Paul's Epistles* (Minneapolis, MN: Augsburg Publishing House, 1961), 497.

6. *Andrew Wommack Bible Commentary,* Ephesians 3:19; http://www.awmi.net/bible/eph_03_19; accessed May 11, 2011.

7. See Jude 1:21 and 1 John 4:9.

8. Strong, *Hebrew and Chaldee Dictionary,* #1820.

9. *Andrew Wommack Bible Commentary,* Galatians 2:20; http://www.awmi.net/bible/gal_02_20; accessed May 11, 2011.

10. Strong, #114.

11. *Webster's New World Dictionary,* s.v. "Identity."

12. *Ibid.,* s.v. "Image."

13. Myles Munroe, *Rediscovering the Kingdom* (Destiny Image Publishers, Inc., Shippensburg, PA: 28. En.allexperts.com/q/easternorthodox-14564/image-us-likeness .htm

14. *Webster's New World Dictionary,* s.v. "Through."

15. *Ibid.,* s.v. "Complete."

16. Thayer, #1421, 160.

17. Strong, *Greek Dictionary,* #2222.

18. Thayer, #1391.

19. Ron McIntosh, *The Greatest Secret,* 112-131.

20. *Ibid.*

21. Thayer, #40.

21. R.C.H. Lenski, *Hebrews* (Minneapolis, MN: Augsburg Publishing House, 1966), 337.

22. Strong, #3306.

CHAPTER 4

1. Francois Fenelon, "The Seeking Heart," quoted in Francis Chan, *Crazy Love* (Colorado Springs, CO: David C. Cook, 2008), 19.

2. This is my unscientific observation through years of ministry work and observation of Christians.

3. *Webster's New World Dictionary,* s.v. "Righteousness"; Noah Webster, *American Dictionary of the English Language*, First Edition, s.v. "Righteousness."

4. Strong, #1344. *Justified* and *righteous* are the same Greek word.

5. Bill Thrall, Bruce McNicol, John Lynch, *True Faced* (Colorado Springs, CO, NavPress 2004), 51-52.

6. *Webster's New World Dictionary,* "Reconciliation."

7. *Andrew Wommack Bible Commentary,* Romans 5:19; http://www.awmi.net/bible/rom_05_19; accessed May 12, 2011.

8. Strong, *Greek Dictionary* #1594; Thayer, #1594.

9. The author in conversation with Dr. James Richards.

10. R.C.H. Lenski, *The Interpretation of the Epistle to 1 & 2 Peter, The Three Epistles of John & the Epistle of Jude* (Minneapolis, MN: Augsburg Publishing House, 1966), 363.

11. *Ibid.*

12. Strong, Greek #3340, 3341.

13. *Webster's New World Dictionary,* s.v. "Steadfast."

14. *Webster's New World Dictionary,* s.v. "Secure."

CHAPTER 5

1. Strong, #4561.

2. *Ibid.*, #2189; *American Dictionary of the English Language 1828,* s.v. "Enmity."

3. *Webster's New World Dictionary,* s.v. "Freedom."

4. Charles Swindoll, *The Grace Awakening* (Nashville, TN: Thomas Nelson Publishers, 1990), 68.

5. *Webster's New World Dictionary,* s.v. "True."

6. *Ibid.*, s.v. "Truth."

7. George Barna, "Young Adults and Liberals Struggle With Morality," *The Barna Group* (August 25, 2008); http://www.barna.org/barna-update/article/16-teensnext-gen/25-young-adults-and-liberals-struggle-with-morality?q=young+adults+liberals+morality; accessed May 13, 2011.

8. Thayer, # 3053.

9. McIntosh, *The Greatest Secret,* 112.

10. Simon T. Bailey, *Release Your Brilliance* (New York: Collins, 2008), 10-11.

11. *Webster's New World Dictionary,* s.v "Con-."

12. *Ibid.*, s.v. "Form."

13. Strong, #3339, 3340.

14. Ron McIntosh, *The Greatest Secret,* 37; in conversation with language expert, William McDonald.

15. *Andrew Wommack Bible Commentary,* Galatians 5:17; http://www.awmi.net/bible/gal_05_17; accessed May 13, 2011; quoting VBS handbook.

16. *American Dictionary of the English Language 1828,* s.v. "Change."

17. *Webster's New World Dictionary,* s.v. "Transform."

18. Strong, *Greek Dictionary* #342; *American Dictionary of the English Language 1828,* s.v. "Renew"; *Webster's New World Dictionary,* s.v. "Renew."

19. Strong, *Hebrew and Chaldee Dictionary* #8176.

20. I.V. Hilliard, *Mental Toughness for Success* (Houston, TX: Light Publications, 1996), 147.

21. Steve Roesler, "Bring Your Emotional Awareness to Work," *All Things Workplace;* http://www.allthingsworkplace.com/2008/11/turn-on-your-em.html; accessed May 14, 2011.

22. IS-USA/attraction2578.phphealthread.net/why-dieters-regain -leibel.htm

23. Strong, Greek #1381.

24. Jack Canfield, *The Success Principle* (New York, NY: Harper Collins Publishers, 2005), 81-83.

25. H.W.F. Gesenius, *Gesenius' Hebrew-Chaldee Lexicon to the Old Testament* (Grand Rapids, MI: Baker Book House, 1979), #7181.

26. *American Dictionary of the English Language 1828,* s.v. "Delight"; *Webster's New World Dictionary,* s.v. "Delight"; Strong #835; Creflo Dollar meeting at the Mabee Center, Tulsa, OK.

27. Strong, *Hebrew and Chaldee Dictionary,* #1897, 1899; *Webster's New World Dictionary,* s.v. "Meditate."

28. Lou Tice, *Investment for the 90's Tape Series MCMLXXX1X1* (The Pacific Institute, Inc., 1201 Western Ave., Seattle, Washington, USA).

29. See my book *The Greatest Secret* for a full explanation. Also check out my website www.ronmcintosh.org for biblical meditation manuals and CDs. We have nine biblical meditation CDs to help you transform your personal belief system in the most important areas of your life.

30. Ron McIntosh, *The Greatest Secret,* 62.

31. *Webster's New World Dictionary,* s.v. "Conation."

32. Strong, *Greek Dictionary,* #5485.

33. *Webster's New World Dictionary,* s.v. "Intention."

34. Strong, *Hebrew and Chaldee Dictionary,* #7503; Gesenius, #7505.

35. *Ibid.,* #7495, #7503.

CHAPTER 6

1. Strong, *Greek Dictionary,* #4152, 2129.

2. John F. Walvoord, *The Bible Knowledge Commentary* (USA, Canada, England: Victor Books, Scripture Press, 1983), 616.

3. *Andrew Wommack Bible Commentary,* 1 Corinthians 1:20-21; http://www.awmi.net/bible/1co_01_20; accessed ?? [[could not read pdf of remaining correction on this]].

4. Strong, #4100; *Webster's New World Dictionary,* s.v. "Faith"; *American Dictionary of the English Language 1828,* s.v. "Faith."

5. John Assara and Murray Smith, *The Answer* (New York: Atria Books, 2008), 48.

6. *Ibid.,* 50.

7. John F. Walvoord, *The Bible Knowledge Commentary,* 492.

8. Andrew Wommack, *The Balance of Great Faith,* Andrew Wommack Ministries, 2.

9. Strong, #5285; Thayer, #5285; *American Dictionary of the English Language*, s.v. "Substance"; R.C.H. Lenski, *Interpretation of the Epistle to the Hebrews and the Epistle of James* (Minneapolis, MN: Augsburg Publishing House, 1986), 375.

10. *Webster's New World Dictionary*, s.v. "Inventory."

11. *Webster's New World Dictionary*, s.v. "Substantiate."

12. Kenneth Wuest, *Word Studies in Greek New Testament Vol. 2* (Grand Rapids, MI: Wm. B. Eerdman Publishing Company, 1973), 94.

13. *Webster's New World Dictionary*, s.v. "Hope."

14. R.C.H. Lenski, *Interpretation of St. Mark's Gospel* (Minneapolis, MN: Augsburg Publishing House, 1961), 493; Kenneth Wuest, *Word Studies in Greek New Testament Vol. 2*, 94. New Testament scholar A.S. Worell states, "If 'Have faith in God' would have been the thought, it would be easily expressed in Greek. Faith, however, originates with God and those who have real faith, have His faith. Similarly, this is true of Galatians 2:20. Jesus uses the Greek phrase 'exete pistin theo' not 'exete pistin en theo' thus the phrase should read have the faith of God. Since this phrase is subjective genetive this phrase is perfectly doable. Theologians and grammarians cannot with certainty call this phrase subjective or objective in Greek. Perhaps, the foremost modern Greek grammarian, A.T. Robertson, agrees with the 'faith in God' phrase, though the genitive must mean 'in' but only the God kind of faith. (Robertson, A.T., *Grammar of the Greek New Testament in the Light of Historical Research*). While Robertson agrees with the "faith in God" translation he emphasizes that 'in' doesn't mean 'in' as we in English speak of it. He points out that the genetive inculcates 'genus' or 'kind' and helps Jesus' phrase involve the God kind of faith, and the subjective genetive is preferred."

15. Strong, Greek #2472.

16. There is some dispute as to whether this verse should be translated *"faith of the Son of God"* or *"faith in the Son of God."* The idea of the God kind of faith (faith of the Son of God) has a lot of support. Multiple translations take Mark 11:22 and Galatians 2:20 in this manner. Such translations include the King James Version, *Young's Literal Translation, Literal Translation of the Bible, Douay-Rheams Bible,* the *Worell New Testament, 1599 Geneva Bible, R.A. Torrey's Treasury of Scripture Knowledge, The Bible in Basic English, The Jewish New Testament* by David Stern, as well as such noted scholars as A.T. Robertson. See "The God Kind of Faith: A Biblical, Historical, and Theological Defense" (Part 1) by Troy J. Edwards for a thorough discussion. victoryword. com100megspop.com/godkind2.html.

16. Wommack, "God's Kind of Love," http://www.awmi.net/extra/article/gods _love; accessed May 14, 2011.

17. *Webster's New World Dictionary,* s.v. "Acknowledge."

18. *Ibid.*

20. Thayer, #1252.

21. Strong, Greek #1537.

22. Thayer, #191.

23. R.C.H. Lenski, *The Interpretation of St. Paul's Epistle to the Romans* (Minneapolis, MN: Augsburg Publishing, 1961), 668.

CHAPTER 7

1. John Bevere, sermon at Word Explosion 2009 at Victory Christian Center, Tulsa, OK, August 2009.

2. R.C.H. Lenski, *The Interpretation of Acts* (Minneapolis, MN: Augsburg Publishing, 1961), 128.

3. Walvoord, *The Bible Knowledge Commentary,* 381.

4. *Webster's New World Dictionary,* s.v. "Manifold."

5. Thayer, #5485, 5486.

6. Dr. James B. Richards, *Grace: The Power to Change* (New Kensington, PA: Whitaker House, 1993), 12.

7. *Ibid.,* 17.

8. William Barclay, *New Testament Words* (Louisville, KY: Westminster Press, 1964), 118-125.

9. *Ibid.*

10. *Ibid.*

11. *Andrew Wommack Bible Commentary,* Romans 5:21; http://www.awmi.net/bible/rom_05_21; accessed May 16, 2011.

12. *Andrew Wommack Bible Commentary,* Romans 6:1; http://www.awmi.net/bible/rom_06_01; Romans 6:2; http://www.awmi.net/bible/rom_06_02; accessed May 16, 2011.

13. Strong, #3049.

14. Richards, *Grace: The Power to Change,* 38.

15. *Zondervan Parallel New Testament in Greek and English* (Grand Rapids, MI: Zondervan, 1975), 545.

16. Strong, Greek, #32.

17. Jack Cantrell, *The Success Principle* (New York: Harper Resource Book), 107.

18. Strong, Greek #3875; Thayer, #3875.

19. Thayer, #2886.

20. The author in conversation with Dr. James Richards.

21. Strong, #266.

22. *Ibid.,* #264.

23. *Webster's New World Dictionary*, s.v. "Obsolete."

CHAPTER 8

1. *American Dictionary of the English Language 1828*, s.v. "Joy."

2. *Webster's New World Dictionary*, s.v. "Therefore."

3. *Ibid.*, s.v. "Access."

4. Thayer, #1391.

5. Strong, *Hebrew and Chaldee Dictionary*, #1382.

6. *Andrew Wommack Bible Commentary*, Romans 5:4; http://www.awmi.net/bible/rom_05_04; accessed May 16, 2011.

7. George Barna.

8. Strong, #3045.

9. *Webster's New World Dictionary*, s.v. "Di-."

10. *American Dictionary of the English Language 1828*, s.v. "Stress."

11. *Ibid.*, s.v. "Rebuke."

12. *Webster's New World Dictionary*, s.v. "Dis-."

13. *Ibid.*, s.v. "Disgrace."

14. "1.6 to 2.8. million teen run away from home every year in America" *National Runaways Switchboard;* http://www.1800runaway.org; accessed May 16, 2011.

15. Bill Hendrick, "Traffic Accidents Are Top Cause of Teen Deaths," WebMD Health News; http://www.webmd.com/parenting/news/20100505/traffic-accidents-are-top-cause-of-teen-deaths; accessed May 16, 2011.

16. "Child Abuse and Neglect by Parents and Other Caregivers," *World Health Organization;* http://www.who.int/violence_injury_prevention/violence/global_campaign/en/chap3.pdf; accessed May 16, 2011.

17. According to divorce rate.org, divorce statistics are 50 percent of first marriages, 67 percent in second marriages, and 74 percent in third marriages. "Divorce Rates in America," *Marriage101;* http://www.marriage101.org/divorce-rates-in-America; accessed May 16, 2011.

18. Strong, *Greek Dictionary,* #2293; *Webster's New World Dictionary,* s.v. "Good cheer."

CHAPTER 9

1. Strong, *Hebrew and Chaldee Dictionary,* #3374, Encyclopedia Wikipedia.org/wiki/aw

2. See Psalm 33:8.

3. Strong, *Greek Dictionary,* #1718, 28.

4. *Ibid,* #4561.

5. Walvoord, *The Bible Knowledge Commentary.* 607-608.

6. http://www.biblestudytools.com/commentaries/gills-exposition-of-the-bible/galatians-5-21.html; accessed December 7, 2011.

7. R.C.H. Lenski, *St. Paul's Epistles, to the Galatians, Ephesians & Philippians* (Minneapolis, MN: Augsburg Publishing House, 1961), 289.

8. Lenski, *The Interpretation of St. Paul's Epistle to the Romans,* 575.

9. *Webster's New World Dictionary,* s.v. "Through."

ABOUT RON MCINTOSH

Ron McIntosh has dedicated his life to helping people find the life they were born to live. He has a gifting to help people unlock the door to their potential and maximum productivity. Ron is a noted speaker, writer, teacher, and life coach. He has travelled the world conducting services, seminars, and conferences of all kinds to help people step into their destiny. Ron's books and resources have helped countless thousands find their dreams and maximize their potential. Ron is the president of Ron McIntosh Ministries and I.M.P.A.C.T., a leadership and coaching ministry. He is also the Executive Director of Victory Bible Institute in Tulsa, Oklahoma.

A former Campus Pastor of Oral Roberts University, he has authored three books of powerful impact. His latest book, *The Greatest Secret,* has created much "buzz" as this work helps people to transform their personal belief system, and to maximize productivity in their lives. His previous best-selling book, *The Quest for Revival,* has been translated into four languages and distributed the world over. Ron serves on several boards, including Impact Productions, as well as serving on the board of three churches. He has been a guest of many radio and television programs and is a gifted communicator to this generation.

Ron has two degrees from Oral Roberts University. He and his wife, Judy, live in Tulsa, Oklahoma. They are the proud parents of three children, David, Daniel, and Jonathan. You can access Ron's website at www.rmmimpact.com or www.onmcintoshministries.com.

IN THE RIGHT HANDS, THIS BOOK WILL CHANGE LIVES!

Most of the people who need this message will not be looking for this book. To change their lives, you need to put a copy of this book in their hands.

> *But others (seeds) fell into good ground, and brought forth fruit, some a hundred-fold, some sixty-fold, some thirty-fold* (Matthew 13:8).

Our ministry is constantly seeking methods to find the good ground, the people who need this anointed message to change their lives. Will you help us reach these people?

> *Remember this—a farmer who plants only a few seeds will get a small crop. But the one who plants generously will get a generous crop* (2 Corinthians 9:6).

EXTEND THIS MINISTRY BY SOWING
3 BOOKS, 5 BOOKS, 10 BOOKS, OR MORE TODAY,
AND BECOME A LIFE CHANGER!

Thank you,

Don Nori Sr., Founder
Destiny Image
Since 1982

DESTINY IMAGE PUBLISHERS, INC.

"Promoting Inspired Lives."

VISIT OUR NEW SITE HOME AT
WWW.DESTINYIMAGE.COM

FREE SUBSCRIPTION TO DI NEWSLETTER

Receive free unpublished articles by top DI authors, exclusive

discounts, and free downloads from our best and newest books.

Visit www.destinyimage.com to subscribe.

Write to: Destiny Image
              P.O. Box 310
              Shippensburg, PA 17257-0310

Call: 1-800-722-6774

Email: orders@destinyimage.com

For a complete list of our titles or to place an order
online, visit www.destinyimage.com.

FIND US ON FACEBOOK OR FOLLOW US ON TWITTER.

www.facebook.com/destinyimage   facebook
www.twitter.com/destinyimage   twitter